Kent Ph

MW00711949

# Memoirs of a Jesus Freak

**EVP**

## Earthen Vessel Publishing

San Rafael, CA

# Memoirs of a Jesus Freak

All rights reserved
Copyright © 2014 by Kent Allan Philpott

Published 2014 by
Earthen Vessel Publishing
San Rafael, CA 94903
www.evpbooks.com

Book Design and Layout by
Katie L. C. Philpott
Bios Research and Composition by
Stephanie Adams

ISBN: 978-0-9898041-1-0 (print version)
ISBN: 978-0-9898041-2-7 (ebook version)

No part of this publication may be reproduced, stored in a retrieval system, or transmitted in any form or by any means, electronic or mechanical, including photocopying, recording, or any information retrieval system, without the written permission of the author or publisher, except by a reviewer who wishes to quote brief passages in connection with a review written for inclusion in a magazine, newspaper, internet site, or broadcast.

All Scripture quotations, unless otherwise indicated, are taken from the Holy Bible, English Standard Version® (ESV®), copyright © 2001 by Crossway Bibles, a publishing ministry of Good News Publishers. Used by permission. All rights reserved.

# Dedication

This book is dedicated to the families of those involved in the leadership of the Jesus People Movement. Awakenings are not always pleasant; there is 'collateral damage', and that was certainly the case with the JPM. While there is glory accrued to God, there is also tragedy. Why this happens is little understood, and there are no easy answers.

In my own case, I want to dedicate these memoirs to those who lived through them with me directly and personally, my former wife Roberta Kay Philpott, my oldest daughter Dawn Doreen LaRue, middle child Grace Marie Reed, and son Vernon Robert Philpott.

# Acknowlegments

**W**hat began as a simple personal story of my involvement in the Jesus People Movement morphed into something much larger. Friends encouraged me to include biographies of those mentioned in the memoirs, and what I thought would be perhaps a dozen or so swelled to thirty-five at last count. Thanks to all of you who took the time and effort to compile a bio and find old photos. This is not something easily done, because it forces the writer to talk about difficult realities.

For Stephanie Adams who collected and wrote many of the biographies, we owe a great deal. Some bios she compiled by means of internet sites, some were submitted to her via email, and others she collected in direct contact via the telephone. Many bio submissions required revisions along the way (some by the named subjects themselves), and Stephanie handled them with aplomb.

My own thinking about the Jesus People Movement started with two visits by Larry Eskridge, the first seven years ago and the second, two years later, when we talked about the JPM. Larry's book, *God's Forever Family: The Jesus People Movement in America*, published by Oxford University press in 2013, stirred up a great deal of interest in the movement. Larry also contributed a foreword to these memoirs, for which I am very grateful.

To Michelle Shelfer, gifted with many talents, one of which is catching the smallest grammatical or spelling flaw - thank you.

For Katie, my wife, who is the editor, cover designer, format maker, constructive critic, and prime mover and shaker of Earthen Vessel Publishing -- thank you very much.

If you are wondering about the photos on the front cover, here are the answers:

The background is a camera photo of one page of the manuscript for *Two Brothers in Haight*, an unpublished book that I co-wrote with David Hoyt. More than any other character in this book, David deserves an extra amount of thanks for contributions over several years - stories, photos, and discussions about our times together on the streets of the Haight-Ashbury, throughout the Bay Area of San Francisco, the East Coast of the U.S., and over the 'pond' to England and Europe.

The group photo is one of Joyful Noise performing in 1971 at San Quentin State Prison in Marin County, California. We changed personnel often during the band's tenure, and I no longer remember every name. We had great fun bringing a folk-like brand of Christian music to audiences around the country. I describe more of our escapades in chapter 13. Suffice it to say, I wish I could thank each member of the band for making such a joyful noise amidst the adventure that was the Jesus People Movement.

# Table of Contents

# Photos . . . 176-199
# Bios Section

# Foreword

The Jesus People movement that began in the latter part of the 1960s and stretched well into the 1970s was, in retrospect, one of the pivotal episodes within the American church in the second half of the 20th-century. Hundreds of thousands of Baby Boomers ranging from hard-core hippies to Middle American church youth group members were swept up in an enthusiastic riptide of revival that swept across the continent. Street corner preaching, Jesus rock bands, coffeehouses, communes, bumper stickers, and underground "Jesus papers" became a part of the cultural furniture in North America.

At the time, many observers – both secular and Christian--thought the onset of the "Jesus movement" was fraught with significance for the future of the Church and American culture. During 1971 and 1972 the movement received extensive (and usually positive) media coverage, racking up articles in almost every newspaper in the country, even making the cover of Time magazine. Nearly a hundred books celebrating, describing, and analyzing the movement made their way into print. At the same time a small armada of companies sprang up to supply the young Jesus People with goods – posters, books, study Bibles, records and tapes, buttons, jewelry – for their devotional, evangelistic, and consumer needs.

The "Jesus Generation" appeared locked and loaded, ready to charge into the future. Then a funny thing happened – as soon as they had appeared, the Jesus People seemed to disappear. By the late '70s there was very little in the way left of any kind of a visible Jesus movement. And by the time the '80s had come and gone they were virtually forgotten by most churchgoers as well as the pundits and scholars who had once hailed their arrival as signaling a change in business-as-usual in the American Church.

Of course, the Jesus People hadn't really gone away – they had matured (or at least gotten older) and moved on with their lives and been absorbed as leaders, workers, and supporters of thousands of local congregations and parachurch ministries across the land.  In fact, the changes that the Jesus movement brought to the evangelical subculture continued to shape American Christianity well into the 21st-century in terms of music, congregational life and style (think "seeker sensitive" here), and the way the Church approached its relationship to popular and youth culture. The reality of this continuing legacy have, after decades of historical amnesia, begun to stir a new interest in the Jesus movement and a quest to understand its roots, its history, and the nature of its impact – positive and negative – on the evangelical church.

As part of the renewed wave of interest in the Jesus People, this volume that Kent Philpott has brought together explores the pivotal stories surrounding the beginnings of the movement in the San Francisco Bay area.  Before 1967's "Summer of Love" sent the hippie movement into full-throttle overdrive, there may well have been a few isolated encounters that took place around the country involving lone evangelical pastors or Christian workers and members of the developing counterculture. If so, they remain largely buried in the memories of those involved or tucked away in dusty boxes of personal memorabilia stored in garages and basements.  In terms of direct impact upon the development and spread of what would become known as the Jesus movement, the events and personalities that were part of the Bay Area "scene" were foundational. The experiences there, the connections formed, and the first rumblings of publicity that emerged in that time were crucial to there ever having been such a thing as the Jesus People. And while the happenings in San Francisco and its environs never achieved the flash and mass of what would shortly take place in Southern California (and some of that is covered in these pages as well), it is hard to imagine the latter ever occurring without what took place to the north in Haight-Ashbury, Mill Valley, Berkeley, and elsewhere around the Bay. *Memoirs of a Jesus Freak* is an important, first-hand, reminiscence about those pivotal early days of the Jesus People movement and its development that will be helpful to scholars, pastors, and laypeople as they reflect upon the past, contemplate the present, and think about the future.

Larry Eskridge, Author:
   *God's Forever Family: The Jesus People Movement in America*
      Wheaton, IL
      March 2014

# Introduction

**M**emoirs – a fancy word and perhaps misapplied to this rather brief and simplistic account of my personal involvement in the Jesus People Movement of the late 1960s and early 1970s – is a relating of events as I experienced them from 1967 to 1978. Though, according to my reckoning, the JPM was virtually gone by 1972, at least in Marin County, California (San Francisco Bay Area), the effects of the awakening impacted me directly until 1978, and to a lesser extent to this day.

The term 'Jesus freak' is somewhat theatrical, since we did not use that term to define ourselves. The first tag applied by those of us who were active was 'Street Christian,' since we mainly worked on city streets. 'Freak' was a term generally used for the sex, drug, and rock and rollers, plus those who made up the hip scene in the large metropolitan cities, who were seriously hoping to discover themselves. Jesus freak was an obvious designation for young people who carried big black Bibles around and were 'pushing' Jesus and nothing else.

Most of the people who were part of the Jesus freak scene in the Bay Area are still with us, and my dominant concern is to 'get things down' while we are still able. I have in mind future generations of researchers into awakenings and revivals in general, that they might have primary source material to examine.

Three sections make up the book: (1) forty-five short chapters that chronicle most of what happened to me in the JPM, (2) black and white photos of JPM events and persons, along with more recent portraits of participants, and (3) thirty-six biographies of those participants. There is an index to help the reader find a favorite subject or person of interest, but, since so many of the books on the JPM are just being written, there is no bibliography. (Be on the lookout for David Hoyt's account coming up soon.)

# Chapter 1

# Some Background

This is the first chapter in a series about my life as a flaming Pentecostal; well, maybe not flaming as in Holy Roller, just about my life in the Charismatic/Pentecostal fold. It all began, strangely enough, with what happened down at the local Odd Fellows Hall in Portland, Oregon.

One block from the family home in Northeast Portland was the Odd Fellows Hall on Deacon and Durham Street. Many different groups rented it for their meetings and events. It no longer exists, and I suspect the huge, old, wooden, two-story structure probably burned down. During the 1950s, Pentecostal meetings were cropping up all over the country, and one came to the hall around the corner. We kids – my brothers, a kid named Topsy, and I – would sneak in and watch. We slipped in the back door, found seats in the back, and enjoyed our entertainment. Since that day I have never seen anything quite like it; there was actual rolling around on the floor.

My dad said nothing too bad but nothing too good about it all. I don't know that he ever went in there, but he definitely went to the North Baptist Church about a mile from the house. My dad had not yet become a Christian, a real one I mean, and I think he attended church out of tradition, because his folks were the quiet, serious kind of Baptists.

I'll jump now to 1963 and the First Baptist Church of Fairfield, California and my conversion at age 21. I will not walk us through the details here, but I will say that after a period of nine months of sporadic listening to the Gospel preached by Pastor Bob Lewis, I experienced the new birth. It is still mostly a mystery to me. Pastor Bob was in his mid-thirties and was serious about discipleship. A book he gave to all of us new believers was on the Bible-based American cults. It was a small volume and covered only five such groups: Mormons, Jehovah Witnesses, Christian Science, Adventists (Seventh Day), and Pentecostals.

Back then Pentecostals were rightfully included in such a book, but today the 'cult' distinction is missing for most such groups. In the early years of the 20th century Pentecostals earned the designation of cult, because they believed that they were the only ones really filled with the Holy Spirit and that speaking in tongues was the only sure mark of a real born-again Christian. This thinking took them into the cultic realm.

So then, reading that book I was convinced that Pentecostals were cultic, and I gave them and their doctrines wide berth. This was my mind set all the way until 1967 and the Jesus People Movement.

# Chapter 2

# The Call to the Hippies

During my years at Golden Gate Baptist Theological Seminary (Southern Baptist), I was anti-Pentecostal and did not yet know what was meant by 'charismatic'. As far as I was concerned, speaking in tongues was of a demonic origin, and short of that it was at least wrong doctrine. We had little or no fellowship with Pentecostals. In Marin County that would have been limited to the Assembly of God churches or maybe a Black Pentecostal church of some kind.

One night in February of 1967, while I was driving home from my part time job as shoe salesman at the J.C. Penny store in Corte Madera and while listening to Scott McKenzie's "When you come to San Francisco, be sure to wear some flowers in your hair," it was as though God spoke directly and personally to me: "Go to the hippies in San Francisco." That was it and that was all. The very next day, a rainy Thursday evening, I did just that and the adventure began.

That night, while peering through the window of Hamilton United Methodist Church on Waller Street, a young hippie approached me and wanted to know if I wanted to meet someone who knew a lot about religion. I jumped at the chance, thinking, "This is the hand of God," and said yes. He brought me just a few doors away to an old Victorian house and introduced me to David Hoyt. David was living in a house full of lesbians; he was the token male and bodyguard for the ladies, and his room was under the stairs that climbed up to the second floor. It was really just a janitor's closet, but David had made it into a bedroom that was probably the same size as his jail cell at Lompoc Prison from which he had recently been released. David had entered prison at age 19, a biker convicted of drug smuggling from Mexico. He had become a jailhouse guru of sorts and had decided on Hinduism as his religion of choice. By the time I met David that evening, he had risen in the eyes of Swami Baktivadanti to one of the chief devotees at the Hare Krishna Temple on Frederick Street, just blocks away from where David was then living.

We began a Bible study under the stairs, just David and I, but in a few weeks David moved his living space to the basement of the Hare Krishna Temple. To continue the studies, I had to get permission from the swami.

I recall meeting with Swami Baktivadanti in his sparsely furnished second story apartment a few doors down from what we called the Hare Krishna Temple. He asked me, "Why do you want to come to the temple?" Not expecting to be asked this I replied, "Because David asked me to." "Are you a Christian?" he asked. "Yes," I answered, "and I am learning about Hinduism." "What do you know about it?" "Not much," was all I could honestly say.

It seemed to me that the Swami was conflicted; he knew it would be applauded if he let me do the Bible study, since he was trying to appear ecumenical. But deep down I was convinced he was afraid of me in some way; more importantly, he did not like what I represented.

"You must attend the Kirtan. If you do that, you can have your study." I agreed to the terms, and the very brief meeting was over.

Once the Bible study started at the temple, more people started attending, which continued for some months. The devotees were all white, young hippies and were extremely serious about all things religious. I was rather shocked that they had such a keen interest in the Bible. Though I disliked having to sit through the Kirtans, still the chance to tell the growing group of seekers about Jesus overcame all else.

So it continued week by week until a particular Saturday morning when I received a phone call from David asking me to rush in to meet him at the temple. I jumped in the old Ford and did just that. My life was about to change dramatically.

# Chapter 3

# Fire
# in the Temple

I raced into the City, down 19th Avenue, left on Fulton, right on Stanyon, right on Fredrick, and then I saw the fire trucks and smelled the smoke. I parked just up the street next to old Kezar stadium (original home of the 49ers pro football team), jumped out, and ran to the door of the Hindu temple.

Fire hoses snaked into the temple from the fire truck, and people were running in and out. The place was chaotic. I stepped back and saw, in almost foot-high letters painted on the walls, Christian phrases like "Jesus is the Way," "Lord Jesus Christ," and more.

As I began to move in the direction of the basement where most of the activity was happening, David suddenly appeared carrying bags of his personal belongings and shouted at me to take the bags he was carrying, so he could dart back down the stairs to the basement. In a moment he was back carrying more bags, and we ran out onto the sidewalk and down the street to my car, into which we threw David's few possessions. We hustled back to the temple, David disappeared again, and I simply stood in the middle of the room contemplating this place of the Kirtan rituals and studied once again the altar for the offerings to various Hindu gods.

Then I noticed a little cluster of Hare Krishna devotees huddled in the back behind and to the right of the altar near the kitchen, which had been the source of some really good Indian food fed to the devotees and visitors like me. The little group of former hippies turned Krishna worshipers moved toward me and began yelling at me.

"You did this, you caused this" one guy was yelling at me. He never attended the studies in the basement, but I recognized him. "I just got here. How could I have done this?" I yelled at the guy. I was stirred up; the old fight or flight adrenaline was taking charge.

I was a young man, not big but not small, and I stood my ground and faced them. At that point David rushed by carrying more stuff. As I turned to follow him, two of the devotees grabbed me from behind and shoved me up against the door of the temple. One had his hands on my throat and was squeezing as hard as he could. I was almost out of breath when a fireman ran up behind us and swatted them away. I fell down gasping for breath and saw the devotees lying around on the floor after their brief encounter with a San Francisco fire fighter. Gathering myself up quickly, I headed out the door and up the street to the car. David was already inside it, so I jumped in, quickly started the engine, wheeled down the street, and somewhat dazed, headed for 10A Judson Lane, Mill Valley, my home in the student housing section on the campus of Golden Gate Baptist Theological Seminary. There was no place else to go, nothing else to do. I was excited, and I was also scared.

The adventure had only just begun.

# Chapter 4

# Bible Study in the Temple

What happened at the temple – the fire and David's coming to our little apartment at the seminary – was preceded by an event that I never clearly understood, but I will relate it as best I can now, although it takes us back a little in time.

Timothy Wu was a young and very evangelistic student at the seminary. Since we shared a passion for personal evangelism, we became friends. I was feeling overwhelmed and inadequate as I now faced holding a Bible study in the Hare Krishna Temple, and I thought it would be good if Timothy came with me. He readily agreed, and we set a time to go into the City.

My relationship with David was naturally strained; he was wary of me and me of him. Other devotees were polite but guarded and defensive. David and company would throw questions at me that I could not answer, although I was learning as much as I could about eastern religions. To make things more uncomfortable for me, I could find nothing at all on Krishna Consciousness in the seminary library.

As was my agreement with the Swami, Timothy and I had to sit through the Kirtan before heading down to the basement for the Bible study. After a prayer, I introduced Timothy and asked him to give the teaching. He started with how he had become a Christian and moved right into a very fine account of the Gospel message. He was speaking rapidly and passionately.

After the meeting broke up I headed upstairs, and after discussing the study with some of the devotees for a while, I looked around for Timothy but didn't find him. I went back down the basement steps and saw Timothy and David engaged in animated conversation. They were both yelling, and it looked like they might be headed for a fistfight. When they noticed me watching them, they calmed down and backed away from each other. Timothy approached me, and we both turned and climbed up the stairs and up and out of the temple.

On the ride home we did not talk about what happened with David at the end of the Bible study. Timothy was silent about it for some reason, and all my attempts to find out failed. The best I could get out of him was, "Wait and see." Something had happened, that was for sure. "What do you mean? I want to know what you guys were arguing about." For some reason, he refused to tell me. Years later I figured it out. Timothy did not think that I, a good Baptist guy, could understand that he had received a 'word' from God or a vision. It was almost three weeks before I found out what transpired between David and Timothy.

A little less than a month later I made another trip from the Hare Krishna Temple to Mill Valley. This time David accompanied me on the way back to the seminary. He was silent for most of the ride, but as we were crossing the Golden Gate Bridge, he told me what had happened between him and Timothy that night. Timothy had given him a prophecy, a word of revelation that within three weeks God would take David out of the temple. All I did was listen.

Driving north on Highway 101, now in Marin, David told me about a dream he had had the previous night. He saw himself in a very large open space with peoples of the world all around him. All of a sudden he heard a trumpet blast, and looking up he saw Jesus in the clouds with a host of angels. People all around him were lifting up their arms to receive Jesus, and as they did they floated up and joined Him in the air. David said that he looked at his own feet, and they were firmly stuck to the ground. Fear rushed through him, and he woke up to find that his makeshift basement altar was on fire. He tried to put it out, but it was already too large to extinguish. He grabbed what he could and raced up the stairs. Then he ran down again, picked up some paint cans and a brush – supplies he had used to paint out the basement prior to his using it as a bedroom – and began writing in large letters those Christian slogans I saw on the walls of the temple. As the fire trucks started to arrive, he found a phone and called me.

Now his life was going to be very different.

As an endnote: Timothy Wu and I remained friends. He was the youth pastor at a Chinese Church in San Francisco, and he invited me to preach to their rather large assembly from time to time – and this was while he was at the seminary. I remember now the last time that we did evangelism together. Dr. Francis DuBose, professor of missions and evangelism at Golden Gate Seminary, had become a friend and mentor to me. Sometime in 1968 I asked him and Martin (Moishe) Rosen, who later founded Jews for Jesus, to be on the board of directors of Evangelical Concerns, a vital group composed of mostly American Baptist pastors. Around that time that Dr. DuBose asked me to conduct a tour and evangelist foray into the Haight-Ashbury. I did this several times, and on the first of these Timothy Wu came along.

Timothy and I met the students on the corner of Haight and Ashbury streets, divided up into teams of two, and agreed to return in two hours, bringing any converts with us. At the appointed hour the students began to arrive back at the appointed place. I brought two with me, and none of the students brought any, but Timothy came walking down the street with a whole group of hippie kids, twelve being the number I recall. We held a prayer and discipleship meeting right there on the street. Timothy preached and taught, and so did I. A larger crowd gathered, and several more professed faith in Jesus.

This was the Jesus People Movement. And this was not the last time I would see something similar happen on that very street. But descriptions of some of those events will emerge when I talk about Lonnie Frisbee.

# Chapter 5

# David Comes to Seminary

riving back across the bridge into Marin, now with David Hoyt in the car with all his worldly possessions, I started thinking what I was going to tell my wife Bobbie. David still had on his Hindu religious garments, and he had that look in his eye, expression on his face, and body language of someone who had totally imbibed eastern spirituality. I frankly worried how this would work. Here I am bringing a stranger into the house where my family and I lived, all in a really small two-bedroom apartment with one bathroom and a dinky kitchen, and now this weird looking guy dressed like Mahatma Gandhi takes up residence. I guessed he would have to sleep on the couch.

"Bobbie, this is David. Hey girls, this is David, come and meet him." It went something like that. No cell phones existed at that time, so our arrival was not pre-announced, and it was a shock for them, especially Bobbie, to lay eyes on David. Bobbie quietly said hello, stepped up and shook hands, then retreated a bit and just looked at the strange house guest. It was quite uncomfortable, and we stumbled about for a bit until we all came in and sat down. The time was 1967 and the place was a Southern Baptist Seminary. Everyone on campus was Caucasian, the professors mostly spoke with Southern accents, and no one looked like I did, with a mustache and slightly longer hair, and certainly no one looked liked David Hoyt. Now he would be living there among them.

What with my wife Bobbie, about as straight an arrow as you

could get, plus my two little girls, a first grader and a kindergart-ner, Dory and Grace, with neighbors on each side, there was no place to hide David.

I was working part time, and Bobbie worked as a sales clerk at the Thrifty drugstore in Corte Madera. We had the G.I. Bill, without which I would not have been able to afford a seminary education, but I was also pastor of Excelsior Baptist Church in Byron and making $10 a week.[1] We barely survived as it was.

David ended up making our tiny front room his bedroom, and we managed as best we could, but the pressure was on Bob-bie. My dear, sweet daughters made the best of it and got along with David just fine.

How it all worked out is kind of blurry to me now, but I recall David coming to classes with me, and I would hear stories of his wandering around the campus and talking to students. He spent some time with Timothy Wu, who was living in the men's dorm. Due to David's strange appearance and presence in the admin and academic buildings, a ruling was made to the effect that stu-dents could not have non-relatives living with them. (This rule is still in force.)

My job was to disciple David, and I did the best I could. All my life it seems I have been constantly busy but especially then. Somehow we fit it all in. David and I started from scratch: who is God, what is sin, what was the Fall, and the longish story about what God did about it all. David was nothing else but intense and eager. He was a sponge and grasped complex biblical ideas quickly. After a few weeks he was ready to go with me into the City on what were now routine visits and ministry on the streets of the Haight-Ashbury. It was the 'Summer of Love', which David and three others had actually organized. As I am thinking

---

1    It had been $20 a week but the deacons got mad at me for bringing migrant workers to church and baptizing them. All these years later, and I still wonder how it was that my salary did not ever go back to the starting $20 per week yet our income climbed rapidly and steeply.

through these things, I realize David Hoyt was not only one of the first, if not the first convert in the Jesus People Movement, but he was also one of the chief evangelists for the whole hippie scene in San Francisco. Wherever David went, whatever he did, his impact was outsized.

So our adventures together began. At least once a week we drove into the City, arriving as early as possible and staying as late as possible. We visited David's old friends at the Krishna Consciousness Temple and others like the Buddhist priest, Robert Sutherland, to whom David did his best to tell about Jesus. Added to them was hippie after hippie by the hundreds. Early on we wrote up and passed out flyers, some of which I still have, and we bought hundreds of Campus Crusade's, The Four Spiritual Laws, and other materials to use in our witnessing. Many hippies and others were converted during those days in 1967, but it was only the trickle before the flood that was to come.

One other thing David and I did together: he began coming with me to Byron on Saturdays and Sundays. That story comes up next and may actually be the reason why the deacons of Excelsior Baptist Church declined to restore my money.

# Chapter 6

# In
# Byron, CA

Byron is still a small farming community in a bend in the road between Brentwood and Tracy off Highway 4 in Contra Costa County. A large subdivision was developed there called Discovery Bay, but that was long after I was gone. In fact, the Excelsior Baptist Church disappeared long ago, although the old building is yet standing that once housed the Excelsior School followed by the church.

Toward the end of my first year as a seminarian I had a strong urge to pastor a church. Pastoring was what we 'young lions' were constantly talking about. We were either going to be missionaries or pastors, one or the other for sure. I wanted to pastor.

The seminary often posted announcements of churches looking for a pastor. Someone called my attention to that, I made a call to Joe Smith, the area missionary for Contra Costa County, which was east of Marin, and he offered me the chance to preach at the Excelsior Baptist Church in Byron. Was I ever excited, and I went right to work on a sermon that I was sure would cinch the deal. I was right, and quickly they 'called' me as pastor and gave me a salary of $20 per week.

I think my first day as pastor of the little church was in July of 1966. The congregation was tiny; I remember some of the folks there: Al and Ruby Belah and Hartman Shelton were the deacons. The Belahs had one daughter, and the Sheltons had two, Pam and Rhonda. (When Pam was a senior, she had no one to take her to the senior prom at Liberty High School in Brentwood, although she was a wonderful and attractive person. Harman asked me to take his daughter to it, since I was only twenty-four.) I came to love this family, and they were faithful to me the whole time. There was also Ruby Bauguss, the Lansfords, and especially Lorraine and Myron Williams. They took special care of their seminary pastor, of which they had had quite a few, and I got the chance to preach twice a week, and did not have to attend even one business meeting, which is not small thing.

On October 2, 1966, the church ordained me, and Bob Lewis, my pastor from First Baptist Church of Fairfield, California, preached the ordination sermon. My dad made the trip but my mother did not. Although a staunch Methodist, my mother was never born again, and this is not a charge against her but something she proclaimed loud and long. I never did figure that out.

A few weeks after David's arrival in Mill Valley, he began to accompany me to Byron. My practice was to travel up on Saturdays and Sundays, 75 miles one-way, meaning 300-plus miles per weekend. My 1956 Ford sedan had already been driven too many miles, and it was forever breaking down.

J.C. Penney & Co. allowed me weekends off, and I was incredibly busy with work and classes four days per week.[1] Seminary education was real graduate work. To be accepted as a student one had to have a BA degree from an accredited institution, and the professors loaded their students up with tons of reading and papers.

As I think about it now, I had begun a pattern that would excessively take me away from my family. Here were doors opening up, which seemed to me to be by the Hand of God, yet in walking through them I was also harming my family. It is something I have had to live with and wrestle with, never coming to a

---

1 An M.Div. degree normally required four years but the government money lasted only three years, so I loaded up to take the maximum units in order to graduate in three years.

clear understanding of it.

David and I began to see what inroads we could make in the Byron area. For one thing, we made contact with the local juvenile hall. David had practically grown up in state institutions; California had, in a real sense, been his father and mother. He was quite comfortable visiting there, and before long the entire boys' home was coming to church every other Sunday; the other Sunday they went to the local Methodist Church, the only other church in town.[2]

Oddly, this did not sit well with the deacons, maybe because it took my attention away from them, yet I still visited every single household in the church at least twice a month. Byron was and is so small, that I could park at the church site and walk to most every church member's house.

The situation deteriorated further when David and I started walking through the local migrant workers' camp on Hwy 4 between Byron and Brentwood. One particular family of seven quickly responded to the Gospel. They lived in a one-room shack in the migrant settlement, and I baptized all of those over about age ten. Soon other Mexican people were coming as well, and the church got crowded. Soon after this the deacons cut my salary to $10 a week.

Perhaps they knew more than I did, because trouble followed almost immediately. One Saturday morning I arrived at the church building alone without David to find that almost all the windows had been broken. Tomatoes from the fields that surrounded the building on three sides had found their way into the chapel and schoolrooms. It was a huge mess. I put out a call for help and soon most of the church members arrived to clean up the splattered tomatoes and broken glass.

The next week David was with me, and as we entered the migrant workers' housing area, two large German shepherd

---

2 As soon as the Methodist pastor heard that the boys were visiting the Baptist Church he demanded equal time and got it.

dogs rushed out to attack us. It was a fight for our lives; David and I fought them off, and soon the dogs were whimpering and whining, but David and I were a complete mess – dirty, bloody, and completely scratched up. None of the occupants of the camp, including those who had been attending church, emerged to help us, except one elderly man who told us that the priest at the Catholic Church in Brentwood had put the dogs on us.

We drove to the Excelsior Church, cleaned up, and then headed to Brentwood and the Catholic Church. Both David and I had grown up having to fight and stand up for ourselves. Parking in front of the church, we loudly called the priest out, and when he emerged we verbally let him have it, and in no uncertain terms. He knew we could have made a lot of trouble for him if we had gone to the police.

That was the last time we had any trouble, and the migrant workers continued to come to church while harvesting work was going on.

# Chapter 7

# My Years as a Tongues Speaker

prior to 2 a.m. on a winter night late in 1968 at Soul Inn (the story of which is yet to come), I had consigned anything to do with Pentecostalism to the nether regions, meaning that I thought such was error or even outright demonic. After that night, I was a tongues speaker until 1975. When I ceased speaking in tongues I continued to hold to its validity, as well as the validity of all the other charismatic gifts. It is simply that I stopped speaking in tongues, a ceasing I cannot explain.

I am not a 'cessationist', defined as someone who believes that the charismatic gifts listed in 1 Corinthians 12 and Romans 12 – at least the 'power gifts' like speaking in tongues, prophecy, and miracles – are no longer operative and are also unnecessary after the publication of the Bible. I never bought that idea, because I did not clearly see it in Scripture. I was tempted to advocate it, however, when distortions of the charismatic gifts, especially prophecy, became all too flagrant.

On the other hand, neither am I a 'continuationist'. I am better described, at the present time, as a 'semi-cessationist' and a 'semi-continuationist' and all at once, but I reserve the right to change my mind. What I mean is that the charismatic gifts of the Holy Spirit are operative, but mostly in awakenings, and during 'normal' times they recede. My position is based on two things. One, this was my experience with the JPM, and I am not the only piece of evidence; rather, I have found that my tongue speaking, and the definite beginning and ending thereof, is characteristic of many. Two, I have found in my research into awakenings in America and elsewhere that the same may be observed in some of them.

Early on in the Jesus Movement (a designation originating from where, I do not know), we called ourselves 'Street Christians'. Our fields of labor were the streets of the big cities. For me it was San Francisco, specifically the Haight-Ashbury District, where the young and restless were looking to expand their minds and explore esoteric spiritualities, and where sex and dope could be found in abundance. Sex and dope went hand in hand and likely became motivators for the majority, but there were definitely those who wanted to find God and assumed He was not to be found in the American churches. The causes for this are beyond the scope of this piece, but to identify with a 'church' was not the thing to do then.

I was a Baptist, but I mentioned this to very few people. For a while, I avoided the term 'Christian' as well. 'A follower of Jesus' is how I described myself. Eastern religions were big, Buddhism more than Hinduism, but there was the Hare Krishna thing, and the Beatles[1] made TM (Transcendental Meditation) popular for a time. There were many 'isms' vying for attention, and all of them were foreign and new to me. During 1967, I received so many rejections, beatings, and threats, that I felt like giving up and concentrating my efforts in Byron, but I remained sure that God had called me; I did not discourage easily.

Sometime in 1968 news coverage circulated of what was going on. Some reporter used the phrase 'Jesus Freak', a tag I did not appreciate and rejected in favor of 'Street Christian'. A more friendly term, 'Jesus People', was coined along the way, and I more gladly adopted that one. Later on, the whole awakening

---

1    One day I ran into George Harrison of the Beatles. He was wearing glasses with thick red heart shaped lenses. I said hello and noticing the glasses wondered how he could even see through them. I learned later that day that he had visited the devotees at the Hare Krishna Temple.

thing going on across the country was termed the 'Jesus People Movement' or JPM. This worked for almost everyone.

It is not clear to me when I realized that what I had been involved in was unusual. During my seminary years the great revivals of religion were taught, but I had no idea that the JPM was actually one of those. It was only in looking back at it that I realized that the JPM was an awakening like the great awakenings America had previously experienced, and this realization came primarily through reading the books of David Martin Lloyd-Jones and, above all, Iain Murray.

In my book, Awakenings in America and the Jesus People Movement, I attempt to demonstrate that the JPM meets the requirements for inclusion in America's great awakenings (see www.evpbooks.com).

Jesus freak was not a term of derision, as it turned out. Everyone who sought after more than could be found on main street USA was a freak of some sort, even if it did not involve sex, dope, or far out religion. Artist, poet, musician, writer, occultist, astrologer, psychic, Satanist, monk, wanderer – these and more were considered part of the freakiness that seemed to offer more. I was not really one of these, as I had already found what I had not even been looking for. The fact is that I was a babe in the woods when it came to the hip lifestyle. I was too old to be a 'teeny bopper' and felt out of place at times. I was closer to a would-be beatnik, but I soon learned how the hippie life worked.

# Chapter 8

# Three
# Bizarre Stories

Here I will stop and relate three incidents taking place in three separate years, events that were each bizarre in their own way. They illustrate the outrageous extent to which those involved in the San Francisco hippie scene had sunk into degradation, even evil, and how they desperately needed rescuing. The stories also convey a certain sense of adventure inherent in our work there, although some of it we would have been happy to avoid.

A warning must be issued at this point: the following stories are bizarre, but more than that. I have stopped short of excessively lurid detail, but the subject matter of two of the stories might disturb impressionable readers.

## The 1967 Story

David and I regularly walked up and down Haight Street during 1967, and we were meeting dozens of people every day. One girl we encountered (I will call her Sherrie) hailed from Sun Valley, a town at the northern edge of the San Fernando Valley. She was a seventeen or eighteen year old runaway of Italian descent, and she was beautiful in every way.

One or the other of us came across her several times over the course of maybe two months. We had no idea how she was surviving on the streets and couldn't tell whether our witnessing was making a dent or not. She did hang out with a small group of kids, some of whom we also got to know during our forays.

One afternoon, one of Sherrie's friends ran up to us, agitated, and announced that Sherrie was being initiated into a satanic cult at that very moment. The friend led us to the place, a store front right on Haight Street, but the windows were covered and we couldn't see in. The door was locked; no one answered our knocking, and we didn't know what to do next. Before giving up we went around to the back of the store. Again, we couldn't see in, but we could hear things, weird sounds that reminded us of chanting. Faintly, we could see lights flickering as though candles were burning. We decided to act.

We smashed open the door and rushed in. The room we entered was mostly dark with only a few candles providing any light. My impression is that there were maybe six or seven people huddled around a table in the center of the room. As we approached, most everyone scattered to reveal Sherrie lying naked on the table with someone in a black robe shaving her pubic area.

David and I pushed the people aside, picked Sherrie up off the table, and quickly half-carried/half-walked her toward the front door. We managed to open it, and in a moment we were on Haight Street, in mid-afternoon, on a summer day, with a naked teenage girl in tow. We peeled off our own shirts and covered her as fully as possible. Immediately, we headed for the car, which was parked one block down on Waller Street, and away we went.

No one followed us out of the store. If they had, there would have been a big melee that would certainly have brought the cops, and it would have been a difficult situation to explain. Once back in Marin, we called Sherrie's parents and arranged for her to fly home, which happened the very next day.

Sherrie's friend had been correct; she was being initiated into a mini satanic cult that focused on dope and sex.

About a year later I visited Sherrie and her parents in Sun Valley. They lived in a duplex on Glenoaks Blvd., the street I always took to get to my brother's house in Glendale. I had ridden down on a big road bike, and I have a photo that Sherrie's dad took of me with his daughter posing on the back of the bike in front of their place. Every time I pass that way, I think of the day David and I committed felony breaking and entering and rescuing.

## The 1968 Story

I was alone when this story unfolded. For weeks I had been walking past a store front near the corner of Cole and Haight Streets, close to where the Safeway Market stood on the corner of Stanyon. In the window was a sign notifying readers that a satanic priest was available for consultations.

I could see that in the center of the room was a desk with a chair behind it, and against the opposite wall was another chair. The desktop was bare – no phone, nothing. And there was nothing on the walls. All was empty, drab, and kind of gloomy.

There were businesses on either side and what I thought were apartments above. For weeks I often stopped at that storefront and stood there staring in and knocking on the door. My behavior might have been seen as strange, since it was obvious the place was deserted. But one day a man was sitting at the desk.

It was the middle of the afternoon as I stood at the window and tried to size the situation up. Of course, I had to knock, and when I did, the man at the desk just sat there unmoving.

He looked to be about thirty years of age, not a hippie but clean-shaven with short hair. He simply sat there, with nothing in this hands and nothing on the desk. I couldn't resist, so I turned the doorknob, found it was unlocked, and walked in.

He said nothing. I picked up the chair and moved it closer to the desk and sat down. After a few seconds, I began to question him. "Who are you?" "What are you doing here?" He responded, little by little, not making much sense or really answering my questions.

Then, after a couple minutes of this, I heard a loud explosion, like a sonic boom. Then another and another, maybe a dozen. Loud, really loud, ear splitting loud, and the guy at the desk seemed not to notice. I tried to keep up some kind of conversation while the loud booming went on. One crash seemed to come from the ceiling, the next time a wall, then another wall, then the ceiling again, then the floor – boom, boom, boom, louder that an M80 firecracker going off.

Finally, I couldn't take it any longer and walked out. Stunned, I walked up the street, away from the park, and tried to make sense out of what I had just experienced. I collected myself to some degree and  decided to go back and get to the bottom of it.

The guy was gone, but all else was the same. I began to wonder if I had not been slipped some LSD or something else. I assured myself I was in my right mind and decided to check whether anyone else had heard the booming; I thought it must have been heard for blocks.

What a shock as I went up and down the street and across the street, knocking on doors, describing what happened, and no one, not one person had heard a sound. Over the years, I have turned it around a thousand times in my mind and have been able to come up with only one explanation.

During deliverance ministry, where demons were cast out, there were often times when the demons attempted to frighten us by one means or another – threats, physical violence, and screaming, to name a few. Perhaps that's all it was – the noises were intended to scare me away. And, I must admit, if that was the case, it worked.

## The 1969 story

Steven Gaskin was a spiritual guru type who attracted hundreds of hippies. Down in the Richmond District just up from Ocean Beach, he took up shop in a storefront or some kind of hall and held what was known on the streets as the 'Monday Night Class'.

Gaskin was an eclectic, meaning he gathered his ideas from various places. He was older, educated, street wise, spiritually wise, and a compelling speaker. I had heard of him for some time, but since I never heard of him visiting the Haight, I paid him little heed. Then I heard that he was teaching tantric yoga to the hippies, meaning they were getting naked, pairing off, and having sex while Gaskin instructed them. This I had to see.

One Monday evening, I made the trip by car from Marin where I was living. Sure enough, what I heard was true. Within ten feet of the front door, in the semi-darkness, dozens of couples were having sexual intercourse while Gaskin sat in the lotus position up on a raised platform and coached them. Part of his line was that union with god is approached through human union, and that meant intercourse. So everyone was getting spiritual.

I came back on the next few Mondays armed with a flyer I had written that started shaking things up. It did not take long before I was causing a problem, but I persisted and persisted, until finally I was barred and ignored.

That is not the end of the story, however. It was not long before Gaskin and crew, now called The Farm, moved out of San Francisco and headed east for an actual farm. The strange thing is, they stopped for a rest stop in their big yellow buses in Nashville, Tennessee, at the very moment and at the very spot I was standing that day.

I do not recall why I was in Tennessee at all, probably speaking at a church in the city, and I just happened to be downtown by the Grand Ole Opry, when the first bus showed up. Instantly, I knew who they were by the writing on the sides of the buses, but imagine their surprise and exasperation! I was the first person each one saw as they got off the bus and the last person they wanted to see.

# Chapter 9

# Soul Inn

Shortly after my graduation from Golden Gate Seminary, the Philpotts – wife Bobbie, daughters Dory and Grace, and I[1] – had nowhere to go, so we moved in with my parents on Whitegate Avenue in the twin cities of Sunland and Tujunga, snuggled up against the San Gabriel Mountains in the northern most part of Los Angeles. My parents had moved to this lovely little community from Portland, Oregon, in 1954, and it was where I attended Verdugo Hills High School. I had resigned as pastor from the Excelsior Baptist Church of Byron in 1968, and there were no more options for my working with Southern Baptists, so I was on my own.[2]

Then began a tortuous period where I alternated doing construction work all over the LA area[3] for a couple weeks with my father-in-law, Robert Davidson, then traveled back to the Bay Area. After making some money (Bobbie worked as a telephone operator), I would hitchhike up to San Francisco and continue my work in the Haight-Ashbury.[4] This was the time during which

---

1   Son Vernon would come along about a year later.

2   Though I had been appointed as a missionary of what was then entitled The Home Mission Board, I was denied work as a missionary to the hippies in San Francisco, since the California Southern Baptists would not give a salary to anyone who spoke in tongues.

3   I recall building a barn for horses in Malibu overlooking the Pacific Ocean and remodeling a dentist's office in Hollywood.

4   There were times it would take more than a day to make the trip, and in winter it could be most miserable.

I worked with David, and the Jesus People Movement was in full bloom. This was also the period I often stayed at the Anchor Rescue Mission in the Fillmore District.

Sisters Drayton and Yvonne, large and wonderful and most gracious African American women, ran the Anchor Rescue Mission near the corner of McAllister and Fillmore streets.[5] David discovered the place and stayed there from time to time. Whenever I returned after my two weeks in LA, I would also stay there.

Large numbers of white hippies descended upon the mission every evening for dinner. David and I peeled potatoes, cut up vegetables, preached and sang to the hippies, and cleaned up afterwards. It worked for both the sisters and for us.[6] While staying at the Anchor Rescue Mission, one thing I learned was not to carry a wallet or money with me. More than a few times I was robbed, usually at knifepoint, and after a while the thieves left me alone, because they knew I carried nothing of value.

It was at the mission that I finally became convinced that there was an actual devil and demons. It happened this way: One of the sisters told me there was a man who frequented the place who was demon possessed. I listened to her, inwardly chuckled, and decided to just keep my mouth shut. One night after I thought everyone was gone, I was sitting in a chair in a kind of lounge area in the center of the mission, when I heard a noise deep in the back behind the kitchen. I turned to see the person in question, a fairly tall white guy, walking toward the front door. For some reason it occurred to me to use the occasion as a chance to test whether the guy did have demons or not. And, of course, if he did, it would challenge my worldview. So I said, in a loud voice, "Jesus." The guy jumped straight up in the air, perhaps a foot off the ground, then came down and continued walking. I

---

5 The building that housed the mission was torn down a couple decades ago, sadly.

6    I still have a necktie I selected from the free clothes closet located in the mission; it is beautiful and many think it is brand new.

did this several times, and the result was the same each time. He got to the door, never once looking my way, opened it, walked out, and that was it. I sprang from the chair, locked the door, and spent a rather tense night there at the mission.

I loved preaching to the hippies every evening, but I felt it was wise to find someplace else to live, until I was able to bring my family back up north. That was one impetus for starting Christian houses, though not the primary one.

One of the first Christian houses on the West Coast was Soul Inn, born out of the Lincoln Park Baptist Church. The Soul Inn began late in 1968. The House of Acts in Novato, led by Ted and Liz Wise, Dan and Sandy Sands, Jim Dopp, Steve Heathner, Lonnie Frisbee, Rick and Meagan Zacks, and others was begun earlier, sometime in 1967. It was maybe the first of all the Christian communes of the Jesus People Movement. John MacDonald wrote The House of Acts in 1970, published by Creation House, in which he describes that period and the beginning of the house.

The Way Inn, a Christian house that David began in 1967, not long after his conversion and after he moved out of my place at Golden Gate Seminary, preceded Soul Inn as well.

The Way Inn was in Lancaster, California, where David had landed after an attempt to go to a Bible college in the Los Angeles Area. David wanted to grow in his knowledge of the Bible, which had prompted his move out of our place at the seminary. I recall visiting the Way Inn, a series of dilapidated buildings that had once been a TB sanitarium, and David gave me an old faded blue jean jacket that had been worn by a patient, likely a decade or more before. I proceeded to wear that jean jacket throughout my ministry in San Francisco, and I still have it, with some leftover Gospel tracks we used still in the pockets.[7]

The second time I travelled to Lancaster, David and company,

---

7    Up until then I had worn my field jacket from my military days, but as we began to engage, in various ways, with the anti-war demonstrations, it became painfully clear that I needed a change of clothing.

which included Gary Goodell and the members of a Four Square Gospel Church pastored by Gary's father, had utterly transformed the place into a thriving community filled with hippie converts. How I wish I had been into photography at that time.

## Back to the Story of Soul Inn

Among the many young people who were becoming Christians were a significant number of the homeless, mostly because they had walked away from their parents to live the hippie life. Many of them had burned bridges or were so enraptured by their new lives in Christ that they preferred to stay where that had happened.

Al Gossett was pastor at Lincoln Park Baptist Church, a storefront church in the Richmond District of San Francisco. Al was a graduate of Golden Gate, and he and his wife Letty were so very friendly, accommodating, and eager to reach out to the hippies. The major influences and driving forces behind the Lincoln Park church were really Dr. Francis DuBose and his wife Dorothy. It was Dr. Dubose who, through his classes and his personal involvement in what I was doing in the City, made a very large impact on me. He was a great preacher of the old time Southern Baptist style, and in class after class he focused on the passage in John 20:21 where Jesus told His disciples, "As the Father has sent me, even so I am sending you." He hammered that verse in every class, and I got it. I saw myself as one being sent, and sent directly by Jesus. My dear old friend Dr. DuBose is gone now, but I will never forget that kind and generous man.

Little by little, I spoke to various folks at Lincoln Park about the need to house new converts, and the topic of starting a live-in place came up at a business meeting. They gave me the green light to move ahead with adapting the few small Sunday school classrooms into a kind of dormitory and gather those things necessary to care for new believers, chief of these was a shower arrangement that eventually found a home in the back end of the kitchen.

Soul Inn's opening night was quite unforgettable. The Salvation Army had donated bunk beds and blankets to us, we scrapped up a few kitchen implements, paper plates, and plastic spoons and forks, and we were ready to open the doors.

On the corner of what I think is Haight Street and Clayton, at about four p.m. each day, a grass roots organization of Hippies called the Diggers[8] set up a card table and tried to steer people into finding food, shelter, and medical help. For weeks I had been stopping by and telling them the Soul Inn would soon open. Finally the day arrived, and I made the grand announcement.

That evening, four of us were sitting around a makeshift table, a sheet of plywood sitting on the backs of four metal chairs. Dave Palma, Paul Finn, Roy,[9] and I were talking about spending our first night at the Soul Inn. It was late—a winter's night—and our only remaining food, a quart can of pork and beans, had just a small amount left in it. That was it, no other food, but we did have some Lipton tea bags. It must have been about ten o'clock, and there was a knock on the door. Outside stood twenty-six hippies, mostly young, who had just walked several long miles from the Haight to Balboa Street between 41st and 42nd Avenues in the Richmond District.[10] The Diggers had given out the address as requested, but now what? Paul Finn and I went back into the kitchen or what passed for one, and we started scooping pork and beans into paper bowls. Within a very short time, both of us realized we were in the middle of a miracle. There was enough in the can to feed all twenty-six people, with as much left as when we started. I scooped, and Paul carried the bowls in. Twenty-six bowls filled with pork and beans that came out of

---

8    There was also a group called The Haight Defense Committee operating at that time and it may have been this group of hippie activists instead of the Diggers I notified about the opening of Soul Inn.

9    I have a photo of Roy but his last name escapes me.

10    The location is now a restaurant.

what had been a nearly empty quart can.[11] That was only one of what would be many miracles, no two identical, but happening when we least expected them. There were also miracles of healing that were plain and incontrovertible – not a large number, and they did not happen as seen on television. I tended to play down the miracles, knowing from the biblical Gospel writers that Jesus had done the same. As time went on, I realized why Jesus did not publicize or sensationalize miracles – strange and dangerous results often follow. But there were indeed miracles.

Soul Inn did not last long, and the primary reason was that I needed to move my family up from Los Angeles.

In late 1968 the Philpotts, David Hoyt and wife Victoria, and David and Margaret Best (Margaret and Victoria were sisters) moved to San Rafael and shared a rental on D Street. This was the beginning of a Christian house we called Zion's Inn.

---

11   After not talking to him since about 1970, Paul Finn called me from his hometown of New York a few years ago, maybe 2008, and we talked about the old days. He and Dave Palma, also from New York, had gone home when Soul Inn closed, and each started their own Christian House, one of which was called Philadelphia House and the other, The House of Philadelphia. (The word Philadelphia must have meant a lot to them.) Paul and I talked, and I thought it was a chance to see whether or not I had been wrong about the miracle of the food multiplication. I asked Paul what he remembered about the evening all the hippies showed up on our first night. He said, "Oh yeah, the big miracle. Yeah, I remember it, and it is like I am right there now." We went on for a while, but I had the confirmation I was hoping for. Funny how it is that miracles impact us; even when we see them, it is often hard for us to admit they actually happened.

# Chapter 10

# Zion's Inn

The Soul Inn did not last for long. It was under the direction of a Baptist church, with its congregational, democratic form of government, so the house was subject to the will of too many congregants who did not especially like our use of the storefront church. Toward the end, there were only a few of us left living at Soul Inn, and one by one the residents moved on to various places. Some even returned home.

San Rafael, the largest town in Marin County and also the county seat, still had reasonable rental prices. The smallish home we rented was a bit too small, and this was the time that David and I began painting houses to support our ministry work, but only on rare occasions did it provide sufficient money for us.

Three couples living in the same house did not work out for long. After about six months, the Hoyts and Philpotts moved to a larger house on Greenfield Avenue, also in San Rafael. David and I transformed its large basement into living quarters, adding three additional bedrooms. We didn't care much about permits; we only cared that it worked.

Our consistent problem was what to do with young women who became believers in Jesus and had nowhere to go. Many times we simply placed them homeward bound on trains, planes, or buses. Some had no home to go to, so we had to do something.

David had the idea first. He bought a VW van – yes, a real hippie-mobile – and painted "Zion's Inn for Girls" on the side. David and I used that van for our painting business and also drove it for the street evangelism in the City. It was extremely useful.

Soon girls began to move in, mostly for short durations, but some stayed long enough to get stabilized once again. During this period we somehow made friends with a Marin County judge, Peter Allen Smith, who began sending girls to us as a kind of diversionary practice, rather than sending them to jail. He required that Bobbie and I become foster parents, and we did this for a number of girls. It also meant that some court-provided money was coming into the house.[1]

It was here on Greenfield Avenue that I began a Tuesday night Bible study, a tradition that has continued to this day, although in different locations.[2] Someone who began attending the meetings and occasionally leading them was Martin Rosen, who was then with the American Board of Missions to the Jews (now Chosen People Ministries) and who later became 'Moishe' Rosen of Jews for Jesus. This connection with Rosen lasted many years, and he and I often worked together doing various kinds of ministries. My oldest daughter Dory was an administrative assistant to his first secretary while she attended high school.

Within a short time, the front room of Zion's Inn could not accommodate the crowd, so we moved the study just one block down the street to John Wesley Hall at the United Methodist Church of San Rafael. It was at this Bible study where miraculous events began to occur again, mostly healings. I was shocked at this, seeing it happen right in front of me and fairly often. Those who know me know I am a terrible skeptic, and it takes a lot of evidence to convince me.

---

1    Our contacts with Marin County and the City of San Rafael and the good reputation we were able to build with these local governments allowed us to open two 'Christian Houses' especially for drug addicts and alcoholics - again a sort of diversionary assignment rather than to jail. This ministry worked out wonderfully well, and some of our top leaders emerged from these houses.

2    Son Vernon now leads this Tuesday night Bible Study in the fellowship hall of Miller Avenue Church.

## Family Miracle Story

I will tell the story of one rather incredible miracle. It was about a week after David and Victoria moved to Walnut Creek. My painting work had not been going well; it was before I developed a real painting business employing some of the young men and women living in our houses (yes, many more houses were to come), and one morning we had nothing to eat.

At the breakfast table sat Bobbie, Dory, Grace, and Vernon, who was either an infant or about to be born. In addition, there was Kathy Granger, Linda Patton, and Sher Keaton. Bobbie had boiled some water for the few tea bags we had left. And that was all we had. I can still see us, a motley crew for sure, and we prayed and asked God to take care of us. As if on cue, there was a knock on the door. I answered it, and there stood two people, a man and a woman, both about my age, and they were holding several white bags. They held out the bags toward me, and I took them, carried them back to the kitchen, came back, and received another bag or two. They turned to leave, and I thanked them as they retreated down the stairs and climbed into a newish white panel van (I did not yet know what was in the white bags). They drove off, and I returned to the kitchen. There on the table was a full breakfast of eggs, bacon, potatoes, and milk - the works - exactly enough food for the lot of us. We thanked God for His provision and loved every second of that meal. When we finished, it began to dawn on us what had just happened. Somehow we did not get it right away. But then we realized that someone, perhaps angels, had appeared to answer our prayer.

We examined the bags and the food containers, top and bottom. Even on the bottom of the paper plates there was no indication by whom or where the cups and plates had been made. Nothing. Not a clue. I had never seen the people before and I never saw them again. After all these years I am still amazed. After that event, I rarely worried about our needs being met.

That was breakfast; there was still no money for lunch or dinner. I do not recall how it was we survived, but we did. Never again would Zion's Inn for Girls ever suffer want. And it was not pennies from heaven that turned things around it was ads placed in the Marin Independent Journal that read, "Seminary Student and Crew," that God used to bring us what we needed.

It was after about one year at Zion's Inn that David and Victoria moved to Walnut Creek to begin a new work. David and I were both type-A leaders who knew how things should be done, and thus we had times of conflict. I have often wondered what might have been, if we had been able to continue working closely together.

My daughter Dory reminded me just recently of one memory from the Zion's Inn days that needs to be told. My daughters Dory and Grace shared a bedroom that David and I had constructed in the basement. One mid-morning, I returned to the Greenfield house or Zion's Inn and saw fire trucks blocking the street. A jolt of fear ran through me as I realized the trucks were parked right in front of our house. As I rushed to the scene, I found my family – Dory, Grace, and Bobbie – standing in front of the house, watching smoke billow out of the basement. Dory, who was crying and shaken, told me that when the girls went to school a space heater must have been left on and started the fire. She was scared to death I would blame her, and I did my best to let her know it was all okay.

The smoke from the fire made the entire house uninhabitable. The landlady, Gloria Ladd, graciously stepped in and offered us the use of a house she owned in Ross, a mansion really, that happened to be vacant. We lived in that sprawling Victorian type house until the Greenfield place was ready to reoccupy.

Until more recently, I forgot about this incident, perhaps because it brings up my lack of caring for my own family during the turbulent years of the JPM. Times of awakenings are wonderful, but there is a price to pay. Those involved will often go through very trying times at minimum, and some of the stories I hope to relate toward the close of these memoirs are not comfortable to recount.

# Chapter II

# Berachah House

Two of the seminary students of the newspaper classified ad, "Seminary Student and Crew" were Paul Bryant and Oliver Heath. They were first year students at Golden Gate Seminary; both had established ties with Southern Baptists and were, in fact, raised in SBC churches. Perhaps because of that, they wanted something new and different, and they found it with our Christian House Ministry, as we called it then.

It was in 1968 that Paul and Ollie joined with us. The requirement was singular: a desire and willingness to follow Jesus was it. Ollie went on to start a Christian house in Mill Valley, but Paul established Berachah House in San Anselmo, a town in Marin next door to San Rafael.

Berachah means 'blessed' in Hebrew, therefore a house of blessing, and it definitely was. Gloria Ladd owned both houses, the Greenfield house called Zion's Inn and the house on Knoll Road in San Anselmo we called Berachah House.[1]

Every bedroom in the house was claimed days before we acquired possession of it. Each of the four small bedrooms had two occupants. No one paid rent, no one turned over their money to Paul, and there were no demands. But here were now

---

1    Gloria, sadly, ended up with a wild Pentecostal cult, and due to strange prophesies, murdered both of her teenage sons and wound up spending the rest of her life in a psychiatric prison. It was a horrible event that shook the tiny Christian community, and it still impacts it to some degree.

eight young men who needed to go to work. So was born a house painting business. At one point we had three crews going, and I spent my time giving estimates and making sure the crews were properly equipped. Wages were $5 an hour per painter; that was how I figured the cost estimate. We could paint most houses in one week, and we did good work. With three painters per job, a customer got a house painted for around $600 plus materials, which was a good deal then.

A young man who came to the Tuesday night Bible study on Greenfield in 1968 was Mark Buckley, who later married a young woman in the ministry and also started a construction crew. Mark contributed greatly to our Christian House Ministry and became a house leader and a pastor – really an amazing man. I still have the hammer Mark gave to me back then (some forty-five years ago now), when I worked with his crew putting shingles on the sides of a house he was working on in San Anselmo.

Mark married Chris Kenner, and together they operated Solid Rock, our Christian House in Novato. Mark later became the founding pastor of the Church of the Open Door in Novato and oversaw the Christian bookstore there.[2] Mark and I, along with Kenny Sanders, whom I will discuss soon, became very close and essentially guided the JPM in Marin.[3] Mark later moved to Phoenix, Arizona, and founded what soon became a large church.

A tall, thin, longhaired hippie named Greg Beumer lived in Berachah House, as did Malcolm Dawes; they both played guitar and became key members in our band Joyful Noise. Most of the practices for the band in its early days were at Berachah House.

---

2    In many of the cities where we established houses we also opened up a Christian bookstore. The first was the Christian General Store in San Rafael, where I had my office for a decade and operated the Marin Christian Counseling Center, a ministry that became amazingly significant.

3    The importance of Mark Buckley and Kenny Sanders, along with their wives, deserves much more attention than provided here. They were in fact some of the major players in the Jesus People Movement as a whole.

Greg wrote his first song with a Christian theme entitled, "You'll Never Get to Heaven on LSD," and it became the most popular of all the songs Joyful Noise ever performed. Everyone liked to think up new verses with substances or behaviors well suited to the hippie life but ill suited to a Christian one.

At the house, Paul taught a Bible study for a gathering of kids who attended Drake High. I recall an incident that occurred at the house, which reflects some of the trials and tribulations of running such a place.

It must have been Easter, 1970, and one of the occupants of the house had arranged for the people who showed up at the regular Tuesday night Bible study to gather Easter Sunday morning wearing nothing other than sheets. He made it clear: even under garments were not acceptable. No, everyone was going to greet resurrection Sunday with nothing on besides a sheet.

The mother of one of the girls who attended the study at Berachah House called me. Her daughter had told her mother what was afoot. Not too pleased, I rushed over to the house, learned that Paul was away in San Diego with his family, gathered the occupants, and let them have it. The instigator would not back down but tried to justify himself with weird, icky-gooey, spiritual talk. Seeing that he was about to prevail, I was forced to utter a phrase that served me well during those years: "You have two choices – 101 South or 101 North." Highway 101 cuts through the county north and south and was the main way in and out. His choice was south, meaning San Francisco, so I dropped him off at a freeway onramp.

Berachah House survived for a couple of years but folded when Paul married. It was one of the first of its kind, and perhaps thirty or more young men lived there. One of these was Kenny Sanders. When I first met him, I could not see his face for the longish, tangled hair that obscured it. Kenny, whose father had been one of Martin Luther King's attorneys, was one of the first black hippies to show up, and he became a major part of our ministry in Marin County and later on in Petaluma in Sonoma

County.

Kenny later led a painting crew, was a fabulous painter, a part of Joyful Noise, the founding pastor of Church of the Open Door in Petaluma, and along with Mark Buckley and me, a director of the entire ministry. He married Mary Jensen, who was a student at San Rafael High School and led the small Christian group there; Mary was a tireless evangelist whose witness led to the conversion of Bob Burns, who became one of the pastors in the Church of the Open Door family. Kenny and Mary later had three children, and Kenny became a medical doctor with Kaiser Permanente. Now retired, Kenny is attending seminary[4] and doing mission work along with Mary.[5]

---

4    Most of the leaders in our Bay Area ministry never attended seminary or Bible college. They were self-taught people who took advantage of the continuing stream of discipleship programs we involved ourselves in.

5    Mary Sanders became an artist, and her consistent testimony and witness saw many come to Christ as a result.

# Chapter 12

# Early Leaders in Marin County

## The Hippie Scene Degenerates

The hippie thing was done by the summer of 1968, and by 1969 the Haight-Ashbury had utterly changed. Long gone was the 1967 Summer of Love, but despite the radical change, the unabated influx of kids from all over the country continued, likely because the hippie thing had moved eastward over the previous year. They were easy to spot with their sleeping bags and suitcases and were the kids I approached and shared the message of Jesus with. They were often runaways, and what they found in the 'liberating mecca of love' disillusioned and discouraged them. Now they were scared, broke, and desperate. The girls had often been molested in one way or another, and the guys often turned to drug dealing and prostitution.

The Switchboard was a hippie organization set up to assist America's youth looking for a new way of living and provided 'trip masters' for those wishing to expand their minds by taking LSD. Owsley was the favorite brand then, and several trip masters turned out to be little more than rapists. One day, angered by tales I had been hearing from both young men and women,[1] I walked into the old Victorian on Fell Street, where the Switch-

---

1    On Haight Street I was known as someone to turn to, and it was not unusual for emergency cases to find their way to me. I found that the local police and medical people were extremely helpful and competent in those days.

board was housed, and standing in the large front office I began calling them out, challenging them all to a fight, right then and there. I cut loose with, "You raping, robbing jerks, you need to go to prison, and I'm going to see to it, if you continue, you %$#*&+$s." Not too Christian, perhaps, which is debatable, but considering my size and physical condition in those days, few would have wanted to accept the challenge.

The predators had descended into the district by the middle of 1968. Even the motorcycle gangs were there in large numbers. People's minds had indeed been expanded by marijuana, LSD, peyote, magic mushrooms, and mescaline, so that heroin and meth were becoming the new drugs of choice. No one wore flowers in their hair anymore. Drug dealers were everywhere, as were the pimps and the porn makers. Good-looking young flesh, mostly white, was up for grabs. This is not racist in any sense, just true.

The kids kept coming, and once in a while we were able to rescue some. We sent many young people home on buses, trains, and planes. Sometimes parents traveled long distances by car to claim their children.

I must relate a story, since I have included her biography in this book. We called her Mary K., and she had sunk to real lows by the summer of 1968. She had been a high class business professional but heroin did her in. There she was, standing on Haight Street, flagging down cars. I called out to her, she stopped and listened, and as I presented the forgiveness we have in Jesus, she was immediately converted right in front of me. I took her to Zion's Inn, and she lived with us for about a year, until she married a young man who attended the Tuesday night Bible Study. Mary K. was one of the original members of Joyful Noise, and through her testimony at our concerts in high schools and churches around the state, I would estimate that several hundred kids' lives where changed. She is someone special, and so is her husband Chuck Mancebo.

Sometime in 1970, I turned my attention exclusively to

Marin County where I was living, since the work there was in full bloom.

## Leaders Emerge

In 1969, I had met Mike Riley and Roger Hoffman, both students at Golden Gate Seminary. Like Paul Bryant and Oliver Heath, they were attracted to a different kind of Christian ministry and were also interested in the charismatic part of the Jesus Movement. They soon saw that we were in desperate need for some theologically trained people, so Mike and Roger led the opening of a new Christian house in Mill Valley on Ethel Avenue. At one point they asked me to come to the school they attended, my old alma mater, to meet a friend of theirs who had expressed interest in working with us. His name was Bob Hymers.

Bob, whose full name is Robert Leslie Hymers, Jr., would play a very large role in the ministry we were developing in Marin. He was one of the best preachers I had ever heard; yet he was quite different in many ways. A Southern Baptist, not the slightest charismatic, but a real fighting fundamentalist, he loved evangelism and was tireless in this area. A brilliant man of the highest IQ I had ever met (during his high school years in Los Angeles he would be the lead in several plays at once and could memorize all the lines without confusing them), he and I became close friends.

Bob, Moishe Rosen, and I became fairly well suited to different kinds of ministry: demonstrations, protests, infiltrating antiwar demonstrations, book burning events, picketing the Russian Consulate in San Francisco, and other forms of street evangelism, including street preaching and the use of tracts, known as broadsides. It was Moishe who, being older than Bob and I and with experience and inventiveness we could not match, spurred us onto these new approaches. Led by Moishe, we quickly organized many demonstrations. We regularly managed to get leaflet materials composed and prepared for printing, placards made by the dozen, and the call put out to be at a certain place at a certain time. Hundreds of Jesus freaks would show up, marching and handing out flyers. It was a wild and exciting time.

Moishe taught me how to get media coverage from radio, newspapers, and television stations at whatever event we were up to; it worked wonderfully well. The attention we received served to inspire other Jesus freaks all over the country to try the same things; thus it served as a kind of cross-pollinization process, and the same sort of strategies began to spread across the nation.

Bob was an exciting preacher, and we brought together many of our Bible study groups and material to new Sunday evening gatherings. We met in San Rafael at both the Lucas Valley Community Church, pastored by Dale Nystrom, and The Christian Church, pastored by Chuck Boman. We also rented out the Episcopal Church in San Rafael's suburb of Lucas Valley.

I was attracted to the Presbyterian form of government as opposed to either the congregational style I had learned as a Baptist, or an episcopal, hierarchical style, like the Catholic or Episcopal churches. As a result, we developed an eldership structure within our Christian House Ministries. By the time Mike, Roger, and Bob came along, our eldership consisted of Mark, Kenny, and me. Some other key leaders, who later became elders, were Bob Gaulden, Bob Burns, and Cliff Silliman. Paul Bryant and Oliver Heath had already moved on to other things, so Mike, Roger, and Bob joined Mark, Kenny, and me to form a group of elders; I served as the senior elder, but this was all informal and not recorded in any way. This came about in 1971, but I am getting ahead of my story.

# Chapter 13

# Joyful Noise

Music, predominantly guitar music, was prominent in the JPM. Early in 1968, I began learning to play the guitar, never picking up bass or lead, but learning just enough chords to play most of the Jesus songs. During that period I wrote a few simple choruses, and I notice that some of them are still sung to this day.

At Excelsior Baptist Church in Byron we sang hymns with a piano accompaniment. The same had been true at First Baptist at Fairfield. At the Bible studies, however, the guitar was the mobile instrument of choice, and the music was modeled on the rock and roll we had all grown up with. Bands quickly emerged that wrote and played their own songs, and the band we formed out of my Tuesday night Bible study was called Joyful Noise. Greg Beumer, Rick Ricketts, Kenny Sanders, Jeanine Wright, Donna Hays, Malcolm Dawes, Tommy Gaulden, Gary Bartholomew, Jimmy Ayala, Linda Fritz Patton, Mary Kay Herb, Mark Buckley, Chris Kenner, Kenny Hopkins, and others made up Joyful Noise over a period of four years. I played rhythm guitar and sang lead. (My childhood severe ear infections served me well in Joyful Noise and as a preacher, because to compensate for my hearing loss I developed a loud, strong voice.)

Undoubtedly, the most productive and fun years of my life were those spent in the ministry of Joyful Noise. We were not musically polished, but we wrote most of our own music and were equipped to play anywhere, anytime. We played at nearly all the high schools in Marin County, at many churches, and on the street, in parks, in private homes, and even once in San Quentin State Prison.

Joyful Noise had a growing reputation for performing and preaching at drug abuse assemblies in high schools. We would set up and quickly play a song or two – songs like You'll Never Get to Heaven on LSD; Oh Holy Joe; The Christian Way of Life; There's a Great Day Coming; One Name; Jesus, Jesus, When I Hear that Golden Name; and This Little Light of Mine. Then one of us would give a testimony, followed by another song or two, then another testimony, until I would finally preach a short sermon and give the standard appeal. Time and again, nearly the entire audience to whom we were singing would respond and be apparently converted. One event stands out in my mind.

Glenn County school system in Northern California invited us to spend an entire day at their high school of 95 students. After the assembly, where we played our music and gave testimonies, we split up into groups of two and visited every classroom for more testimonies and Q and A. At the end of the day we added up lists of names totaling 96 people who had made a commitment to Christ, one more than the student body. I sent these names and addresses with phone numbers to a local ministerial association for follow up. It was quite a joyful ride home for Joyful Noise.

## We Travel Afar

Due to the influence of Cora Vance, a wonderful Christian lady I had met at a Women's charismatic meeting where I had spoken in Atlanta, Georgia, the Atlanta school district hired us to conduct drug abuse assemblies at each of their high schools. It took us three weeks to complete the circuit, holding at least two assemblies each day. On one such occasion, we were scheduled for an assembly during first period in the school's gym. En route, we lost our way and arrived late. When we opened the door to the gym we found it packed wall to wall with kids sitting silently, patiently on the benches, at least 2,000 of them. In silence we set up the band. Guitars were not in tune, we had no time to warm up voices or tune instruments, and the time was slipping away. We were introduced, I made some sort of apology for being late, and we opened up with a couple of songs, which we performed badly. It was apparent we had to shut down.

One of our Joyful Noise crew, a seventeen year old newcomer named Kenny Hopkins, stepped forward to sing and play Jesus, Jesus, When I Hear that Golden Name. It is a slow, quiet, meditative song, almost like a love song to Jesus, and when Kenny was finished he said a few words and stepped back. The time was gone, the bell for the second period was ringing, and I simply asked anyone who wanted to be a follower of Jesus to stand up. The entire place responded, teachers and students alike. No sound, no excitement. My few sentences lasted less than a minute. Even today it thrills me. At this point in my life I would not count all those who stood to have been converted. Yet, in the JPM the Spirit of God was poured out in unusual ways. Times of awakening are not like normal times.

Besides the assemblies at the Atlanta area high schools, Joyful Noise played at churches in the evenings and walked onto the campuses of prominent colleges such as Emory University, presenting our typical song and testimony formula. The results were mixed or unknown, but whenever we set up and started, crowds gathered.

Cora Vance had arranged for us to play somewhere south of Atlanta – Rome being the name of the city I think – at a Southern Baptist school whose focus happened to be music. We arrived mid-morning and walked around the campus. I recall taking advantage of extra time to do some running. At noon they invited us to lunch in the student cafeteria, where many students joined with us for conversation. They were curious to see the hippie-looking Christians, not the usual appearance on that campus. Taped to the walls in the cafeteria we found flyers about our arrival that showed a picture of our band playing at the Protestant Chapel in San Quentin Prison.

The 'concert' was scheduled for 3 p.m. We began practice around 2 p.m. and were overwhelmed by the beautiful, old music hall we found ourselves in. At 3 p.m. we looked out to see the hall utterly packed with students and faculty. A bad case of nervousness overcame all of us, and Malcolm was so impacted he had intestinal problems and wouldn't come out of the bathroom. Time was slipping away. With no lead guitar we decided to do a few easy choruses. I was rarely nervous at high school presentations, but here I was almost shaking. We tried to open with There's a Great Day Coming, a tune written by David Hoyt in 1967, but on my very first downward stroke on the guitar, I broke the bottom E string. I handed the guitar down to Gary Bartholomew and said a few things while the broken string was replaced. Then, starting again, I broke the very same string first strike down on the D chord.

Fighting panic, I smiled and said something like, "I guess the Holy Spirit wants something else." So it was testimony time as usual. I was not able to gauge the impact of our work, but ever since that day I have often imagined our little band playing some of our songs in that rarified atmosphere.

For four years requests for Joyful Noise came in. We turned down more invitations than we accepted, only because we lacked the time. We never charged for this ministry, but money for food, gas, and lodging had a way of showing up. Once we spent a week at the University of Texas in Austin for a student-led religious week, sponsored by the Southern Baptist Student Union there. Also there that week was Maranatha, the lead band from Calvary Chapel, led by Chuck Girard. They were musically very good, and we were not, but it did not matter, as we saw many conversions during that week.

Requests for Joyful Noise slowed and finally stopped altogether, so we disbanded. That was 1972.

# Chapter 14

# On the Road with Paul and Oliver

In the spring of 1969, Paul Bryant, Oliver Heath, and I set out in Ollie's new, red Volkswagen bug for Mobile, Alabama. The little car was stuffed with printed material ready for handing out along the way. On the road we stopped at every college or university we came across. I would haul out my guitar, set up someplace on campus, sing some songs, and preach short little sermons when a crowd gathered. Our California license plates were usually enough to attract attention, and I looked somewhat like a hippie, which few had ever seen up close in many of the places we visited. After the short preaching, we would hand out literature and talk individually with those who were interested. Paul and Ollie were exceptionally adroit at personal evangelism during such times.

My friend, Prince Altom, arranged our visit to his Southern Baptist alma mater, Hardin-Simmons University in Abilene, Texas. Word had not trickled down to the campus police, and we were ordered off the campus and threatened with arrest. But after some pressure from the students, the school officials understood we really were Christians and not troublemakers. They made an abrupt turnabout, welcomed us, and gave us freedom to do our ministry.

Secular schools all along our route received us to some degree. I doubt this would happen now, but it was characteristic of the Jesus Movement to be welcomed on campuses of all kinds. Of course, the 'One Way' theology we constantly proclaimed ruffled some feathers, but it seemed to us then that God's hand was upon us.

In most places we visited, no one was aware of a spiritual awakening or revival happening. However, the news media knew about it to some extent and alerted many to the events taking place in California, and that opened doors for us as we went. Some churches welcomed us, and some did not, but the group most open to us was youth who were trying to emulate the hippie thing. In almost every town we visited there was someplace where the kids hung out, maybe a coffee house, a café, or a park. We only had to drive around a short while to find the spot.

Paul, Ollie, and I were not exactly outgoing people naturally, but during this period we were able to easily approach a group of kids and start handing out literature. Conversations ensued, and almost always some would trust Jesus as Savior. Since we were meeting the kids mostly on the street, on the campus, or in a hangout, we didn't give an altar call or invitation of any kind, which was what I practiced in my pastoral ministry. Instead, while we talked, people simply experienced the new birth. This, too, was typical of the Jesus Movement; people seemed to be specially brought to us, and then, in some way, were touched by the Holy Spirit.

## A Texas Story

I will relate an event, one of the many wild and crazy things that happened on that trip. We were in Houston, Texas. Dr. Francis DuBose had arranged for us to visit several churches he knew from having lived there. Somehow, we were also invited to one of the flagship churches among Southern Baptists, First Baptist Church of Dallas, where Dr. W. A. Criswell was pastor. While we were in Houston, we discovered a scheduling error: we were to be in both Dallas and Houston at the same time. In fact, on that one Sunday morning we were supposed to be in two Houston churches and the one in Dallas. We had to split up. Paul and Ollie covered the Houston churches while I drove the 'bug' to Dallas.

It was a dark and stormy night, however, and the windshield wipers were not working on Ollie's car. Over two hundred miles separate the two great Texan cities, and I left after a Saturday evening youth gathering in a huge Houston church. For hours it poured, and I was scared to death. Every car on the road seemed to be traveling at top speed, and I had to lean out the window and use my left hand as a wiper blade in order to see the road ahead. I finally made it to Dallas about four in the morning, found the church I was to speak at, parked across the street, and tried to get some sleep. In a while the rain stopped, but soon the police pulled up behind me and made me get out, while they questioned me, patted me down, and checked the inside of the car for contraband. I explained what I was doing and why I was parked there, but they made me move. I circled around for a while, found another spot, but soon they were back and I had to move on. To kill time I simply drove around the downtown area of Dallas and waited for the sun to come up. Tired, dead tired, and partially wet, I was in no shape to do any preaching.

Around seven a.m., and right on the same block as the church building, I happily entered a little café and took a chair at the counter. The place was packed, and I waited as the guy behind the counter kept going back and forth in front of me, serving other customers. Though I tried to smile at him, he would not serve me. Finally I got up some courage and asked for a cup of coffee. He stopped in front of me, put his hands on the counter, leaned forward, and in a loud voice said, "We don't serve your kind here."

I was wet; I was tired, and now I was mad. Sliding off the stool I stood there and said, "I am a Southern Baptist preacher, and I am preaching at the church next door. You can bet I am going to be talking about this little incident." With that, I walked out.

After a couple of hours, folks began to arrive for the Sunday school gathering I was to address. (I was also to give a testimony at the main worship service later on.) When the young man who was leading the class saw me, it was evident he was taken aback. He hesitatingly allowed me to speak to the college age group, which was really large, and before I spoke I was able to get some coffee and donuts down me. With a simple explanation of what was going on in San Francisco, I emphasized how God was working things in a way I had never heard of before. I basically talked about a miracle-working God.

Those young men and women, who were not much younger than me, received me warmly and mobbed me when I was finished. As I was preparing to go to the main auditorium, the contact person, the guy who was somewhat startled at my appearance, told me there had been a change and I would not be able to give a testimony after all. I accepted that, said I understood, and instead of leaving to head back to Houston, I found my way into a balcony and got to listen to the great Dr. Criswell preach. It was worth the trip to Dallas.

# Chapter 15

# Charles Simpson
# in Mobile

Ollie Heath had migrated to California from Mobile, Alabama, where he had attended the Baptist church pastored by Charles Simpson. In the early days of Soul Inn in San Francisco, Ollie invited Pastor Simpson to visit us and preach and teach. This was an experienced pastor who was kind, generous, and encouraging. In no time, he became a mentoring influence for us, especially since he was the first person I knew who actually spoke in tongues.

By that time, I was newly charismatic, the story of which is coming up in the next chapter. Pastor Simpson was one of the few charismatic Southern Baptist pastors at that time, meaning that he claimed to receive the 'baptism of the Holy Spirit with speaking in tongues'. The Catholic charismatic movement was still a really big deal in 1968, and, along with the resurgence of the Pentecostal phenomenon, significantly impacted the fledgling Jesus People Movement. Until then, evangelicals were generally resistant to anything Pentecostal and thus shied away from the tongues-speaking Jesus freaks. Lacking acceptance from mainline evangelicals (with the exception, at least in my own circumstance, of a number of American Baptist pastors and just a few Southern Baptists), the Jesus People therefore listened to the charismatics. Charles Simpson came along side us and was admired and appreciated.

The trip that Paul, Ollie, and I made across the country terminated in Mobile. Pastor Simpson invited me to preach at the church he pastored, Bay View Heights Baptist Church. He later joined with others to form the group we called the 'Fort Lauderdale Five' that included Bob Mumford, Derek Prince, Don Basham, and Ern Baxter, all men we would learn to value and regard highly. (The details of this, and what came to be called The Shepherding Movement, will be presented in a later chapter.)

It was around this time in 1968 that a dangerous mind-set began to develop in me. Since tongue speakers were, for the most part, not well received by evangelicals and were outright rejected by most fundamentalists, defensiveness regarding the spiritual experiences took hold of many, including me. Perhaps to counter the rejection, I began to think that those of us who were 'baptized in the Holy Spirit' were spiritually superior to those who were not. I and those like me did not necessarily hold that speaking in tongues was the evidence or even a sign of conversion, like many mainline Pentecostals did, but our trouble was more subtle than that. We thought we were moving 'in the Spirit' and empowered by the Spirit. A 'we-they' mentality developed, which I later admitted to be a cultic or toxic mentality. But I thought there were two types of Christians, those who were being used by God to do miraculous works on the one hand, and the rest who sat in the pews doing next to nothing, on the other. Charles Simpson did not teach this, but a separation was taking place, a division that grew as time went on.

My own view of the 'Baptism of the Holy Spirit' was that it was indeed a second working of the Holy Spirit, but not for becoming holy or for speaking in tongues. My reading of Acts, chapter one verse eight, was that the Holy Spirit empowers the witness of the Christian. The primary work of the Holy Spirit, as I saw it then and continue to believe today, is to convict a person of sin and reveal to the person who Jesus is and what He did, showing the person that they are lost and hopeless without Him. I believed, then and now, that the Holy Spirit works conversion, the new birth, regeneration, and salvation, and that the individual can do nothing to save him or herself.

## Awakened by Speaking in Tongues!

The day I began to speak in tongues in 1968 marked a turning point in my witness. I had graduated from seminary, my family was staying with my parents at their house in Sunland-Tujunga, a suburb of Los Angeles, and I lived sometimes at the Anchor Rescue Mission in San Francisco. After joining Lincoln Park Baptist Church, I regularly stayed there at night with my sleeping bag rolled up and stashed inside the pulpit. And there I slept. One night at 2 a.m., having spent all day on the street evangelizing, followed by walking all the way back to the deep Richmond District and the church, I awoke loudly speaking in tongues. I was absolutely shocked.

Acquaintances had previously tried to get me to speak in tongues, but I had resisted. The most notable example of this took place some months prior at the Clayton House, a ministry run by Dick Key, who was an Assembly of God minister. I visited there from time to time for fellowship and a cup of coffee and donuts. One day a group of the young people who ran the ministry literally pushed me onto a table and tried to work my mouth to get me to speak in tongues. I had to fight myself away from them, gather my coat and Bible, and flee from the scene. I never came back, and I felt a significant sense of loss, since these Christian brothers and sisters were the only other evangelicals reaching out to the hippies in the Haight-Ashbury at that time. It wasn't long before Ted Wise and friends opened The Living Room on Page Street, but until then I was alone.

Nonetheless, now I was a tongues speaker, and I continued to be one for many years, slowing down in 1972 and eventually ceasing all together in the mid to late 1970s. What tongues speaking triggered for me was a dramatic change in my ministry. Prior to this, a steady but small stream of conversions followed my ministry; but now the number began to grow significantly.

There was such a marked difference, that I could only account for it by assuming I had been empowered by the Holy Spirit that night I woke up speaking in tongues.[1]  It was Charles Simpson who helped me understand what had taken place.

---

1    Writing this book forces me to once again consider what happened then. I am doubtful that the conversions and sometime miracles had anything to do with me. Of course, it could not be so, since only God does these things. Perhaps it is that Acts 1:8 was operational – God's Spirit empowered the witness, and that is the beginning and end of it.

# Chapter 16

# Evangelical Concerns

This memoir is not strictly chronological; rather it weaves in and out. It is necessary to backtrack now and recall a group of men who made a great deal of difference in my life and in the lives of many others – Evangelical Concerns.

Ted Wise, Danny Sands, Rick Zacks, Jim Dopp, Steve Heathner, Richard Haskell, Lonnie Frisbee, and others began a ministry in the Haight on Page Street, one block from Haight Street, called The Living Room. Quickly after they opened in 1968, I discovered it and began showing up, especially around lunchtime. These were the first Christians of a like mind and passion for evangelism that I encountered in the Haight. Later, after the media began covering the Jesus freaks, lots of Christian groups showed up. Behind Ted and the gang was a group of men who mentored their outreach to the hippies.

Ted, Danny, and most of the others, except for Lonnie Frisbee, were a bit older than the general hippie, even a couple years older than me, and they were all part of a group called Evangelical Concerns, headquartered at the First Baptist Church of San Francisco on Octavia Street. John Streater was its pastor, and John MacDonald was pastor of the First Baptist Church of Mill Valley, where Ted and the rest attended. There was also Howard Day, a leader at the San Francisco Church, and Ed Plowman, pastor of Presidio Baptist Church in the City. All of these were American Baptist Churches.

Soon enough, they invited me to the regular monthly meetings of Evangelical Concerns, which was some time in 1968. Before that year was up, I invited both Dr. Francis DuBose from Golden Gate Seminary and Martin (Moishe) Rosen, who later founded Jews for Jesus, to attend the meetings with me. Before the end of 1968, the three of us, along with David Hoyt, were on the board of directors of Evangelical Concerns (EC).

EC acted as an umbrella organization, especially for Ted's ministries: The Living Room and The House of Acts, which was a Christian commune in Novato, a town in northern Marin County.[1] Financial contributions for these ministries were funneled through EC. Larry Hoyt became the treasurer after EC began to connect with Christian World Liberation Front in Berkeley, a ministry headed up by Jack Sparks, Pat Matriciana, Billy Squires, Brooks Alexander, and others. Soon, nearly all of those who were involved in street ministry to the hippies in the Bay Area were somehow connected with EC.

David Hoyt and I, however, chose not to use EC as an organizational covering; we developed United Youth Ministries instead. Later on, we formed an actual non-profit corporation called Christian House Ministries, and Chuck Kopp of Greenbrae was the attorney who drew up the legal papers.[2]

As the years have gone by, I am increasingly aware of what EC meant to me. Without it, I might have made a bigger mess of things than I did. These wonderful servants of God were able to prevent some of us freaks from being completely taken over by the Pentecostal/charismatic emphasis that came to characterize

---

1    John MacDonald wrote The House of Acts, published by Creation House in 1970. It is one of the first stories of the Jesus People Movement.

2    There were so many people who came along side us in those days, and many of them, such as Chuck and Nancy Kopp, were parents of kids that became a part of what we were doing. A flood of names and faces are coming to mind right now, and I realize I will not be able to give them the notice they are due. In my mind, it was the hand of God that brought so many well-meaning people to us during those early days, and most of them did not fully realize what we all were a part of. They just knew that their kids liked us.

the Jesus Movement. While I am not casting disparagement on charismatically oriented Christians – I was one myself – I was made aware of the dangerous errors that come along when the charismatic is accentuated. For the most part, the EC directors were mainline, solid Christians in the Baptist tradition.

## In the Long Term

An interesting side note is that John MacDonald served as the second pastor of the First Baptist Church of Mill Valley and lived with his wife Marilyn and their children in the parsonage, which was also the home to several of the early leaders of Jews for Jesus.[3] Into that same parsonage later came John Streater to pastor the Mill Valley Church after he resigned from First Baptist San Francisco. (Streater, while a student at Wheaton College had introduced Ruth Bell to Billy Graham.) Then in 1984, I became pastor of that very same church, though we changed the name to Miller Avenue Baptist Church of Mill Valley. For twenty-six years I lived in that parsonage, and now the privilege belongs to my son Vernon and his wife Libby. I am still pastor of the church, along with my wife Katie and son Vernon. My goal is to continue doing so until I drop dead!

In October of 1968, John Streater, John MacDonald, Howard Day, Larry Hoyt, Ed Plowman, David Hoyt, Francis DuBose, and Moishe Rosen were the directors of Evangelical Concerns. They and the ministries they served then are now gone, yet their labor was not in vain. Ed Plowman is still going strong and writes for a number of Christian journals and magazines, including one of my favorite publications, World Magazine. Ed visited me some years ago, and I had enough sense of history to arrange for a photo of the two of us.

I must confess that I did not value those men to the extent I

---

3   Moishe Rosen made First Baptist of Mill Valley his home church during John MacDonald's tenure as pastor. Some of the founding members of Liberated Wailing Wall also lived in the parsonage.

should have; I did not know what I had in front of me. Many of us, and especially me, were blinded by the success we were enjoying and had no idea that we were part of a special outpouring of the Holy Spirit. We therefore were unaware that the so-called success had nothing to do with us.  It is with some pain that I am recalling this now; I did not esteem those men as I would now. I never even bothered getting a photograph of them.

# Chapter 17

# Frisbee, Smith, and Wimber

O ne of the young men who had been part of The Living Room outreach with Ted Wise was Lonnie Frisbee. Lonnie was younger than the rest of the group, several years younger than me, and he loved to talk theology and the Bible. Ted and the others were quite philosophically oriented, and I would often complain to them that I could not follow what they were saying. The reply was that they had been influenced by their mind-altering experiences, especially via LSD.[1] But I could understand Lonnie and he understood me.

Lonnie was thin and below average height, with longish brown hair and a smattering of facial hair. He looked much like depictions of Jesus seen in art throughout the centuries. His soft, easy manner drew people. He was not a dynamic or loud preacher; he was serious yet conversational. He identified with those who had lived a hard life and were searching for answers.

Lonnie loved to roam the streets of the Haight and witness to the hippies about Jesus. On many occasions, I watched him begin a simple conversation with one hippie, which then turned into a preaching event, as people stopped and listened in. On some occasions, the crowd of hippies who gathered around Lonnie resulted in cars stopping and blocking streets. It was plain

---

1    In subsequent years I would bring up this communication problem I had with them and I would receive the same answer - they would lapse into word associations that I was not able to grasp.

there was something about him – perhaps an anointing, a gift of evangelism, certainly a passion – but whatever it was, many were coming to Christ through his witness and testimony.

I did not know much of Lonnie's past, but I talked with him about his girl friend, Connie, and his plans to marry. They lived at the House of Acts in Novato with Ted and Liz Wise, Danny and Sandy Sands, and Rick and Megan Sacks. I did not know until years after his death from AIDS that he had ever been involved in homosexuality. He never once talked about it with me nor did anyone at the House of Acts mention it to me. Maybe he thought I would judge and reject him had he told me, or maybe he thought the past would remain the past. It seemed to me that he had a genuine love for Connie and looked forward to having a family.

After awhile, Lonnie expressed a desire to return to his hometown, Costa Mesa. At the Living Room we would talk about this and were divided as to what we thought about it. But Lonnie was determined to return home and start reaching out there. Shortly after his move, he called and asked me to gather up some of the old bunch and travel down to the House of Miracles, the Christian house he had opened in Costa Mesa, in order to interview some Christians with whom he was thinking of joining forces.

David Hoyt, Danny Sands, Rick Sacks, and I drove down to Costa Mesa and met with Chuck Smith and a number of his elders or deacons. Pastor Smith wore a shirt and tie, as did the rest who were with him. They sat on the furniture, while we Jesus freaks sat on the floor. For some period there were questions and answers, and theology was discussed. After Pastor Smith and his folks left, and after much discussion and debate, the four of us advised Lonnie that he should develop a relationship with these more experienced men and cooperate with them. This subsequently turned out to be a significant event in the history of the JPM.

Shortly after Chuck Smith and his leaders left, Lonnie wanted to drive to Huntington Beach to look at a group that had opened a kind of Christian nightclub. It was that very night we encountered David Berg, who soon developed a cult known as The Children of God – a Bible based cult that became a scourge to the Jesus People Movement.

From time to time, Lonnie would call to talk over events, but after a while we lost touch. I knew he became enmeshed with Chuck Smith and his church, Calvary Chapel. Reports of many coming to Christ, with miracles occurring, drifted up north to us.

Only later on did I learn of the trouble Lonnie ran into. I heard from people who were close to Lonnie at the time, that a kind of jealousy developed, primarily over Lonnie's notoriety, and an attempt was made to curtail the characteristic independence that Lonnie clung to. Then, after the arrival of John Wimber at Calvary Chapel, in 1970 or 1971, there was an open break, and Lonnie joined with Wimber, who had split off from Pastor Smith. Lonnie connected with Wimber's new church, The Vineyard, until certain conflicts arose. In my view, Lonnie was essentially 'thrown under the bus'.[2]

Now that the Jesus People Movement was ending, human engineering would be employed in order to attract crowds and create excitement and interest. That is what commonly occurs, as the outpouring of the Holy Spirit diminishes and everything changes. It happened in Marin and the entire Bay Area as well. The power and the miracles actually did not reside in or with us, and they faded little by little, although they did not entirely disappear. As I see things now, I think Lonnie – along with so many others, including me – simply did not understand the difference between 'normal' times, when we do all the same things like preach, pray, and plan, but the results are not so dramatic and encouraging. It's not nearly the same as during the exciting times of awakening and revival. God has His reasons for this, as I will propose in the next chapter.

---

2    I have struggled over this somewhat harsh treatment of fellow Christians, but I thought it necessary to tell it like I saw it or the account of Lonnie Frisbee would be incomplete or appear doctored to please others.

# Chapter 18

# Awakenings are Exhausting

A question I ask myself now that I am seventy-plus years old is: Could I survive an awakening like that of the Jesus People Movement now? My answer is, I am not sure.

In the research I conducted in preparation for the writing of my recent book, *Awakenings in American and the Jesus People Movement*,[1] I found that most of those who carried leadership roles were young men and women. None of them lived through two awakenings, and if this is a pattern, then I am safe. In answer to a consistent question I receive on this particular issue – Do I expect another American awakening soon? – I can only reply that I do not know. I would love to see one, love once again to see an outpouring of God's Spirit bringing vast numbers into His kingdom, but it is an unknown.

As I study histories and news of awakenings throughout the world, it seems to me that there are awakenings (or revivals, which is a synonym) going on all the time somewhere on the planet. Some are quite small, others larger, and some even national in scope. Apparently, there are no two alike.

The three major American awakenings agreed to be such by the majority of historians are so designated because they were national in scope. The first, 1735-1742, when the population

---

1   Some may be interested in this book, so please excuse what might appear to be a sales pitch, but at www.evpbooks.com you will find the book available in print and ebook formats.

was in the neighborhood of one million, was national. The second, 1798 to 1825, was also national and the population had grown significantly. The third, 1857 to 1859, again was national and the population was tens of millions. The JPM, a national event when the population of America was far greater than all the other awakenings combined, prompts the question, was its impact on a par with the others? In my estimation, this is a significant question, but one that is likely impossible to answer at this period in history.

In an email I received from Charles Simpson, which quote is contained in his bio at the end of this section, he suggests that one million were converted. Then comes the question, which awakening saw the most conversions? My thinking is the JPM would be the answer. And this conclusion is based on the fact that the focus of the JPM was personal evangelism. My observation is that in Marin County, with a population then of about 170,000, there were probably 500 conversions just in the central area. Extrapolating that yields some large numbers.

Awakenings are exhausting for those involved in Gospel ministry. There was never a day off for me, not that I didn't want one. I needed to rest and refresh, but those times were few and far between. Those who know me well say I am a 'Type A' personality. How valid this might be I am uncertain, and I am not sure whether there is any real science behind such a label, but I have always enjoyed, really love, working hard. There was just so much opportunity, so many open doors, and this was the JPM, with the constant need and constant press of people, which was very difficult to ignore.

I worried about my family, my wife Bobbie and my children, Dory, Grace, and Vernon. From time to time I realized that I was not being the husband and father they needed me to be and that I wanted to be.

The years passed speedily, and the pressure to do and go and worry was consistently upon me. I had little ability to examine myself and reflect on what I was doing, especially after the 'dark sides' of the awakening began making their appearances. (Stories about these dark sides are coming up.) Once the trouble started, once the camel's nose was inside the tent, and the wolf emerged from the sheep covering, my life became one of continual strife and anxiety.

One comfort I receive is knowing that what I experienced in the JPM and its aftermath is not atypical; in fact it is usual. That knowledge does not, however, compensate for the losses sustained.

Could I go through an awakening again? Maybe. Would I make the same mistakes? Hopefully not. And one of the reasons I wrote the book on America's awakenings, and a reason I am writing these memoirs, is to perhaps hold up a warning sign, a cautionary flag, that some of what happened to me might not happen to others.

# Chapter 19

# High School Bible Studies

In 1968, when we were living on Greenfield Avenue in San Rafael, I wrote Gospel flyers and began to hand out dozens of them at San Rafael High School. Often, I positioned myself on the sidewalk and passed out leaflets to the students as they left for home. If I attempted this now, I would see a police car pull up within a few minutes.

One of the marks of the Jesus Movement was an acceptance on the part of the secular world of spiritual things. Transcendental Meditation, Satanism, Zen Buddhism, and more were common topics of conversation, particularly among young people. So was Jesus. There was this hunger, perhaps a curiosity, almost like a fad, and the sight of someone holding a Bible was sure to start up some interaction. One of the characteristics of awakenings is that people other than Christians talk about spiritual ideas. This was certainly the case in the JPM, and consequently even school officials, students, and their parents were receptive to a Christian presence. This was not so before the JPM, and it was again not so when the JPM ended. I did not grasp the implications of this phenomenon for several decades.

Very often I carried a big black Bible under my arm as I strolled down Haight Street in San Francisco. There were certainly some derisive comments, yet the sight of that Bible triggered openings for a little sermon about Jesus. Such a conversation on the street tended to grow as passersby heard what was being discussed and wanted to join in. The same happened at San Rafael High.

It started with a couple of kids who regularly looked for my arrival. Mary Jensen was one, and she brought along Hugo Catanden, Byrne Power, Keith Fink, and Bob Burns. The group of five grew larger, and they proposed we start a lunchtime Bible study in a classroom at the school. The students approached the vice principal, got an initial approval, and I received a telephone call to come to the school and discuss it.

The result was a weekly lunchtime Bible study. Most of the kids came and went, but some stayed and became part of the group. In the beginning, I arrived early to pass out flyers, but eventually the kids themselves began to write their own one-page flyers and distribute them.

We also started Bible studies at Redwood High, Drake High, Tam High, Dominican High, College of Marin, Terra Linda High, Novato High, and San Marin High. At first I conducted them all, but when the number reached six I had to have help. In time the students led the studies, but for a fairly long period I continued at San Rafael, Drake, and Redwood.[1]

In 1968, in order to better serve the kids and others, I began a Tuesday night Bible study at our Zion's Inn on Greenfield Avenue in San Rafael. Then, due to the press of people, we moved it to Wesley Hall, a large room belonging to the United Methodist Church of San Rafael, which was just up the street from the Greenfield house. That Tuesday night Bible Study grew and grew, and it was there that I saw so many healings, real healings of surprising proportion.[2]

---

1   In recent years, I have continued visiting these schools but instead as a baseball coach, visiting each of the Marin County public high schools with a baseball team, first from Tam High and then from Terra Linda High.

2   A young woman was healed of a serious eye disease the night before she was scheduled for an operation. Her father, a high ranking San Rafael City employee, called me to complain that his daughter did not need the surgery. This was discovered just prior to the surgery and after she had been anesthetized. And to make matters worse, she was saying it was because of Jesus. The father said this was impossible, because they were Jewish.

The format was simple: we sang a few songs, had the study, which was verse by verse through a book of the Bible, then a time of prayer for those who wanted to believe in Jesus, and last, prayer for healing. A line would form, and I would sit there and pray for each one until the line was exhausted. It often took hours.

In 1968, that group of kids bought me a guitar to replace my old shabby one, and I still have it and play it every week. It is a Gibson Humming Bird Japanese imitation called a Conqueror. At that time it cost $225.

The Bible studies, both in the high schools and on Tuesday nights,[3] were the primary engine for the growth of the JPM in Marin County. Some of the kids who were converted in those studies became church leaders and still serve Jesus to this day. Parents began showing up to simply check things out, and some of them stayed as well.

What characterized that time was an extraordinary desire to talk about God; it seemed perfectly normal to me, and I was not surprised to see people being converted right and left. Out of necessity, we started baptizing people. Sometimes in swimming pools, or at Stinson Beach, or in San Pablo Bay at Paradise Park in the area alongside Tiburon and Corte Madera. Things were moving quickly, and none of us understood that we were in the midst of a national outpouring of the Holy Spirit.

---

3   Tuesday night was chosen so we would not be in competition with the regular Wednesday night prayer meetings so many churches held.

# Chapter 20

# The We/They Mentality

Perhaps we were trying to cast ourselves as New Testament disciples. One of my favorite Bible passages was then and still is Acts 2:42-44:

> And they devoted themselves to the apostles' teaching and fellowship, to the breaking of bread and the prayers. And awe came upon every soul, and many wonders and signs were being done through the apostles. And all who believed were together and had all things in common.

We began to think we were living the same life as the early church experienced close after the outpouring of the Spirit at Pentecost. And it began to produce in us a dangerous, indeed a cultic-like notion, that we were more spiritual than other Christians.

After all, we were seeing miracles. We saw people healed of real disease and medical problems. We saw many dramatic conversions. Our meetings were jammed with people. We were speaking in tongues and seeing other gifts of the Holy Spirit. We were witnessing on the streets when no one else was, just like Jesus, Peter, and Paul. All of these things were real and apparent, leaving us with a view of the 'churches' being by-passed. We were the elite, and we started being treated as such.

How I was living from 1967 to 1972 was nothing like what I had known at First Baptist Church of Fairfield or the Excelsior Baptist Church in Bryon. Even at Golden Gate Baptist Theological Seminary, where I was a student, I heard of no reports of great workings of God among the students. Sad to say, I developed an elitist attitude, a silly arrogance that I regret now.

Without the influence of the wonderful folk of Evangelical Concerns, it might have been worse. Real life would eventually be a teacher also, but we were blinded by what we thought was God's favor, a favor bestowed on us because we were, of course, so sold out for Jesus.[1] And although we had no personal wealth, our needs were continually being met, either by our own labor or by unexpected and large gifts. It was, without doubt, an unusual time.

## Awakening vs. Normal Times

Not until I read Iain Murray's book, *Revival and Revivalism*, did I understand the difference between 'awakening' and 'normal' times. At no time in my ten seminary years did I run across the concept, and that was much to my detriment, indeed the detriment of so much of the JPM. Murray, who inherited the mantle of David Martin Lloyd-Jones as a world-class expert on revival and awakenings, pointed out that in awakenings God pours out His Spirit in special and powerful ways. During normal times, however, although Christians pray, prepare, and plan, there are few conversions and miracles.

Without knowing it, what I had previously experienced were normal times, and now I began to actually judge others who were not 'walking in the Spirit' as somehow failing. We commonly said, "Well, they are not Spirit filled." This was the language and the mentality of the Pentecostal/charismatic folk, and the Jesus People quickly adopted it. Another of our statements was, "They are not flowing in the move of God." And it actually got more

---

1   Actual favor or grace is a sovereign work of God independent of any merit on the part of the recipient of the grace. For instance, Mary, the mother of Jesus, found favor with God, which had nothing to do with her personally.

ungracious than that, but we were full of ourselves and saw ourselves as special and thus without need of correction. We were moving in the Spirit and no one could tell us anything different.

Going over this chapter for the last time prior to handing it off to the editor, I am reminded of Dr. Fred Fisher, a renowned professor of New Testament at Golden Gate Seminary during the early days of that institution. He called me sometime in 1970 and asked me to visit him in his office at the seminary. The next day I arrived, and he spoke kindly to me but warned me of the trouble I was heading for. I listened patiently to my former teacher, but when I walked out of his office, I left behind all the good counsel I had just received. After all, he was not baptized in the Holy Spirit with speaking in tongues like I was.

The fruit of this mentality was undermining me and my ministry at the time and would bear much worse fruit in the years to come. Little by little, I will recount that process.

# Chapter 21

# More
# Christian Houses

Expanding the number of Christian houses was not a strategy as such; rather, their addition was driven by necessity. Through our continuing street evangelism in San Francisco with the hippies, we constantly took on newly born again youth who wanted out of that hell hole but had nowhere to go. It seemed to us it was like the early church, having 'all things in common'.

First was Soul Inn in San Francisco, then Zion's Inn in San Rafael. Berachah House in San Anselmo followed, Solid Rock in Novato, a house in Mill Valley, more houses in San Rafael, and on and on it went. We rented these houses, and I was usually the one signed on the lease as the tenant. The first house in Sonoma County was actually the Berachah House moving to Petaluma. It was a rustic farm, sort of, and the landlord was sympathetic to what we were doing. We turned its A-frame house into living quarters for about ten people. When that was full, we turned an out building into a bedroom as well.

Cliff Silliman was in charge of Berachah, and he did a wonderful job of it, being a solid Christian and a hard worker. He loved the young people coming to stay there, and some were not very easy to deal with. I showed up every other week to teach a Bible study, and I recall standing by the back door of the place teaching from the Bible. Residents sat on the floor of the kitchen and spilled over into a dining area just beyond that. (In addition to the farm we opened up a Christian book store right in the heart of town which Cliff also operated and looked after. But that story follows soon.)

Gradually, youth from the surrounding community began to attend the Bible study. Cliff and the guys (it was for men only) made evangelistic forays into the lovely little town of Petaluma, handed out flyers containing an invitation to the Bible study, and news spread about the Jesus freaks in town. We also twice held 'concerts' featuring the band Joyful Noise in a park in the town's center. Lots of kids showed up and we told them about Jesus.

Beginning to circulate on the East Coast was a Jesus People publication, a kind of funky newspaper. In one edition it listed the addresses of Christian houses around the entire country, and our houses were included. Traveling hippie types began showing up on a regular basis, almost using the houses like bed and breakfast inns. And it was partly due to this phenomenon that the Jesus Movement was cross-pollinated. The year that this reached its peak was 1970. It became obvious that what God had done in the San Francisco Bay Area was happening all over the country.

## A Silly Decision and a Big Gift

On one of my visits to 'the farm,' as we called it, Cliff and I discussed what to do with a tiny red foreign car that had been left behind by someone. There was no paper work, and the car's engine was shot, but there it remained. Money was always in short supply, so we thought the best way to dispose of it was to bury it. Cliff created a great plan and oversaw the work, except the hole the guys dug was not deep enough. The next time I showed up I asked to see the burial spot, and even from a distance I could see the red roof of the car jutting up about one foot above the ground. There was no way it could be dug up, so we got some sledge hammers and beat the roof down as far as possible, piled up a little hill of dirt around what was still showing, and left it like that. When we finally had to move off the land, however, our lack of foresight meant we had to dig up the little red car and have it towed away.

Barry Elegant, a Jewish man, visited the house after riding a motorcycle across country from New York and was converted under Cliff's preaching. When he left, he gave Cliff a check for three thousand dollars. Cliff called me, and I came up to the farm, so we could plan what we would do with the money. Our decision proved to be a good one.

# Chapter 22

# Christian General Store

The $3000 dollars Barry Elegant gave to Cliff became the seed money for a Christian bookstore.

Up to that point there were only two places in Marin County to buy Bibles and other Christian literature: Golden Gate Seminary's bookstore and a small one in San Rafael, operated by some staunch, conservative hardliners who did not care much for the Jesus People. This store closed sometime in 1968 or 1969, and I had it in the back of my mind to start one myself, so the timing of the gift of $3000 may even have been the hand of God.

I'm not sure how or when these ideas had come to me, but for some years I had entertained hopes of doing certain things in my life. (1) Open a Christian bookstore, (2) Write books, (3) Have a missionary-sending ministry, and (4) Start a Christian publishing house. This was the time for the store.

Our group of elders came mostly from the leaders of our Christian houses – Mark Buckley, Kenny Sanders, and Cliff Silliman primarily. They met together, discussed what to do with the money, and agreed to the bookstore, no doubt due to the influence I had at the time. Two things needed to be done: Find someone to operate the store itself, and find a location.

Kristina ('Kris') Kenner began trusting in Jesus as a student at Redwood High School in Greenbrae/Larkspur due to our witnessing at that school. Soon I met her mother, Betty, and in a rather short time both Chris and Betty became residents of

Christian houses. Kris moved into our Zion's Inn and became the best help with me in painting houses, our chief way of earning money at that time.

Betty had been suffering with alcohol and marriage problems, but she turned out to be an exceptional Christian and was soon placed in charge of a new house. Her Christianity blossomed, and she was well regarded by us all. She was the natural choice to be manager of the store and did an excellent job. She was a real gift to many of us.

Once Betty consented to manage the store, Cliff, Betty, and I began a search for a location. There had been an Arthur Murray dance studio at 2130 Fourth Street in San Rafael for years, but it had closed. It was a large space on the second floor of a commercial building, and on the first floor was a Japanese restaurant. An aging Italian couple owned the building, and we were able to work out a deal with them to rent the space. The place was beautiful and was divided into three spaces. Mirrors covered the walls of the main room, and behind that was a second large room that we were not able to rent initially, but there was a third large room in the back. Here I made my office, the first I ever had, and I occupied it until 1980. It was in that office that one of the more significant ministries of my life began to unfold. But that is another story.

The store did not do well at first. Cliff and I, along with a few others, painted the walls, made signs, built book shelves, and so on. However, we made a bad buy – hundreds of a poorly printed paperback edition of the King James Bible that did not sell – but we had made a start. The $3000 did not go far, and there were not nearly enough books to fill up the shelves. The house leaders found ways to put money into inventory, Christians in Marin supported the store as best they could, and slowly we took hold.

The store in San Rafael was the first of many. Soon there was one in Novato, then Petaluma, San Francisco, Pt. Reyes, Sonoma, and Redwood City. None of the bookstores was highly successful; in fact, most of the time, they had to receive help from the churches we had planted in the nearby area. The real benefit from the stores was their being a base for generating other ministries.

One by one, these stores closed; not one of them exists to this day. This was probably due to my inability to promote them, although very few 'brick and mortar' Christian stores exist anywhere in this region of the country anymore, overtaken by the ease and selection of items available on the Internet.

The Christian General Store – my memories of it are yet vivid and mostly pleasant. The building is still there, with a McDonald's next door to it now, and tears sometimes well up in my eyes as I drive by. On an occasion or two, I have parked in the old familiar spot in back of the building and walked around the neighborhood where I once walked with counseling clients. It was within that store that the Marin Christian Counseling Center operated.

# Chapter 23

# Marin Christian Counseling Center

### Educational Preparation

My college degree was in psychology. When I started out as a freshman at Glendale Junior College in Glendale, California, I was going to be pharmacist. But then I got a D in Chemistry 1 and followed that up with an F in Chemistry 2.

In a health class at Glendale I got my first exposure to psychology, and I was captivated. I had already figured out that I was a bit off. When I was sixteen, a school buddy, Bill Johnson, said I was a hypochondriac. What I found in Webster's Dictionary rather shocked me, but after thinking if over for some time, I agreed that I had been using illnesses such as a headache or an upset stomach to get out of things and attract attention. There were a few other little things about me I began to notice, little superstitions and obsessive/compulsive behaviors, and I concluded I had learned these things from my mother. After reflection, now many years later, I think my evaluation was fairly right, both about my mother and myself. So, knowing I was no rocket scientist and a bit strange, I chose psychology as my college major.

Since I was not able to stay in one school for long (due to the military), I ended up graduating with a BA in psychology, with minors in cultural anthropology and sociology. I entered a master's program, had completed the course work, and was starting the unit involving observed counseling. Suddenly, I realized I would never be able to bring up the Gospel of Christ as a school psychologist, which had become my career goal. For a week or so I pondered this, talked to my Pastor Bob Lewis, and decided to quit college and go instead to seminary. My whole point here is that I appreciated psychological counseling and was actually prepared to do it but not with the strictures that would have been imposed in a school setting.

## Getting to the Work

My office at the Christian General Store in San Rafael was spacious and quiet, perfect for a counseling office. Betty Kenner, the book store manager, kept my appointment book, and for ten years I accepted clients. I had no license and no insurance, and I did not charge any fee. My work was completely free, but sometimes people would slip me a twenty or so. For the most part, no one paid a dime.

Most weeks I had appointments Tuesday through Friday, anywhere from four to six per day. Sometimes I saw couples, but most often single individuals; a few times I did small groups. Churches all over Marin County sent people to me, and after a while, people from other counties made appointments as well. During my college studies, I had learned and appreciated both directive and non-directive counseling theories, so I combined the two, which worked out well over the years. I could both listen and speak to a situation.

In 1972 we began Church of the Open Door, and a great many of the folks who ended up there came through the Marin Christian Counseling Center. 'Center' was a popular word then; if I had it to do over I would not use the word, as it seems rather arrogant. But I have already indicated that I was arrogant, buoyed with the notion, 'We have the Spirit'.

What I learned during my counseling period I could not have learned elsewhere. People, most of them Christians, were desperate to talk to someone who would not condemn them. They wanted to talk to someone who would not call their pastor on the phone and make a report about them.

## Pastors Came, Too

Pastors from churches all over the Bay Area even made appointments for themselves. It was then I learned the plight in which many pastors found themselves. Churches, I discovered, were like battle grounds with buried mines dug in just below the surface; thus arose one of my favorite phrases, "Churches are mine fields." I eventually found this out for myself at our Church of the Open Door. What I learned found its expression in what is commonly echoed by other pastors: "If you can do anything else at all, don't go into the ministry."[1]

Pastors made appointments as did associate pastors, especially youth pastors. I began to wonder if there was something wrong with the whole institution. Sadly, professional ministers had then and continue to have a high rate of attrition, especially in a 'one person, one vote' congregational form of government. If something went wrong – for instance, if a power person became offended at something that a paid ministerial staff member did or said, well, that person was gone fairly quickly. And these ministers were usually younger people with few or no assets to fall back on.

What I realized (maybe rationalized), for me personally as well as for those I counseled, was that there was a price to pay for being in the professional ministry. And the reality was that the opportunity to preach and teach the Gospel almost always required pastoring a church. There was no alternative forum, for most anyway, although a few managed to acquire enough recognition to make it as travelling evangelists or guest speakers. It

---

1    During that time of the mid 70s, I wrote an unpublished book entitled, *The Care and Feeding of Your Pastor*. That manuscript formed the basis of a book jointly published by Evangelical Press and Earthen Vessel Publishing in 2008 – *How to Care for Your Pastor*.

was during this period that I would announce, "I pastor in order to preach."

A final note based on long experience: there is, in my opinion, a problem with being both a pastor and a counselor. If the counselor is competent, people will open up their lives. But how can this be a comfortable arrangement, if they are then regularly around the one who knows the deep, dark, and sometimes terrible truths? My advice for pastors and other church leaders who need therapy for themselves for whatever reason is: be sure to see someone in another county, and use an alias if necessary.

# Chapter 24

# How Love in Action Began

**M**y counseling work at the Marin Counseling Center is the nexus for telling the story of Love in Action.

Generally, I had appointments Tuesday through Friday, four to six each day. During one week in what I think was 1972, Betty scheduled appointments for three men on three different days. I had never met any of them before, and as it turned out, none of them knew one another either.[1]

Each of the three men said they were homosexual and had been all their lives. Each claimed to be Christian, and all three were quite conflicted about the contradiction between what the Bible said and their behavior. Two of the three were living with lovers; the other had intermittent lovers. Two of the men were regular church attenders. One was a school teacher, one an artist, and the other a businessman.

The businessman was Frank Worthen, who owned the Black Market in San Anselmo along the Miracle Mile. Frank, a sincere Christian, had begun an outreach to gay people. He made a tape of his testimony and sent copies of it to those who responded to his ad, which Frank placed in the San Francisco Chronicle. It was an outreach he called, Brother Frank's Ministry. Frank and I

---

1    The exact date of the beginning of Love in Action has long been in dispute. The appointment books could not be found, and for a number of reasons, researchers will find different people saying different things in regard to when, how, and who, regarding the founding of LIA.

became good friends and co-partnered the new ministry. Frank is still doing the work under a new name, now married for many long years to a former lesbian, and together they do a wonderful and faithful ministry to those with same-sex attraction.

In turn, each of the three told me that they wanted out of their homosexual lifestyle.[2] Now I was wondering what in the world I should do. It went through my mind that this might not be accidental or coincidental – it might be the hand of God.

Homosexuality! I knew little of it. The closest I had gotten to it was knowing a couple of fellow medics in the military who got caught in the barracks, very compromised, and it was a big deal. It took awhile before I pieced it all together in terms of what kind of sex they could have. Now I was getting acquainted with, at least from a professional point of view, three men who told me they were homosexual and were looking to me for some support and guidance.

The next Tuesday I asked Betty for the phone numbers of the three, and I called each one and set up a meeting for the end of that week; that first meeting was likely on Saturday morning. We met in my office, and after a couple hours or more of intense conversation, we decided to meet together on a weekly basis to discuss issues, pray, and lend mutual support and encouragement. So we did, and after a few weeks, the artist said he knew of three women, all lesbians, who would like to join us. They did, and after two or three meetings of the six self-described homosexuals and me, we decided to open it up to others. One of the women thought it would be good to give the group a name, one she had already thought of out of 1 John 3: "Love in Action." Everyone liked the name so, that was it.

---

2    During my time with Love in Action no attempt was made to convert homosexuals into heterosexuals. LIA was so accused, but that is not the truth. In every case, people came to us declaring they were gay and wanted help to get away from the 'life'.

## How the First Book, *The Third Sex?* Came to Be

After several months but less than a year, there was a general consensus that we should write a book. Since I had one book previously published, the task of writing it fell to me. It seemed logical to me to begin with the stories of those people already in our little group. I simply taped a conversation with each one, starting with what each remembered of his or her early childhood, and we worked through defining life moments all the way to the present.

Without exception, each of the six, both the men and the women, were convinced of being born homosexual. It was as though there was a third sex, men attracted to men and women attracted to women. I was completely naïve about all this and did little more than listen to what was being said and make sure the tape recorder was working properly. From time to time, one of the six gave me a book on the subject, which I studied, but none of it made much sense to me.

Surprisingly, as time wore on and the tapes started piling up, the idea that each one had been born homosexual began to break down. I was as shocked as the rest, when it became evident that certain circumstances evolved, primarily with the nuclear family, which were largely instrumental in the development of their sexual identities. I had assumed from the outset that what I had been told was accurate, that they were born with their homosexuality. Now, one by one, and without exception, it was clear that the same-sex attraction developed over time.[3]

The result of this 'turning things on their head' was to give our book the title, The Third Sex? It was as though I was simply a reporter of what had been discovered. Beyond the six interviews, I added a handful of chapters to give the book a biblical foundation.

---

3   Later on, what I have just written was denied by three of the six, namely that it was discovered that none of the six was born homosexual.

## Logos International and Dan Malachuk

Once the book was ready we had to find a publisher. Zonder-van Publishing House had published my first book, but this book did not fit for them. As it turned out, it did not fit for a number of other publishers either. The whole topic was a hot potato in the 1970s, especially for Christian publishers.

A favorite publisher for those of us who were in the charismatic movement was Logos International. Most of us knew of Dan Malachuk, the president of the company. I sent a letter off to him, and someone at Logos sent me a favorable return letter. I immediately made a plane reservation to fly to White Plains, New York, where Logos was headquartered.

Mr. Malachuk received me cordially in his office and allowed me to present my book. He had, of course, read a copy of the manuscript beforehand. As gently as possible he let me know that he did not think Logos would publish the book. Stunned and shaken, I would not let it go. I recall pacing around his large office making a case for the book, its importance, the potential scale of its outreach, and the groundbreaking impact it might have. After what seemed like a long time, Mr. Malachuk came toward me, shook my hand and said, "Okay, we will do it."

And they did do it, and my life quickly changed as a result. The ministry grew, and there was real change in people's lives. I was fearful that it was moving too fast, as more and more people became involved. As a pastor of a fairly large church that was also growing, Love in Action was threatening to overwhelm me. Over and above those feelings, however, was the sense that this was the direction God wanted for me.

## The Sequel—*The Gay Theology*

It was not long, perhaps just under two years, that the need for a sequel to *The Third Sex?* became apparent. The pattern for the second book would be the same as the first, except there would be four instead of six interviews. Two men and two women volunteered, and I prepared this material exactly as I had for the first book. Following the interviews I added some theological content, this time focused on the kinds of objections and questions we were receiving from the gay community, a segment of which was very close by in San Francisco.

Logos also published *The Gay Theology*. It was very courageous of them to publish both of these books, and at royalty time I always asked them to plow the money back into their work. I never received a dollar from Logos, because they went bankrupt sometime later. Many people owe a great deal of gratitude for the courage of Logos and Dan Malachuk.[4]

The events that followed the publication of *The Third Sex?* in 1975 and two years later its sequel, *The Gay Theology*, could be described as analogous to a whirl wind. At times, I have regretted the publication of these books, because the grief that descended upon me and my family at that time continues to some degree even to the present day.

Though I had been trained as a counselor, I was not prepared for dealing with people who had the misfortune of being involved deeply in homosexuality. It was difficult for me to understand the pain and frustration they were enduring. Though I could present Bible truths and listen to life stories, I struggled to get inside the hearts and minds of those who were showing up. As a heterosexual, I did not have a clear understanding of the gay life, so my role was limited. Others were better suited for the real work of Love in Action, mostly Frank Worthen.

## On the Door Step

From all over the country people were arriving, hoping to find a way to leave their homosexual conduct behind. There

---

4  Logos International closed, but another Logos emerged later on, and the present Logos publishing house is not the same as the Logos of Dan Malachuk.

were, in the broad sense, two motivations that brought them to San Rafael and the Love in Action ministry. First, as Christians they wanted to follow Jesus more carefully, and they knew that homosexual behavior was neither biblical nor pleasing to their Lord. Some of them had been to pastors and other ministers who saw nothing wrong with homosexuality and who then attempted to confirm or affirm them in their sinful ways. Usually, such unbiblical counsel worked for a season only. The Holy Spirit, we found, would not endorse homosexuality, so any cover-over or 'fix' was merely temporary.

Second, non-Christians were motivated, simply because they were desperate to leave the gay lifestyle. From these people I learned that the designation 'gay' did not accurately describe the day-by-day life of the homosexual. Many of them were older, both men and women, but mostly the men called 'aunties,' whose bodies were not what they used to be, found that the gay life was one of repeated rejections or just unacceptable sex. And this was all before the days of HIV and AIDS.

Often I would hear a knock at the door, open it, and find a poor, desperate individual, sometimes without baggage or money in the pocket, wondering if he or she had found Kent Philpott and Love in Action.

## Exodus

Frank Worthen, one of the three men whom I counseled during that first ground breaking week, was the real leader of the ministry. I served more as a pastor and teacher for Love in Action, and I withdrew from hands-on ministry in 1978. Before this time, however, a group that would be called Exodus was forming elsewhere. It acted as an umbrella organization for ministries like ours, groups that were springing up spontaneously in many different places. I have a photo in which I am speaking to one of the first national gatherings of Exodus in Minneapolis in 1975.

Love in Action was not the only group that had come into being in order to meet a growing need. There were groups all across the country operating with the same goal – to bring the message of a liberating and loving God to people who wanted out of the gay life.

It has been repeatedly said that ministries like Love in Action were out to turn homosexuals into heterosexuals. Nothing could have been further from the truth. No, people with same-sex attraction were lined up outside the door, seeking support and encouragement to turn from their sin and help them live new lives. There may have been some groups out there who were perceived as intent on sexual identity change, but I never encountered such an organization.

# Chapter 25

# The CWLF and Holy Hubert

When Moishe Rosen showed up in 1968, in the days before he founded Jews for Jesus, he and I organized large-scale events involving hundreds of Jesus People. Moishe was the actual brains behind the demonstrations; I served as his lieutenant.

I remember the time that Moishe (I knew him as Martin then) and I agreed to descend on San Francisco's Broadway Street in North Beach[1] to create a stir and promote an event where Hal Lindsay of *The Late Great Planet Earth* fame was to preach in front of Big Al's. In two days we mustered a couple hundred Jesus People from our Marin County base alone and set them to creating dozens of placards and hundreds of 'broadsides' (tracts).

At another of these evangelistic demonstrations, we picketed and marched in front of Adam and Eve's on Broadway in North Beach on a Friday night. We persisted for a long time, and it was plain we were interfering with customers entering the strip joint. Toward ten o'clock some goons came out of the place and began yelling at us. I stepped forward aggressively and started 'talking' to a guy, not knowing he was the owner, Michael Savage.[2] He took a swing at me, hit me in the face, and knocked my

---

1    The area is where all the strip clubs operate, bordering Chinatown, it has long been a mecca for various sorts of thrill seekers. Carol Doda, Big Al's - real sleaze stuff but made to look glitzy.

glasses off. Having been alerted, cops had already arrived, seen the scuffle and then jumped in. We were both taken to the North Beach Police Station, where we ended up declaring the incident 'mutual combat', making it possible for us to avoid further difficulties. When I got back to Broadway, the demonstration was still underway.

## Enter the CWLF

Sometime in 1969 a higher degree of organization crept into the JPM. There were conferences and large campouts featuring music and preaching. In the Bay Area there were several times when JPM leaders met together to plan evangelistic outreaches, much of which was stimulated by or held in conjunction with the Christian World Liberation Front (known to us as CWLF), led by Jack Sparks, Pat Matrisciana, Brooks Alexander, and Billy Squires, among others.[3] I believe CWLF started up in early 1969. Moishe and I both loved working with these folks, fellow travelers who were, in terms of background and education, much more like us than many of the other Jesus People leaders.

The flagship school of the University of California system was located in Berkeley, which was sometimes referred to as 'Berzerkeley,' not a flattering term. Berkeley was the absolute center of not only leftwing political thought in the U.S., but also of the East Bay's hippie movement. People's Park, just off Telegraph Avenue and a few blocks away from the university, was the place where the action took place. Here the hippies camped out, smoked dope, and tried to live the free and enlightened life.

Berkeley's hippies were definitely not the same bunch as the university students, but we attempted to evangelize both groups. CWLF lead in this effort, with Jack and Pat, who were

---

2    No relation with the Michael Savage conservative radio personality.

3    One of the very best gatherings of Jesus People in the Bay Area was held at the KOA Campground in Petaluma. Jim Durkin from Eureka was much involved in this one and brought a hundred plus Jesus People with him for the event.

both at that time connected with Campus Crusade for Christ, focused on the university in particular and the hippie element as a sort of tangential target group. They gathered around them a capable and dedicated group that included the above-mentioned Billy and Brooks. Many others, including very talented women, contributed their efforts, and they established what became the most read publication of the JPM, *Right On*.

*Right On* was political yet non-political at the same time. Some of the best articles for the Gospel could be found in that newspaper, although it was sometimes hard to tell at first glance if Right On was even Christian. A careful read, however, made it clear it was and very biblically so. It was *Right On* that Ollie, Paul and I handed out on college campuses from California to Alabama in 1969. We must have stuffed a couple thousand of the papers into the red VW bug.

From time to time, I drove over to Berkeley to visit Jack, Pat, and the others at their offices. Afterward, I liked to walk over to the gate leading into the university at Telegraph and Bancroft Way. Maybe seventy-five yards inside was Sproul Hall and the famous 'steps of Sproul Hall,' where many of the sixties radicals delivered fiery anti-establishment speeches to the crowds who stood and listened in Sproul Plaza. Ludwig's Fountain bordered the plaza, and in its pool we conducted baptisms. The pool was shallow, and I had to get down on my knees along with the person to be baptized, gently laying the new believer's head under the water. This usually attracted a crowd of students, and we took advantage of this by handing out copies of *Right On*, while honing our open air preaching skills.

The student union opposite Sproul Hall was a large building with a café and rest rooms, and it was the perfect place to retreat, freshen up, and spend precious moments instructing new Christians. It is now called the Martin Luther King Student Union, but I don't recall it being called that then.

## Enter "Holy" Hubert

An amazing street preacher who would place himself at the gate leading into the university, right there at Telegraph and Bancroft Way, was Holy Hubert. He would climb up on a portion of the large concrete gate and hold forth. Hubert was well into his fifties, or so I thought at the time, and was small of stature and large of heart – maybe courageous is a good description of him as well. Hubert had no front teeth, and that was because he was regularly punched in the face by angry listeners, most of whom where hippie street people. To say Hubert was a throwback would be an understatement. He was John the Baptist, Elijah the Prophet, John Wesley, and George Whitfield all rolled into one. Whenever I was there I would stand in front of him as a kind of bodyguard. Things got ugly once in a while.

It was claimed, but not by Hubert, that he had memorized the whole of the Bible. On a couple of occasions I tried to find out about this without directly questioning him. There were a couple of times, however, when right in the middle of an impromptu sermon out would flow, and perfectly, chapter after chapter of Scripture, even passages in the Law that were rough going at best. I guess the legend was true.

Holy Hubert yelled at the hippies and students things like: "You dirty filthy fornicating drug addicts," or "You brood of vipers, whores and whore mongers, you will burn in hell." Easy to see why he had so few teeth. Oddly, people would be converted, sometimes right on the spot, and I baptized a few of those who apparently needed to hear what Hubert had to proclaim. It takes all kinds, and Hubert was able to penetrate the defenses some of the hippies used to justify their behavior. It was nothing short of miraculous to see some of those who were yelling for Hubert to be crucified suddenly drop to their knees and begin to repent.

After a few years Hubert stopped showing up, and I never learned what happened to him. Like many used of God in the JPM, he suddenly appeared, and just as quickly he disappeared.

The CWLF also dissolved, but not as quickly. When Jack Sparks embraced Eastern Orthodoxy,[4] many of the young kids who had started showing up at CWLF to serve the Lord were thrown into a precarious place. The leadership was divided also, and gradually the whole thing ground to a halt. Some of those involved continued to do what they could, but it was over. Actually, it morphed into another ministry, which proved to be very important, a ministry centered on apologetics lead by Tal Brooke, a very capable and interesting person.

This, too, indicates a crucial characteristic about the JPM. There was a time of its beginnings and a time of its endings. As I have often indicated, no one knows exactly when it began or when it ended, and you get different opinions, depending on where a person lived. The very same can be said of the first, second, and third awakenings in America. This seems to be a mark of a genuine outpouring of the Holy Spirit who, like the wind, blows when and where He will.

---

4   I talked to Jack about the situation, and it seemed to me that he wanted to see order and a predictable theology instead of the chaos and confusion that became the hallmark of much of the JPM. His motivation now strikes me as being very similar to what characterized the leaders of the Shepherding Movement.

# Chapter 26

# Antioch Ranch in Mendocino

Jerry and Pat Westfall lived about six miles east of Mendocino off the Compte-Ukiah Road on a beautiful tract of forested land they called Antioch Ranch.[1] This wonderful Christian couple made space for others to stay there and turned the place into a kind of Christian retreat.

At some point in 1968, Jerry heard of us in some way and visited us at Soul Inn. His retreat ranch was ready for guests, and Jerry wanted us to know that we could send folks up his way. We did just that.

I will never forget the first trip I made to the ranch. It was October 31, 1968, Halloween Day. I was hitchhiking, and it took me all day long to get to Mendocino. It was raining hard, and I was thoroughly soaked. My last ride took me right into the town of Mendocino, where I stepped out of the car door and into a driving rain. A bell somewhere chimed midnight, and I wondered how in the world I was going to make it the last stretch to the ranch. The town was dead quiet, with no one around, but I didn't have time to fret, as I heard a voice calling out my name. It was Jerry, and he had been waiting for hours for me to show up. It was a happy ride down the twisty country road to the safe haven of Antioch Ranch.

One of the first to go up to Antioch Ranch was Ira Monroe, a Canadian, who had come to America to avoid military service

---

1   In Antioch of Syria followers of Jesus were first called Christians.

there.[2] He came right off Haight Street, a brand new Christian with long blond hair and a serious demeanor. Ira was a real hippie, and everybody loved the guy.

A number of others followed, and I made the trek myself a number of times, sometimes to teach and baptize, and one time to help tear down an old building in downtown Mendocino. We did the job for free, just to get the old redwood out of it to build dorms on the ranch's property. That was one of my favorite memories. It was a bright but brisk day, and we were up on the second floor, with the Pacific Ocean behind us, the wooded hills opposite us, and the white and glistening little town all around us. How I wish I could go back or at least have photographs of that day, as I can still see myself carefully pulling out the hundred year old square nails, gently handling the long planks of redwood siding, and working alongside a bunch of ex-dopers singing Jesus songs.

Money was always tight on the ranch, and one way we made money for it was to cut down redwood and pine trees and make coffee tables from the wood. I had the great pleasure of making a number of these myself, even cutting down smaller trees for the legs. We carted them to Marin and sold them to the parents of the kids who came to the Bible studies. I still have four of those tables. The legs are pine logs, the tops usually three-inch thick slabs of gorgeous redwood, and on each I laid seven layers of clear varnish. They are as solid and beautiful now, really more so, than they were then.

Jerry and Pat were members of a Presbyterian Church in Mendocino, and I attended there whenever I spent the weekend. At that time, I was not pastor of a church, so it was possible for me to do this. That congregation welcomed the hippies and provided a real church home for them. I do not remember the name of the pastor, but he and I got along very well.

---

2    After his conversion to Christ, some years after, Ira went back home, turned himself in, and spent some time in prison.

Jerry himself was a wonderful and competent Bible teacher, and I still recall one of his studies. Seated in a deep leather chair in the large, rustic front room of the main house, he plainly, lovingly, taught verse by verse through long passages of Scripture, and we stayed there as long as he cared to go on, not noticing the passage of time.

Jerry and Pat were a great gift to me and to many others. At the time of this writing, they are still up there at Antioch Ranch in Mendocino welcoming folks to their beautiful retreat. You can find it by means of a Google search.

## Other Jesus People in Northern California

As time went on, we began to hear of other Jesus freaks in other places. Of course, in our various journeys around the country, we discovered other folks engaged in the same or similar ministries as ours. We knew of things going on in Los Angeles, mostly in Hollywood, but of special interest was what we heard was going on in Eureka and Chico.

Jim Durkin was a real estate agent in Eureka, and a rather large flock of young believers formed around him. (Jim's son, Jim Durkin, Jr., wrote a piece about his father, which appears in the Bio section of this book.) We knew of the work in Eureka as Gospel Outreach, but also as the Lighthouse Ranch. There was some cross-pollinization, but I never made a trip up north to visit these people.

Sometime in 1970, however, we worked out a plan via telephone to have a gathering of the Jesus People in Petaluma. We rented out the KOA campground just north of Petaluma and went about inviting Jesus People from far and wide. Gospel Outreach was a big part of it, and it was here I finally got a chance to meet Jim. The Eureka bunch arrived fully organized. They set up a large white tent, put in Army style cots, and had nurses and medics ready with all the necessary equipment. Everyone was amazed. They also brought about two dozen young guys wearing armbands with "SERVANT" on them, and they patrolled the grounds ready to help out with anything that needed to be done.

It was a special time as the 'tribes' gathered from San Jose to Eureka, with hundreds of Jesus people all having a wonderful time. Several leaders spoke at the teaching times, and I can still see Jim Durkin, a quiet, thoughtful, patient, loving, big man, full of years and experience, being a kind of father to the rest of us. This one event was the only time I can recall when we were together, but it was something I will never forget.

A leader I had only heard of was Gaylord Enns of Ivy House in Chico. The first time I met Gaylord in person was recently in the summer of 2013. Scott McCarrel and I had gotten to know each other a couple of years previously, and Scott was a close friend of Gaylord and arranged for the three of us to meet for a lunch in Mill Valley. My son Vernon and I had a wonderful lunch with Scott and Gaylord at the India Palace, and as soon as we sat down, I asked Gaylord when he first experienced the JPM. He said, "1967." I was shocked to hear someone else make that identification; I said nothing but went on to a follow-up question: "When did it end?" He said, "1972."

Not able to contain myself, I burst out, "That is exactly my experience, too!" This confirmation was stunning, as it corresponded with what I had thought over the years; but here was a person, a leader in the JPM living not far from the Bay Area, who held the same impression. Gaylord is a special guy, who wrote a wonderful book entitled, *The Love Revolution*, which I keep a supply of to give away. He reminds us of the command of Jesus to love one another, a message that resonates with all who read it.

Scott, Gaylord, and a close friend of Scott's, Randy Sager, and I have teamed up under Scott's leadership to have conferences for people who lived through the JPM, in order to talk about that time of the outpouring of the Holy Spirit, encourage those who made 'shipwreck' following the JPM, and think and pray about another awakening in the future, if God would so will. I will bring this up once again at the end of the book.

# Chapter 27

# George Müller
# of Bristol

Before my days as a Jesus freak, a fellow student at Golden Gate Seminary gave me a book by Arthur Tappan Pierson about George Müller, the German Christian who began an orphanage in Bristol, England.

What impressed me about the life of Müller was how God met his financial needs. Müller wanted God alone to be thanked and praised for this, so he would not let others know of the content of his prayers or otherwise broadcast the often dire circumstances the orphanage faced. His prayer requests would be specific about the amount needed and when it was needed. The prayers were answered just as specifically. The answers to prayer were a continued source of strength and encouragement for him and a clear and unequivocal statement about the God who answers prayer.[1]

After I left the seminary and began my work in the City, I also had to leave my job as a shoe salesman at J.C. Penney, and the money I received each month as part of the G.I. Bill came to an end. I had no income, no savings, no credit card, and a family of four. Müller came to mind, and I began copying his approach.

My experience mirrored Müller's. I told no one, not even my

---

1   In more recent years I have read that Müller was not as quiet about his needs as presented in the book about him. I have not fact-checked this, but I suspect there would be those who had some sort of reason to doubt Müller's testimony.

parents, of what I was facing, but I instead simply asked God to meet the needs. He did, and right on time. I know it sounds incredible, and I would not be upset if someone doubted the truth of it all.[2]

So I prayed, and praying has never been a strong suit of mine. I am a reluctant prayer, but in this period I set aside time, usually in the morning, for what I called 'devotions'. I adopted the Billy Graham practice of reading two chapters in the Old Testament, three Psalms, and at least two chapters in the New Testament. In the back of my Bible I had a prayer list divided into columns, with the date on the left, the request in the middle, and the answer with date on the right. I could then track what was going on.

I continued the practice when the Christian houses started. Today we read in the newspapers about a 'fiscal cliff', and I faced many of them, one right after the other, yet we never one time fell over the cliff. I thought it might be nice if God would simply lay on us a large lump of cash, but it never happened. For most of that time, actually all the way to 1980, I had no checking or savings account. I lived month to month, and even today it is not much different.

## A Shift in Procedure

I hope this does not sound pretentious or otherwise haughty, but about 1969 I started being noticed by the media, and invitations began to arrive. So I began to travel about the country, sometimes alone with my guitar, other times with Joyful Noise, flying here and there like a celebrity of sorts. What I did on these travels was collect names and addresses of people I met along the way who seemed interested in the work in California. My recollection is that in 1970 I began to send out a monthly news-

---

2    Somewhere in my archives I have prayer lists I kept at the time which give credence to how our needs were met. I feel a little like I am betraying what I set out to do by writing this but then I thought that Müller eventually had to describe what happened as well.

letter to people I thought might be interested in following what was going on with me and might even contribute some money.

We did have a non-profit corporation, Christian House Ministries. Chuck Kopp, an attorney whose wife Nancy was involved in our work, did the paper work. So I was able to send out tax deductable receipts. With over two hundred on the mailing list, we were able to get a bulk mailing permit. I had a big, old Royal typewriter, and eventually a mimeograph machine, and the letter went out, and money started coming in. By 1972, the average income from the letter was $800 a month. Bobbie was working at Marin General Hospital, and though it was still month-by-month, we were doing fine. It was about this time that I ceased doing the Müller imitation, but I missed it. My thinking was that the newsletter was God's way of meeting our needs, and it also meant I was developing an account of my years as a Jesus freak by way of the monthly newsletters.[3]

---

3    I have not looked at these newsletters or the journal I wrote from 1968 onward, but one day I will. Then I'll be able to fill in some of the blanks found in these memoirs.

# Chapter 28

# Victor Paul Wierwille and The Way International

At some point, likely in late 1968, Lonnie Frisbee began asking me some questions about specific doctrines like the deity of Christ, the Trinity, and speaking in tongues, among other issues. After some period I learned that a Bible teacher named Victor Paul Wierwille[1] was visiting the House of Acts in Novato, and his teachings were causing division among both the members and those attending the weekly Bible studies held there.

Someone living at the house had stumbled across a series of tapes made by Wierwille entitled, *Power for Abundant Living*, and the thirty-six hour course of instruction was drawing a lot of interest. At that point, I asked Ted Wise if it was okay for me to come to Novato and speak with Wierwille face to face.

On two separate occasions, two afternoons when just a few people were at the house, I debated him. What had been troubling Lonnie was Wierwille's insistence that smoking marijuana was permitted for Christians. It also seemed that he advocated open marriage. I had wrongly assumed his theology was orthodox. These were only the first of many troubling doctrinal issues.

At that point, I defended speaking in tongues, as I had begun speaking in tongues myself, but Wierwille carried it to the

---

1   Wierwille was born in 1916 and died in 1985. After his death power struggles splintered The Way International. Loy Craig Martindale emerged as the leader of the faction that most closely adhered to Wierwille's doctrines.

point of being the absolute proof for the resurrection of Jesus. Though I did not accept it, I knew that many Pentecostals were convinced that speaking in tongues was the primary evidence of being truly born-again, but my mainline evangelical theology would not let me go there.

Wierwille would not budge and I did not push it. (Speaking in tongues never did get too far at the House of Acts.) But then I found that Wierwille denied the deity of Christ, followed by the revelation that he rejected the Trinity. He said the Trinity was introduced into the Church several centuries after the ministry of Jesus and was the result of pagan ideas. An even more severe issue was that Wierwille claimed that the original documents of the New Testament were written in Aramaic, not Greek, and that he alone had the manuscripts, so he alone knew what was true. Over and over I asked to see them or to see a photo of them, but Wierwille had his reasons, ones I have now forgotten, why this was not possible. It reminded me of Joseph Smith and the golden tablets from which the Book of Mormon had supposedly been copied.

Most of what I saw come out of the confrontations with Wierwille was a division occurring in the house; some of the original members of the household left. Among those who left were Jim Dopp and Steve Heathner,[2] who remained with The Way. A competing Bible study then developed in Mill Valley by adherents of Wierwille, and it continued for some time but never really caught on. Those who led the group did not have the tight control necessary to enforce doctrinal conformity, like most of the Bible based cults do, and so there was constant slippage.[3]

---

2    Steve Heathner, known as Steve O'Shay, was a well known D.J. on the most popular of San Francisco's radio station that featured rock and roll music. Steve would slip in Jesus zingers into his radio program and it was no small deal.

3    Former participants in The Way began to attend Miller Avenue Church, where I am yet pastor, and updated me on the developments following the breakup of the House of Acts and the death of Wierwille.

Of course, the cause of Christ was tarnished as a result, and I am aware that some are still impacted by it after all these years. Later, in the mid 1990s, I offered a Cult Recovery Support Group and placed ads in the local Marin paper announcing it. A twenty-six week course developed and drew many from a number of different groups, and included among them were former participants in The Way.[4]

The Jesus People Movement was a mixed bag. On the one hand was the obvious power of God to save, and alongside this, which is actually characteristic of most genuine awakenings of the Spirit of God, were the 'dark sides,' the 'wild fire,' the aberrations and distortions. Toward the closing years of the JMP, as I experienced it, the seeds of destruction and division had been sown and would yield bad fruit. This aspect I will address more fully coming up.

---

4   Some of those who attended the group had been members of the Church of the Open Door where I had been the senior pastor during the 1970s. More of this will appear in a later chapter.

# Chapter 29

# Rise of the
# Children of God

The first and only time I talked face to face with David 'Moses' Berg was when David Hoyt, Danny Sands, Rick Zacks, and I visited Lonnie Frisbee at the House of Miracles in Costa Mesa, California. We had come to discuss the pros and cons of Lonnie joining forces with Chuck Smith and the beginnings of Calvary Chapel. After that meeting, the five of us jumped into my 1964 blue Ford station wagon and drove down to Newport Beach to a Christian nightclub run by the Berg family. That was in 1969.

Little by little, word filtered through the Jesus People networks that there was a new group operating and aggressively so. It was known as COG, short for the Children of God.[1] At some point it was also known as The Love Family or just, The Family. This more attractive designation began to be used around the year 1971, and it emerged as the COG's response to negative attention it received from the media.

The COG targeted the Jesus freaks. Early on the attraction was that Berg's followers were really sold out to Jesus, unlike the 'ordinary' Jesus freak. Members of Berg's group had left worldly possessions behind (of course, if they had anything, it was given to the organization), and they were on the road with

---

1    Don Lattin has written an excellent account of the Children of God, the best out there. The title is: *Jesus Freaks: A true story of murder and madness on the Evangelical edge*, published in 2008.

the true gospel.

Many of the Jesus People had been hippies, or wanted to be hippies, so the radical call to leave everything behind, including work, school, parents, wives, or husbands was a real lure – an escape for the bored and burdened.

I had been a disciple from afar of Jack Kerouac and tried to live out what I read in his books, *On the Road* and *Dharma Bums*, which celebrated the 'beat life'. The beat life melded into or helped spawn the hip movement, at least as I see it. Now COG came along and provided the perfect excuse to be wild and radical, and all for Jesus.

Sex was a big draw as well. I recall the 'Mo' letter that Berg wrote entitled, "Flirty Little Fishies," which was a communication that came directly from a spirit that Berg had in him named Abram. It instructed the pretty young ladies in COG to use their bodies to bring in new converts.[2] And as you might guess, it worked.

That Berg was possessed by a spirit that guided him was not as strange as it might seem. Infused with Pentecostalism, most of the Jesus People thought that anything spiritual had to be from God. Due to my Baptist background, I did not share this view, not even close. What I saw instead was a doctrinal issue that contributed to the confusion over Berg and others like him. It was a propensity of many Christian leaders to strongly argue against the possibility that a Christian can have a demonic spirit. The rationale was: if you are filled with the Holy Spirit, there is no room for anything else. And naturally, the Jesus People were 'Full Gospel' and filled 'to the gills'[3] with the Spirit; Berg fell into this category.[4]

---

2    This bit of engineering was essentially a mask for Berg's own sexual perversions.

3    An expression we would use to describe someone who plainly had a whole bunch of demons.

4    In my own deliverance ministry I attempt to avoid the controversy

A second point that led to confusion was the common presumption among the Jesus People that anyone who claimed to be a Christian must be one.[5] There was virtually no understanding or discernment that someone might be falsely converted. In my estimation, this was a difficulty that would haunt the Jesus Movement and produce much of what I call 'the dark sides' of the awakening. After all, one's Christianity was judged on whether one could move and groove to the beat, all the while speaking in tongues. This may be an exaggerated viewpoint, but it is not far from actual practice. But more of this later.

With the news spreading around about the COG, most of the Jesus People knew what was afoot. David Hoyt and I knew and actively campaigned against Berg and his movement. We knew we would encounter them at some point. Indeed, COG people showed up in the Bay Area, but they had little or no chance of gaining a foothold here. A few stragglers got picked off, but for the most part they left us alone. There were better, easier pickings elsewhere.

---

about the vulnerability of Christians to demonic influences and set theological nitpicking alone, in order to concentrate on the needs of the person in front of me.

5    This particular issue stayed with me for many years and in 1995 I wrote a book on true and false conversion. The title is, *Are You Really Born Again?* and is now in its second edition.

# Chapter 30

# David Moves to Atlanta

The Jesus freak I am talking about in these memoirs is me, and in this chapter I will talk only about those things that I was personally involved in and therefore have some remembrance of. I do have my journal, newsletters, old friends from that era with whom I talk, and other materials that comprise my Jesus People archives, but here I am touching only on my own personal experience. And I caution readers: I may have some details wrong or slightly off.

That said, this chapter is focused (after a bit of detour) on David Hoyt's move to Atlanta, Georgia.

## Another Story First

When David finished his work in Lancaster, he moved back to Marin, and we saw the opening of Zion's Inn. This was in 1968, and David and I started painting houses to make money – of which we had very little. Our first job was right up the street, and it consisted of painting out some rooms on the second floor of a commercial building. On the bottom floor was a business, and on the second floor was a large apartment. (The building is still there in San Rafael, and I drive by it frequently.)

First day on the job (and we had passed ourselves off as experienced painters), we put a water-based latex paint on a wooden door rather than the oil-based paint we were told to use. Frankly, we didn't know the difference; at least I didn't, since

I was the one who messed up. That slowed things down, as I had to sand all the paint off after it dried and lost a whole day. But we learned, and David and I found we were good at the painting. And the money was not bad for back then - $5 an hour apiece.

After painting for a little more than a week, we came to the last room, a large one, and it was crowded with furniture covered by white sheets. David and I never bothered to look under the sheets while working there, but after we finished and peeked out of curiosity, we found a number of pieces of very nice, but old furniture. The owner then asked us to get rid of it, and we quickly said yes. I still have two pieces, a beautiful antique corner table and a kind of club chair. It was the very furniture we needed at the time, and I continued to cart the stuff around for decades. I never could figure out if that was a miracle or not.

Just before concluding the job, we were asked to paint the front of the building. I recall doing this alone, since David was on another job, but one day I was working at the very top of the second story when some guys showed up and started yelling at me. They were from the local painter's union and were angry with me, a non-union worker, for taking their work. Of course, I had no idea how that could be and did not even understand about labor unions.

There was nothing else for me to do but continue painting, all the while trying to ignore them. If I had climbed down off the ladder, a fistfight would surely have ensued. When they saw I was not budging, they started to shake the heavy, old, wooden ladder, the top of which I was perched on. Finally, I had no choice; I descended with just enough aggression in my manner that they could see I was ready to fight. Before I reached the ground they fled. It is not always possible to turn the other cheek – a lesson that stayed with me.

I decided to push my luck and was soon putting ads in the local paper for more paint jobs. Over the years the union caused me some grief by throwing paint on jobs I had finished or intimidating those who had hired me. I had to keep it up, however, as

I had a whole house full of people to feed. Despite all the harassment and threats, the protecting hand of God was upon us.

## Back to David's Move

David eventually moved to Walnut Creek, over in the East Bay. There he began Upper Streams, and soon it was a thriving ministry. After some time there, I think in 1969 or 1970, David packed up with wife and some of the folks from Upper Streams and moved to Atlanta, Georgia. David's ministry grew greatly then, not only in Atlanta, where they managed to rent the large and majestic former French Embassy, but they also spread the Jesus Movement to eight additional states, engaged in street evangelism, founded Christian houses, and started Bible studies. As far as I know, it was David who really took the Jesus Movement to the Southern states.

After some time, David invited me to visit him and the work in Atlanta. I gladly did so, and on one of those trips I met a Roman Catholic priest named Ed Sweeney in some kind of charismatic fellowship in Atlanta, and we became good friends right away. As will be seen in the next chapter, he played a large role in the tragedy that was to follow.

There is much I could say at this point, but I will relate only one memory. It was of an evening at the Atlanta house when I was preaching. I stood with my back against the front door and faced the grand staircase that rose up from the large entry hall. Before me was a minimum of a hundred, maybe even two hundred kids, taking up every square foot of room. I don't think I had ever seen anything like it – a real outpouring of the Holy Spirit, where hundreds were coming to know Christ. It far exceeded anything I had seen in northern California's Bay Area. The ministry in Atlanta was growing day by day, and I knew it all was both a huge privilege and a burden for David to manage.

# Chapter 31

# The COG Moves on Atlanta

The JPM was largely, but not completely, a youth movement. Many leaders had no theological training but were self-taught. It would not be an exaggeration to say that formal education, theological or otherwise, was demeaned by a large segment of the Jesus People. It was considered preferable to be 'taught by the Spirit'.

Over a short period of time, a rather extensive vocabulary grew up that represented the insider language of the Jesus People. It was a mixture of hippie talk and Jesus talk. It reflected a fundamentalist mindset, and some of it was useful in shutting down negative ideas. I find myself still reverting to some of the phrases today. One that comes to mind is, "If it isn't in the Word, I don't want to hear it." Of course, what was "in the Word" was carefully and narrowly defined.

The JPM base theology was either Pentecostal in nature or Dispensational and anti-Pentecostal, but in either case, it was thoroughly fundamentalistic, literalistic, and certain that Jesus was coming tomorrow. The 'authorized' King James Version was the only acceptable translation, and alongside their pocket-sized copy of the KJV New Testament, some also carried a copy of Hal Lindsay's, *The Late Great Planet Earth*.

### Jesus People Leadership

Many of the leaders had little experience in coping with a large number of brand new converts, especially ones from dysfunctional homes who often exhibited serious mental and emotional illnesses, chief among them being drug and sexual addictions. After all, the real attraction to the hippie life, maybe not for all but for most, was the lure of dope and sex. After even a genuine conversion, and even after a space of time when the addictions receded, these temptations would re-emerge. Many were the intrigues and crazy rationales concocted to fulfill the perverted drives, but they were now under some kind of spiritual cloak. For many young converts, it was not a quick or simple process to move from being cloaked in self-righteousness to being clothed in the righteousness of Christ.

The youth and immaturity of most JPM leaders resulted in their utter unpreparedness to deal with heavy responsibility – and I include myself here. No group of Jesus People elected their leaders; the most charismatic, aggressive, and outspoken grabbed at or were shoved into leadership roles. Another take on this was, due to the number of youth coming to Christ, someone had to manage the situation. As I remember some of the leaders in those early days, I recall that few, and I mean very few, lasted in those positions for very long. It was as though God had gifted them, undergirded them, and inspired them, and then when the JPM faded, so did they.

## The COG in Atlanta

David and I often discussed the COG, and we were both aware of the danger this radical mob of zealots posed. The few 'Mo Letters' already written were not yet widely distributed, so no one really knew what the group was up to. We did know that the COG targeted Jesus People gatherings and attempted to persuade people that they and they alone were the really committed followers of Jesus.

We had a faint awareness of the cultic tactics the COG used. The media unwittingly helped Jesus freaks here. At first, most secular and Christian journalists could not distinguish between the good, the bad, and the ugly. But as time went on, and the bizarre stories began to appear in both print and television, most Jesus People had their antennae up.

Despite the threat of the COG, David secretly visited their compound in Texas to check out what they were doing. After David's identity was revealed, he was corralled and courted, and to make it a short story, David invited a COG band to visit the Atlanta ministry. At least he thought he was only inviting a band. The COG had planned things well. Suddenly they burst on the scene, isolated the leaders through one-on-one conversation – divide and conquer – and in a relatively brief time, kids were getting on buses heading for Texas. They had managed to isolate David, making it impossible for him to cope with the situation.

Before that point, Berg and The Family's excesses were not apparent, and certainly David was not aware of their tactics. The circumstances David faced in Atlanta and the responsibility of keeping track of all the other houses in the various states was becoming unmanageable. David was understandably stressed to the breaking point; and raising a family in that environment was virtually impossible. My thinking is that David viewed a melding into COG as a rescue of sorts. He had no idea what he was really getting into.

## Ed Sweeny and a Red-Eye to Atlanta

Late one evening I received a phone call from Ed Sweeny, the Catholic priest I had met in Atlanta some months earlier. He told me about the buses that showed up at David's headquarters in Atlanta and about the dozens of kids getting on board. I called an airline and I was quickly on my way east.

Ed picked me up, and we drove straight to the former French embassy. I jumped out of the car, rushed up the steps to the front door, and encountered a young man who had been in the COG only six months. I was way too late; the bus was on its way to other states to pick up unsuspecting folk at the other houses David had founded.

I was highly agitated, though dead tired, and for an hour the young COG zealot preached the philosophy and mission of The Family to me. In a way I do not understand, I was ready to join up, right there and then. All thoughts of my own family and ministry back in Marin fled from my consciousness. It was like I was being hypnotized. Just at the point I was going to walk into the house and become a member of The Family, Ed suddenly appeared, grabbed me by the arm, and said, "Into the car, get into the car, we are leaving now." He literally pulled me off the porch, across the lawn, and into his car.

Ed is gone now, but I love that man to this day.

The dimensions of the take-over, and that is how I viewed it then and still do, was far greater than I thought. It was some years before I realized the scope of the operation, a realization that came via some of those who had boarded the buses heading for the 'Texas Soul Clinic'.

# Chapter 32

# Two Brothers in Haight

Beginning sometime in 1968, I began to keep a journal. I admit this was after the news media discovered the Jesus Movement, and it occurred to me that it might be important to chronicle things as I saw them.

So I began to write it all down with a pencil and a cheap spiral notebook. I went back mentally to the night I was driving home in the rain from my job as a shoe salesman at J.C. Penny in Corte Madera. The Scott McKenzie song about coming to San Francisco and wearing a flower in your hair was playing on the radio. There it was, like the time it seemed God directly and personally called me into the ministry, that I heard, "Go to the hippies in San Francisco." Okay, I said to myself, and the very next night I headed in as instructed.

That night I met David Hoyt and my whole world changed. I had thought I would be a pastor of a normal kind of church and do the things that I had seen my pastor, Bob Lewis, do. I had no further ambition. I never thought I would write a book or be a great preacher or get involved in the wild and crazy things I did.[1] I paid a high price, and my family, eventually families, also paid a high price. If I had known then what would transpire, I might have become a Jonah and tried to run away from the commis-

---

1    Turns out I did write a book or two and, yes, I have done some wild and crazy things, but I never did become a great preacher, although I do my best every Sunday morning.

sion God gave me.

My idea was to write down my experiences as they happened and not wait a week or so when I might have more time. As best I could, this was the program I followed. I shared with David what I was doing, and there were times when we collaborated and jointly tried to recall the events of the days that we spent together walking the streets of the Haight Ashbury.

I hoped that, at some point, the notes might be turned into a book. I knew I was not much of a writer, but I had an interesting story, so I started sending out letters to publishers about what I was writing about. Much to my surprise I got a letter from Zondervan Publishing House in Grand Rapids, Michigan, and it was, as far as I knew then, the largest and most prestigious Christian publishing house in America.

A vice-president named Bob DeVries sent the letter. I sent a follow-up letter to him asking what he wanted me to do, and his reply was a request for the manuscript, which I immediately sent. Then I waited. Within a few weeks, he flew out to the Bay Area to meet David and me for lunch at the St. Francis Hotel by Union Square. Having grown up in what sociologists of that era described as lower middle class, I had never before eaten in, let alone seen, such a fancy restaurant.

Shocking to us was Mr. DeVries' eagerness for us to sign a contract, which we were also eager to do. Bob DeVries was a most pleasant and gracious man, probably the most important person I had ever met. He remained so throughout the adventure with the story of the hippies.

We had entitled the book, *Two Brothers in Haight.* Zondervan kept the title but said the book had to be rewritten, so they hired a professional, Norman Rohr, who made a living ghost writing as well as teaching writing. When he showed up a couple of weeks later we talked about the book and our story, so he could begin reworking what we had done. After I read his version, however, I called Bob and said something like, "I don't think so."

Not giving up on us, they hired Ed Plowman to do the next

rewrite. I knew Ed, because he was a founding member of Evangelical Concerns and pastor of the Presidio Baptist Church in San Francisco. Things went much better with Ed's version, and the book was placed in line for printing.

The whole process dragged on considerably, and by the time I received the galley proofs, David had long since moved from Walnut Creek to Atlanta. I sent the galleys back and waited for the printed version.

## Halt !

But then it happened; David was swept up into the Children of God. I was presented with a dilemma at that point. If the book came out, I suspected the COG would make use of it in a way I couldn't tolerate. By that time I knew way too much about The Family and was convinced the book should not be published.

I called Mr. DeVries and told him what had happened. I unloaded my worries and, after calming down, said, "We cannot publish the book." He instantly agreed. The irony is that the printing job was nearly complete, and the book would have been in the mail in less than two weeks.

That book, two versions of it plus my own original manuscript, sits amongst my archives of the Jesus People Movement. It might yet see the light of day.

# Chapter 33

# Church of the Open Door Begins in San Rafael

## Earlier movements

It was not until 1968 that I became acquainted with the Charismatic Movement, mainly the Catholic version of it. I connected with the Protestant Charismatic Movement a year later, at Holy Innocents Episcopal Church in Corte Madera, a town in central Marin County. Father Todd Ewald brought a fellow Episcopalian priest, Father Dennis Bennett of Seattle, to preach and minister at Holy Innocents about that time, and many of the Jesus People started attending. I recall an elderly lady named Gert Bohanna who often ministered there as well. Somewhere I have tape recording of a talk she made there. She must have been in her seventies and was so interesting to hear. Every one of us loved her.

The services were fairly charismatic but not wildly so, and while there was healing and speaking in tongues, the main focus was on preaching the Gospel and teaching the Bible. Wherever Jesus was preached and the Bible taught, Jesus People would show up.

We soaked up instruction from the teachers and preachers of the Charismatic Movement, especially from the Ft. Lauderdale Five, as we called them – Bob Mumford, Charles Simpson, Derek Prince, Don Basham, and Ern Baxter. These men were older than nearly all of us, and were experienced, mature Christians. They produced dozens of teaching tapes that we eagerly sought out and listened to for hours and hours. If we heard that one of these men was to be preaching anywhere near us, we made our way there. We also appreciated mainline Pentecostals like Oral Roberts and Kathryn Kuhlman, but they didn't draw us as the Five did. Several other preachers and teachers also caught our attention – names that escape me now.

Jesus People, like those of the Catholic Renewal or the Catholic version of the Charismatic Movement, although influenced by charismatics and Pentecostals, were nevertheless distinct from them, at least in the earliest years. My guess for the origin and chronology of the Charismatic and Catholic Renewal movements is that they preceded the JPM. They may have been a part of the general awakening that developed from various directions, but my experience tells me they were not related.

In San Rafael, where I was living from late 1968 until 1985, there was a Marist seminary, and one or two of their priests/monks visited the Bible studies we conducted. They invited me to their masses, and I occasionally participated in these. There was also in San Rafael a Carmelite Monastery that offered a public prayer service that many Jesus People and charismatics from a number of different churches attended. Still, the JPM was different and distinct from the Catholic Charismatic expression, though many people moved freely between the two.

Our work in Marin centered on Bible studies and evangelistic outreaches at the local high schools and the local community college, College of Marin, which has two campuses, one in Ignacio and the original and main campus in Kentfield. Eventually, we had a Bible study in each school, and that often led to opening up yet another Christian house. I signed so many leases and guaranteed so many utility accounts during that period, it caused me some sleepless nights. As stated earlier, we began then to open up Christian bookstores and even a thrift shop.

On Sunday mornings, my family and I attended local Baptist churches, mostly Southern Baptist-aligned and some American Baptist churches as well. In every case we were warmly received and encouraged. Although we were a para-church ministry that came alongside churches and not leaders or pastors of a church, I felt it important to be a part of a community of faith; evangelistic outreach was not enough. Most of the time, we attended the First Baptist Church of San Rafael on Lincoln Avenue, the Lucas Valley Community Church in a northern suburb of San Rafael, or the First Baptist Church of Novato.

## Pressure to Begin a Church

Among our early leaders, from around 1970, were Mike Riley, Roger Hoffman, and Bob Hymers. Roger and Bob had roots with Southern Baptists, Mike had been with the United Brethren Church, and all attended Golden Gate Baptist Theological Seminary in Mill Valley, the school I graduated from in 1968.[1]

Mike, Roger, and Bob were much more used to regular church involvement than the rest of our leaders. Nearly from the beginning of our relationship they were pushing to start up a church. They had a valid point, since the kids and some of their parents attended all kinds of different churches, while the majority attended nowhere at all. For more than a year, I resisted this move, thinking a para-church ministry was the proper model for us.

Moishe Rosen of Jews for Jesus, who more than anyone else served as a mentor to me during that period, encouraged us to remain a para-church ministry with a focus on street evangelism. I agreed fully, and thus a wedge opened up between the others and me.

## An Evening Gathering in Mill Valley

Mike, Roger, and Bob had assembled together a number of the young people from our ministry for gatherings at the Dow's

---

1    At the time of this writing, my son Vernon is now attending the seminary and my wife Katie graduated from there three years ago with an MDiv.

home in Mill Valley. I decided to attend to see what was happening. Bob, no question one of the best preachers I have ever heard, anywhere, anytime, could hold anyone listening in rapture for long periods. Bob, whose full name is Robert Leslie Hymers, Jr., is a strong leader with a lot of experience in churches, and he was bound and determined to start a church, which he wanted named Church of the Open Door after the famous church of the same name in Los Angeles.

Quickly, the house became too small to accommodate the crowd, and a move was made to Scout Hall in Mill Valley on East Blithedale. That place also filled up quickly, and I was left with a very large dilemma. This was all being done despite my wanting to avoid becoming a church. However, the leaders of our Christian House Ministries – Mark Buckley, Kenny Sanders, Bruce Arnold, Blacky Smith, Geoff Tachet, Bob Gaulden, Bob Burns, and others – conferred together and recognized the church-like entity that had already developed. They also decided to continue the existing model of street evangelism, high school ministry, Christian houses, Christian bookstores, and so on.

A board of elders formed, I served as senior pastor, and we took steps to incorporate. It did not take too long before Scout Hall was not adequate, so we moved into Carpenter's Hall on Lindaro Street in central San Rafael and rented out some office space nearby on Jordan Street. This was in 1972.

As could be expected, the Monday morning elders meetings were stormy, to put it mildly. The egos, including mine, could not easily be contained in the space in which we met, which was my office at the Christian General Store, 2130 Fourth Street in San Rafael. After around one year, Bob decided to go back to Los Angeles from whence he had come and begin another church there. The original name of his first church in downtown Los Angeles was the Fundamentalist Tabernacle Baptist Church. Bob's great preaching soon drew crowds, and the church grew rapidly.

Bob's leaving had an impact on me I did not recognize right

away. He was the only non-charismatic among us, not that we were 'wild-eyed', but we were tending more and more in that direction. The oars were missing, and I was carried along on the current. It was not until 1978 that Dr. Lou Rambo, my major professor at San Francisco Theological Seminary, forced me to make a critical analysis of what we were doing and thinking.

In 1975, the Church of the Open Door had outgrown the space in Carpenter's Hall. On one single Sunday, we divided ourselves up and started four additional churches. One was in Novato with Mark Buckley, another in Petaluma with Kenny Sanders, one in San Francisco with Bob Gaulden, and one in Pt. Reyes Station with Bruce Arnold. At that point there were somewhere between 325 and 375 attending the two Sunday mornings services in San Rafael. The Sunday following the division into four churches the hall in San Rafael was full again, although there should only have been about 125 in attendance. My figures may be faulty, but that is how I remember things. We were forced to continue two morning services, and the later service was always packed wall to wall.

Final note on the founding of the Church of the Open Door in San Rafael: The view of the church's founding above is my own, and I have discovered in the process of preparing these memoirs that my account is only one among several. None of the versions vary enough to cause any alarm, however. Perhaps a more agreed upon story may evolve out of conversation around this book.

# Chapter 34

# Jim Jones and the People's Temple

Another spiritual leader also had many people fooled about the real nature of his group besides David Berg and the Children of God. It has been argued long and hard about which was more damaging to the Jesus People Movement. My opinion is that the COG caused the most damage, since the Jones' business collapsed so completely and was so utterly discredited, any trouble instigated by them disappeared rather quickly. And it must be made clear, despite confusion to the contrary – Jim Jones and The People's Temple had absolutely no connection with the JPM.

Jim Jones did not impact my ministry in Marin County until 1972, the year Church of the Open Door was established. We were a non-denominational, charismatic church built on the ministry foundation several of us had established in Marin's towns. I became aware of Jones from articles in the *San Francisco Chronicle*, since he had involved himself in San Francisco politics, a very strange creature during that period.

Jones began sending buses to our parking lot at the back of the Carpenter's Hall in San Rafael on Sunday mornings, in order to transport anyone wanting to come to his services in San Francisco instead of ours. This tactic revealed Jones' arrogant and aggressive nature. At first, I did nothing to stop this tactic, but after hearing reports of what was taking place at the meetings, I decided to visit The People's Temple myself and attended at least two of their services.[1]

What I recount now may seem rather strange; however, many other people witnessed what I experienced, and over an extended period of time. Here is what happened: (1) Angel's wings (or so it was said) brushed over me; (2) My up-stretched hand was clasped as in a hand shake that could be felt but not seen; (3) I smelled a pleasant aroma, which Jim Jones called 'the sweet savor of the Lord,' wafting through the air; and (4) Drops of oil fell on my Bible held open on my lap. In addition, there was a young black girl from Oakland, maybe aged thirteen, who stood in front of the congregation while the 'stigmata' appeared on her hands and ankles – the places where the Roman soldiers pounded the nails into Jesus' body – and blood, or so it seemed, soaked through her dress at the point where the spear of the Roman soldier pierced Jesus' side.

After this I understood the attraction; there was a powerful presence in Jim Jones' meetings. Despite the spiritual nature of the meetings, and the enthusiasm, the clapping, dancing, and exuberant singing, I heard no gospel preached or Bible taught. Oddly, it was also not the kind of service I would describe as either Pentecostal or charismatic.

After my visits to the People's Temple, I addressed the San Rafael Church and made it very clear that it was the devil at work in Jones' services and definitely not the Spirit of God. The miracles, I declared, were counterfeit, however real, and the whole purpose was to deceive and confuse the faithful. I warned as sternly as I could that no one should attend his services.

When the Jonestown tragedy in Guiana became known to the world, and for some months after that, I officiated at funerals for some of those who died at Jonestown. It was then that I was

---

1    I later climbed on board the bus when it pulled into the parking lot and literally threatened the driver with bodily harm if he ever showed up again. No bus ever came back, and I am thankful for that to this day, without apology.

able to make sense and be certain of what had happened: there was at work at The People's Temple the same force at work with David Moses Berg and COG – a demonic power able to seduce and deceive through counterfeit signs and wonders. I had felt that same power on the morning when Ed Sweeney had to pull me away from being drawn into the COG while listening to a member's pitch. It was that same pull I had experienced during the Kirtans at the Hare Krishna temple in 1967. Now I had seen it at work at The People's Temple.

## A Failure to Discern

I learned a lesson: not all that is spiritual is of the Spirit of God. Due to the charismatic orientation embraced by most of the Jesus People, we were not able to grasp this. This failure was likely the most damaging aspect of the JPM, contributing to its dark side. We simply did not know that prophecy, healings, and miracles could be of a devilish origin. I am still working through aspects of this in my current spiritual walk. I don't want to assign all signs and wonders to the nether regions, because I think that during times of awakening, there are exceptional Holy Spirit gifts given that authentically result in glory to God. Let me be clear, however, that none of what I experienced during the Hindu services, or encountered with the young man on the porch of the former French Embassy in Atlanta, or saw firsthand at the People's Temple in San Francisco had anything to do with the Spirit of God.

# Chapter 35

# Thyatira

**B**ob and Diane Ellison were among the people my age or older who began to show up at Church of the Open Door in San Rafael. Although there was a whole pack of young people involved, few had actual jobs or only had low paying work. What I mean is, for a church our size, our income was below average. Bob and Diane, to a considerable extent, made up the difference.

After Bob and I had met and been friends for a while, he decided to invest in our ministries. I don't have the details of all he did, but one thing I do recall clearly is the small farm in Petaluma he bought for use as a Christian house. The address of the little farm was 1399 Springhill Road, Petaluma. Because Bob's first wife, then deceased, was named Lydia (and students of the book of Acts know that Lydia was from Thyatira, one of the seven cities of Asia addressed in John's revelation), Bob and Diane named the farm they bought Thyatira.

From the beginning, Bob involved me in the purchase. We checked out several places in Sonoma County, but the little farm that had once grown Christmas trees was the most attractive. Our forays into farmland searches were also enjoyable, because Bob loved hamburgers like I do, so when we drove up to Petaluma, we always stopped at a hamburger joint on Washington Blvd. He could have afforded big steak houses, but he preferred the old time little places.

Bob's parents had been with the Salvation Army, and he

learned the thrift store business from them. Later on, he opened a chain of stores he named Purple Heart, and they flourished. He was a faithful tither, and that money was put to many good purposes.

Thyatira had a modest main house of maybe 1,600 square feet, but its best feature was a nice, big swimming pool. Some of my favorite photos are of baptisms we held there.

Kenny Sanders was the first leader of Thyatira. The first time I met Kenny was just after he had come to Berachah House in San Anselmo. His black hair was matted and covered his face. I walked up to him and parted the tangled, greasy mop that shielded his face, and got a look at him. His looks at the time did not give a clue that his father was in the inner circle of attorneys who worked with Martin Luther King, Jr.

The farm's bedrooms quickly received their occupants, and the group next expanded a tool shed and converted it into a dorm of sorts. When the Petaluma branch of Church of the Open Door opened soon after a bookstore, they then needed a parsonage, which the guys promptly built on the property, mostly through the work of Ken Sanders.[1]

Cliff Silliman ran the bookstore in Petaluma, and it was a place where the community could drop in and get to know the Jesus People who had taken up residence in the town. Cliff was always welcoming and cordial, and although the bookstore eventually proved not to be financially successful, overall it was a solid ministry.

One of my favorite escapes from the counseling work and

---

1    I recall days when I would paint on work crews that Kenny and Cliff organized in order to make money for the parsonage on Thyatira. Kenny learned painting on one of the work crews I headed in Marin while he was at Berachah House in San Anselmo. Kenny became an excellent painter. The parsonage was expensive and nicely built, and we had to raise money for it. Kenny was the first pastor of the Church of the Open Door in Petaluma, later became a medical doctor, and recently retired as an emergency care doctor with Kaiser.

pastoring in San Rafael was to drive north up highway 101 to Petaluma. I would visit Cliff at Berachah House and then drive over to Thyatira. Those were some of the most pleasant days of my life. It was so nice to be in that beautiful country and walk around the farms and plan new projects. As I write this I find in me a desire to go back and find the locations of those farms. Perhaps I will someday soon.

# Chapter 36

# How We Got into Big Trouble

It was not long before real trouble struck the Jesus People Movement.[1] A steady stream of 'prophets' started appearing, from Sung Young Moon to David Moses Berg to Jim Jones and more. These were the big names, the big groups; and there were others.

## Kathryn Kuhlman

Kathryn Kuhlman was a lovely, elderly lady in Oakland, who had a healing ministry popular with the local Jesus freaks. She was sweet and kind and impossible to disparage, but from a pastoral point of view, she presented difficulties. Kuhlman was a healer of the old fashioned kind, and when healing of the body is involved, people flock to whatever remedy is being touted. Some of the Marin kids in the Bible studies were driving over to be part of the Kuhlman services. In time, I made the trip, too.

She had rented out what must have been an old-fashioned movie theater, and before the scheduled start time, she would walk between the curtains, peer out at the audience and ask, "Have you been waiting for me?" The audience would roar back, "Yes."

---

1    From my point of view, the year was 1970 when the trouble started. The JPM was still in full flower, but opposing forces had moved in and were winning victories. I estimate that the awakening that was the JPM ground to a halt in 1972, though it may have lasted longer in some places.

Ms. Kuhlman spoke softly, preaching the standard evangel-ical/pentecostal line but without much biblical content, and soon, lines of people hoping to be healed appeared on both sides of the stage. One by one, they walked or were wheeled to the center of the stage to receive Kathryn's healing touch and prayer. Helpers discarded wheel chairs and pairs of crutches, as loud shrieks of praise echoed off the walls of the cavernous building. One afternoon as I left for home after a healing service, I saw people throwing wheel chairs and other stuff onto a pile of like things outside the back door of the theater.

Kathryn was so warm and loving that one did not want to disappoint her. If she claimed a healing, then there was a healing. No one dared to publicly embarrass her. I had studied enough psychology to know about the placebo effect, and as time wore on I was fairly sure I was seeing this played out. We were glad to see people healed, but when the healings wore off, which they most often did, pastoral chores resulted.

Healing is wonderful, and I have seen people healed, been healed myself, and watched as my son Vernon was healed on at least two occasions, but healing began to be a distraction from the core activity of the Jesus People, which was evangelism. What was occurring without our full realization was that distractions, if not distortions, were sweeping into the JPM.

Investigative journalists eventually descended on Kath-ryn, and her whole endeavor was discredited. Kathryn slowly receded from the public gaze; gawk might be a better word. She was a dear old lady and much loved, and she represented a throwback to the old Pentecostal holy roller healers I witnessed in Portland as a kid.

## Other Questionable Persons

Another 'evangelist' who came well before Kuhlman was Wil-liam Branham. His only trouble was that an angel, named Emma or maybe Emily, stood beside him and actually conducted the healing ministry. Branham admitted to it, and despite the fact that he was killed in an automobile accident while drunk, a kind of cult grew up around him, claiming he had been the Messiah or a forerunner of the Messiah. (I ran into little groups dedicated to him at San Quentin Prison.)

It seemed as though one thing after another was insisting on attention. Individuals and groups, it occurs to me now, saw what was going on and jumped onto the bandwagon. David Berg's The Family fits this description. Victor Paul Wierwille and his Way International also fit here. But the healers and the positive-thinking faith people were whom we encountered most of all.

Through arrangements made by a dear lady in Atlanta named Cora Vance, I was invited to appear on Pat Robertson's 700 Club for an interview. In the small, sterile waiting room before my turn, I found myself talking with a guy in a light blue leisure suit. His interview with Robertson was scheduled just before mine, and he asked me what my 'shtick' was. I did not know what he meant, so he explained that he was known for making legs grow. He said he could do it without fail and insisted on giving me a demonstration. Sure enough, he declared that one of my legs was shorter than the other and, boom, he made them both the same length. I just smiled and hoped he would soon be called onto the stage.

## Prophets and Other Problems

In my view, the most dangerous of all were those who styled themselves as prophets. It was heady to know a prophet and, of course, to later be known as a prophet oneself. When we heard the words of the prophets and prophetesses, we yelled out exclamations such as, "Wow! Praise God! Hallelujah!" Once a 'prophet' is accepted into a fellowship or church, however, trouble begins to emerge.

My sense of it is that those self-styled prophets had learned from others how to go about 'prophesying' yet sincerely thought their pronouncements were from the Lord. While praying for a person who was hoping to receive a word of knowledge or revelation, the prophet would receive impressions and announce them: "God is calling you to China." "You are to marry your boyfriend and stop living in sin." "You are being used by God to provide finances for this church, and you must sell your house and hand over the money to the elders." These were typical prophetic words I heard, and some of them came out of my own mouth. At minimum, I was guilty of giving a platform to people whom I thought I could trust, whom I thought were genuine prophets of God, but who eventually proved they were not. It is safe to say that there was a considerable lack of discernment among the Jesus People.

Then there were the sexual predators who showed up surprisingly often. It is too much to go on with descriptions and details, but I saw it all. There were also thieves, only after money. Cultists hung about at our meetings, looking for new believers and other vulnerable people, befriending them, chatting them up, and inviting them to other meetings. I understood then what Jesus said about wolves attacking the flock. At times, it felt like I was being besieged.

It became increasingly uncomfortable to identify myself as a charismatic. Yet I had seen what I thought were genuine spiritual gifts, and I would not let the weird taint the real.

Alongside these difficulties were the disturbing theologies. These were, in the long run, perhaps more troubling than anything else. I had personally gotten started in the Christian life embracing Dispensationalism and had taped on a wall several charts I used to predict the date of the Rapture.[2] I thought any

---

2   While I was a pastor at Church of the Open Door in San Rafael, a young man asked me to prove that there would be a rapture. I said, sure, easy, look here in 1 Thessalonians 4. I looked and looked myself, trying to find proof, but the only way I could do it was to draw a line between verses 16 and 17 and then invert them. I saw for the first time that the second coming and the rapture were in fact the very same event. I was shocked and embarrassed,

other viewpoint was complete liberalistic heresy. We reveled in
the thought that, at any moment, we would be blasted into the
air to meet Jesus. We were also getting ready for the seven years
of tribulation – that is, if we got left behind. We were preparing
for a war with the devil and his legions, and those legions could
include anyone, even family, and there was no time to waste on
getting an education, starting a business, or raising a family. This
was not a widespread and commonly held view, but people such
as the Children of God, for example, used this end time scenario
to recruit, motivate, and retain members. It was another kind
of high; it got the endorphins going and put an exciting edge on
everything.

The JPM existed alongside the 1960s counterculture revolution, which was a real revolution sans guns and bombs. The
Weathermen, part of a student activist group centered around
the University of California at Berkeley, the radical anti-war pro-
testers, and others on the fringe, like the Black Panthers, were
taking the law into their own hands. Rock and Roll had morphed
into a different kind of music – acid rock and finally heavy metal
– and the relatively mild lusts of young people were being perverted. Eastern religions and mind altering/expanding drugs
impacted the baby boomers with a vengeance. The occult arts
were out in the open and admired, publicized, applauded, and
approved. Here it was – minds blown out and open, spiritualities
abounding, and power, power, power, at one's fingertips.

## Arrogance Abounded

Arrogance is what I am talking about, and the Jesus People
were also arrogant. I was arrogant, terribly so, and I later had

because I had preached a pre-tribulation rapture my entire ministry. After a
lengthy time of study, humiliation, and repentance, I had to concede that I
had been wrong, but at the same time, I couldn't see going over to the 'liberal
amillenialists'. What I did was announce one Sunday, from the pulpit, that if
anyone could clearly, plainly, show me there was a difference between the
second coming and what we called the rapture, I would give him or her one
thousand dollars. No takers yet.

a lot of apologizing to do. We were Jesus People, we were filled with the Spirit, God was on our side, and we alone had the 'full gospel.'

Another view of our arrogance was that we were not as grace-oriented as one might expect. The JPM, despite appearances, was really rather moralistic and legalistic. Yes, salvation was by grace alone, but unless one repented and believed in Jesus, and even more, had actually prayed to receive Jesus, then there was no salvation. It was really that we were in control of salvation and grace was not really grace; it was, at most, cooperation with God. Jesus died and rose from the dead, but our job was to repent, believe, and say the sinner's prayer. This then carried over into our feelings about ourselves and others. It was a performance-based gospel we preached, and there was plenty of room to put ourselves and others down.

Even in our houses, new believers were expected to grow up quickly, and if they failed to do so, they were often told to leave. The atmosphere at Church of the Open Door was often the same; people, including the leaders, were on a short leash. Many of the congregants were baby Christians, mostly from dysfunctional families and converted out of all kinds of sin and perversion, just barely rescued from hell itself – and we were worried about a messy diaper. I carry to this day a measure of guilt for how I judged people and treated them rudely when their sin was exposed.

Funny how the truth is right in front of us, yet we fail to grasp it. The 'new birth' is a phrase with a big clue: newborns must grow up in stages and cannot be expected to be mature adults after a five-week discipleship training course.

# Chapter 37

# Deliverance Temple

The Solid Rock is what we called the house on Wilson Street in Novato. It was perhaps the most active and important of all the Christian houses, and its founder was Mark Buckley.

Mark, joined later by Kristina Kenner after their marriage, grew up in a northern suburb of San Rafael called Terra Linda.[1] There were eight Buckley kids, four boys and four girls, and everyone in town knew them. Mark was the first of the family to become a Christian. His conversion took place somewhere in Oregon through the testimony of people from the Manifested Sons of God, a group I considered cultic, but they did tell Mark about Jesus.

Mark and his brothers, John, Robert, and Barry, were star athletes at the high school, playing mostly football. They were all handsome young men and gifted in many ways. Mark got into the hippie thing, and his salvation saved him not only from sin but also from what could have been a devastated life. Instead, he was instrumental in the conversion of two of his brothers and one or two sisters, as well as his mother.

---

1    From the years 1968 onward, to 1975, Mark was my closest partner in ministry. He met Kristina at a Bible study I held on Tuesday nights on Greenfield Ave. in San Rafael. In my mind's eye I can see Mark seated right next to Martin, later Moishe, Rosen in the front room of the Greenfield house, otherwise known as Zion's Inn. Currently Mark is senior pastor of a large church in Phoenix, Arizona.

Mark was a very skilled carpenter and developed a work crew to provide income and learn a trade for new Christians living in some of the houses. He was very energetic, strong, and optimistic, and he taught a number of young men how to work with their hands. A treasure I still have is a hammer Mark gave me in probably 1969, when he hired me to put redwood shingles on the side of a house he was remodeling, in Ross or San Anselmo. During those years I was either working as a janitor or as a painter.

It was not long before Mark moved out of his childhood home and became the leader of Solid Rock. If I were to attempt to relay here all the events of note that occurred in and around that house, it would be an excessively long chapter. But there is one story, maybe two, I will recount.

In the back yard of Solid Rock was a large, unfinished, two-story building. The ground floor was meant to be a three-car garage, and the upstairs – well, we never really found out about that, but we used one of the rooms for casting out demons. We called it Deliverance Temple, from the Lord's Prayer, "Deliver us from evil" (Matthew 6:13).

A little background would be helpful now. I graduated from Golden Gate Baptist Theological Seminary in 1968 with an M.Div. degree; my diploma may say 1969. An M.Div. used to be a B.D. (Bachelors of Divinity). A three to four year program, it is the basic seminary course of study. My ministry in the Haight with the hippies occupied me for some time, but in 1971, I went back for another masters program, this time a Th.M., or Masters in Theology, a two to three year program.[2]

---

2   Earlier, in 1969, I had begun volunteering at San Quentin State Prison, located between Mill Valley and San Rafael. For more than three years, I worked under the auspices of the Garden Chapel (Protestant) under two chaplains. For a time I taught New Testament in the School of Theology and then toward the end, after a new chaplain took over, I facilitated a Yoke Fellows group. This volunteer time ended with the George Jackson shoot-out, in 1972. I returned in 1985 to work with a new chaplain, Earl Smith, and for

After the class work and the seminars, I began work on my thesis. Because of the constant encountering of persons involved in the occult during my years on the street, I had a desire and need to know more about it. Already I had moved away from my earlier college days' concepts that the demonic was merely poor and outdated primitive psychology. By 1972, I knew better, but I did not know as much as I needed to.

By that time, I was already doing deliverance ministry, and my teacher, via tapes and books, was Don Basham, one of the Fort Lauderdale Five, about which I will have more to say later. Casting out demons was a necessary ministry, since so many of the ex-hippies had been involved in or initiated into occult rituals or eastern religious practices where they had literally invited various deities (so-called) to guide them, or had experienced trances or altered states of consciousness through mind-altering drugs like LSD. It was not something that was going to go away; this ministry, in fact, was requiring more and more time.

*A Manual of Demonology and the Occult* was the title of the thesis. For more than a year I spent every possible spare moment working on the manual in the old library at the seminary. My major professor, Dr. Richard Cunningham, signed off on each chapter, and I entered the oral phase of the project with confidence. But I was shot down, and harshly. My favorite New Testament and Greek teacher, Dr. Clayton Harrop, who long after remained my friend, had the task of telling me my thesis failed.

Disappointed, but not ready to give up, I submitted a new proposal for a thesis, which took me four months to prepare. When, however, I gave it to Dr. Cunningham, he decided to tell me the truth. He reminded me that Golden Gate was a Southern

---

about twelve years did cell to cell ministry. Then in 1997 I was asked to coach the baseball team, first the Pirates, then the Giants, which I did until 2012. By my calculation, I volunteered for thirty years there. Presently I am barred for life from the prison, due to power struggles by both convicts and prison officials. I have a treasured photo of Joyful Noise playing music at the prison chapel, in 1971, at just about the conclusion of the band's ministry. It is on the cover of this book.

Baptist institution and that they would never allow a tongues speaker to be awarded a high academic degree.[3]

The thesis, I reasoned, was yet worth something, so I called Zondervan Publishing House in Grand Rapids and spoke to Bob DeVries, the man who wanted to publish *Two Brothers in Haight*. He asked me to send him the manuscript. To make a long story short, the thesis was published in 1973. A second edition came out in 1976; it was even published in Swedish. It sold like crazy and is actually still available; a pirated version can be bought at Amazon.[4]

The publication of that book, however, opened a floodgate of people who wanted demons cast out of them. Many showed up on a regular basis, some even arriving at my front door in Terra Linda with no baggage, no money, and desperate. At one point there were twenty-six people trained to do casting out of demons – thirteen teams of two, just to cope with the volume of requests.

Back now to Deliverance Temple. Once a week I drove up to Novato to join Mark and cast demons out of people. Mostly, I never knew who the people were, never saw them before, and usually never saw them again. They simply showed up, and Mark or someone else did the scheduling. And this went on for a long period of time.

---

3    Moishe Rosen, who thought I should become a seminary professor rather than a pastor, advised me to sue the seminary to get my degree. My thinking was that I should have known better in the first place. The seminary had the right to do as it pleased, but perhaps I should have been informed early on about their view of my tongue speaking. My wife Katie graduated with an MDiv degree in 2009, son Vernon is a student there now, and currently I am mentoring one student from the seminary, one of many over the years. It is a fine school.

4    Hopefully sometime in 2014 a new version of the demonology book will be published by Earthen Vessel Publishing. Some few years ago I was asked to write a brief description of *How Christians Cast Out Demons Today*, and that book is currently available at www.evpbooks.com.

## Two Stories

Now the first of two stories: After an article covering the casting out of demons somehow got into *Time* magazine, I received a call from Nancy, a young reporter from the magazine, who asked if she could come to a session where demons were cast out; she wanted to do a follow-up story. She lived nearby in Greenbrae, so it wasn't going to be a big deal for her to show up. I agreed and scheduled a time for her to witness the 'activities'.

It was a stormy Thursday night in mid-winter when I picked Nancy up and headed for Novato and Deliverance Temple. Mark, Nancy, and I, along with the first person scheduled for deliverance, passed though the house, walked into the back yard, entered the unfinished garage, and ascended the stairs to the second floor. Mark led the way with his flashlight to where he had arranged four chairs underneath the single light bulb, our sole source of light and warmth. Nancy was seated to my right, Mark sat across from me, and the subject, a young man about my age whom I will call Bill, sat quietly on the metal chair to my left.

We talked a while with Bill, discussing details about how he might have gotten demons. Then the praying started, with Mark and I taking turns commanding any demons in Bill to come out in the name of Jesus. There was nothing about him, either his behavior or his past, that indicated that there were or should be any demons present in Bill. But, as we had found out many times before, one really never knows, so we did not easily give up.

It was a miserable night in Deliverance Temple, really cold, and we wore winter coats. Nancy sat quietly watching and making an entry or two in the notebook she had on her lap. Despite the cold, Mark and I began to sweat, not so much with the effort put forth, but due to a certain embarrassment that came over us. Here we were, sitting in a weird dark unfinished room with only studs along the walls, no real ceiling, only a roof far above us in the darkness, with the wind and rain howling outside. We were Jesus freaks, and Nancy was a reporter for *Time* magazine; no doubt she thought we were fools, at best, but more she probably thought we were deluded and crazed cultists.

Mark and I stole glances at each other. Bill sat still and peaceful, not saying a word or even twitching. No demons were showing up. Nancy squirmed a little as the time rolled on. Maybe an hour passed.

Suddenly, without warning, Bill literally flew backward, straight back and up. If there had been a ceiling he would have crashed into it. He hit the wall behind him and slid down to the floor between the studs. Nancy had fear on her face; she had just seen something that was physically impossible. Mark and I were relieved.

We walked over to Bill, picked him up and escorted him back to the center of the room and his chair. We started again, knowing now there were indeed demons in him. After a few minutes it happened again; Bill flew through the air the same way as before. This time Mark and I pulled our chairs over to him and proceeded, with Bill sitting on the floor, to cast out several demons. We continued until there were no longer any demonic manifestations.

Next and last was a young woman, about Nancy's age, and this time it was different, typical really. We talked some, prayed some, and then started to command the demons to come out, based on the power and authority of Jesus. Several demons were cast out, and we spent some more time talking, essentially a counseling session intended to be encouraging and helpful. That was the end of it.

The reporter had little to say on the way home. I asked her to let me know when the magazine with the deliverance story came out. Weeks went by before the edition appeared. I read every word but found nothing about what happened at Deliverance Temple. I called her and asked why not. She said she submitted the story and described accurately what had happened, but an editor found it unbelievable and deleted that part entirely. I never heard from Nancy again, but I will always remember that strange night at Solid Rock.

One more story: Joyful Noise had been invited by a large Presbyterian Church in Walnut Creek to minister to their youth group. The pastor, whom I will call Joe, and I got along well, and I added him to my newsletter list. Perhaps a year went by before I received a phone call from him. He wanted to bring his daughter, aged fifteen, over for prayer. Sue, not her real name, had been acting strangely, and Joe thought it was of a demonic nature and described some strange things going on. Once I heard this report, I agreed with him, and he and his wife, Sue's mother, brought Sue over for deliverance.

Mark, Sue, and I spent many weeks, six or maybe seven, two hours minimum at a time, hoping to cast some demons out of the teenager. She sat quietly and at rest time after time, week after week. Mark and I decided that she did not have demons, and I called Joe and told him so. He did not agree and pleaded for just one more time. Joe was one of the finest men I had ever met, and the whole family was just as precious as could be. I agreed to another attempt.

Once again Mark and I trooped out to Deliverance Temple with Sue and made every effort, did all we could do. As always there was nothing but simple prayer and asking God to cast out demons. Nothing again, and I dreaded walking back into Solid Rock with Sue to face her parents.

Since this was to be the family's last visit to Novato, Joe wanted to have communion. We stood in a circle in the kitchen area. Joe served us with the bread first, and then he began to pass the cup around. Then it reached Sue. As she raised it to her lips, she collapsed to the floor, and the cup and its contents went flying. Mark and I looked at each other and bent over Sue, and just as quickly and easily as anything I had ever seen, we cast out a whole bunch of demons. Finally she was exhausted; we raised her up to her feet, there was some charismatic type of praise, and off the family went.

It was not over, however. Joe called a week later and told me they found out how the demons had gotten into Sue. There had been a mission trip to Haiti, and on the return trip they brought home with them a girl Sue's age, whom Sue had befriended in Haiti. Sue confessed that she and the Haitian girl had been playing around with Voodoo spells late at night when everyone went to bed. Weird things had started to happen, and both girls were scared to say anything about it.

I agreed to have the Haitian girl come over, too. This time, it was fairly quickly done. Indeed, demons were present and were cast out.

Some years ago now, maybe fifteen, Sue showed up just before the morning service at Miller Avenue. I was called out to the front porch of the building and there was Sue, her husband, and two little kids. She wanted to simply say thanks for what had happened many years ago at Deliverance Temple.

# Chapter 38

# Shepherding Movement – Ft. Lauderdale Five

Perhaps more devastating specifically to the JPM than The Family (Children of God or COG), Jim Jones, or any number of other strange teachings and groups, was the Shepherding Movement, because it directly affected our church life.

The Fort Lauderdale Five – Bob Mumford, Charles Simpson, Derek Prince, Don Basham, and Ern Baxter – were all respected teachers in the early years of the JPM. They formed an umbrella type of ministry that seemed to them to be a necessity, given the chaotic and confused nature of the JPM. These five leaders began to accumulate churches and ministries under their authority and over which they became overseers, 'shepherds'. Certain accountability could then be built into the process. It seemed almost a natural kind of progression, a helpful ministry, one borne out of caring, and I think it was just that at first.

One of their publications coming out of Fort Lauderdale was *New Wine*, a magazine with articles that really spoke to young charismatics across the country. In addition to the magazine was a steady stream of cassette tapes and books that communicated new and exciting teachings about the fresh outpouring of the Holy Spirit for the last days. We in Marin became faithful readers and listeners of this material, and it became very influential to our Christian thinking.

Across the country, Jesus People leaders, with their ministries and churches, 'submitted' themselves to one of the five shepherds and would then become 'under-shepherds'. I considered doing the same myself for all of the Open Door churches, because the work was often beyond me and left me wondering what to do next. Here was where my characteristic independent streak rescued me from submitting to one of the five. There was something I rebelled against in the Shepherding Movement, and my stance was misunderstood by many of those who served with me in leadership.

## The Attractions

Many struggling pastors and leaders considered it desirable, even a Godsend, to be accountable to Bob Mumford or one of the other shepherds. And for local JPM leaders, here was a chance for no-bodies like we were to be aligned with big-named and respected Christian spearheads. The identification with men like Bob Mumford was a big attraction. I, too, traveled long distances to hear him and be in his presence. It was a bit like idol or celebrity worship, thus it would be from pride that someone in Podunk could say they were submitted to Bob, or Charles, or Ern, or Derek, or Don.

Additionally, it was thought, though not explicitly stated, that this arrangement of coming under the authority of the Five was what God was doing in the Last Days. The Last Days, a frequent subject of sermons and teachings, was on our minds. For many of the Jesus People who came out of the Catholic Church it was comforting to think they still had a bishop or an archbishop, if not an actual pope.

## The Detractions

My view was that local leadership was a more biblical model of church structure, despite the troubles it involved. Additionally, it did not seem quite right to be part of a very large organization whose leaders demanded that certain policies be carried out, one of which involved money. The tithe was mandatory, and to determine the amount that should be given, they required submission of financial statements for examination. It was the measure of control they wielded to which I primarily objected. It might have seemed proper to many, but not to me.

## The Battle - Go or Stay

The matter of being in or out was finally made clear in 1975. One of our pastors, a former seminary student who had taken over the remains of several Christian houses, a bookstore, and our church in San Francisco, announced he was now submitted to Bob Mumford, was leaving our fellowship of churches, and was retaining the Christian bookstore. The battle lines were drawn.

In response, I asked for a meeting with the Church of the Open Door in San Francisco, now under Bob Mumford. One evening, we met at one of the Christian houses in the City. I invited Bob Hymers to come up from Los Angeles and also Bob Burns, who had earlier been the pastor of the church in San Francisco. It so happened that David Hoyt was in Marin on a visit, and the four of us intended to make our case before the departing church.

The meeting was packed wall to wall. One by one, the four of us made a presentation of what we knew and thought about the Shepherding Movement. I specifically spoke about our labor in developing the Taraval Street bookstore and the other means by which the ministry had been built over the years. Dr. Hymers, Bob Burns, and David Hoyt also made impassioned pleas for the people to reconsider and remain in fellowship with the other churches in our little network.

There was little response from the listeners, most of whom I knew quite well and a number of whom I had baptized. They sat politely silent and voiced very few questions or remarks. A few days later I received a letter informing me that the San Francisco church had unanimously voted to be under the shepherding of Mumford. One thing was granted to us, the return of the Christian bookstore that Bob Burns and I had worked so hard to establish, using thousands of dollars from the San Rafael church and bookstore to build it.

At that point I wrote a pamphlet about the movement and pointed out that the 'Five' liked to 'wine and dine' pastors and others, in order to get them to submit. This little booklet was printed by many groups over the next several years and was particularly used in Great Britain, where the Shepherding Movement was starting to make inroads.

## From Solution to Problem

The Shepherding Movement was the source of a great deal of grief for me and continues to impact me in subtle ways to this day. It fractured alliances and friendships and seemed to me to have been one reason the JPM ended, in our region at minimum, but to some extent throughout the entire nation.

The Shepherding Movement eventually imploded somewhere in the late 1970s or early 1980s. In my view, and from what I heard from some of those who had seen the devastation, the problem looked like the following: A leader of a church full of Jesus People, who has no real experience as a pastor, finds the job to be overwhelming. Out of desperation, this new pastor submits to one of the Fort Lauderdale Five. Changes come down the pipeline, which are not easily implemented. The congregation is divided up with 'under-shepherds' appointed over small groupings of them. Now hours and hours of listening to tapes, mostly from Bob Mumford, and more controls and new revelations are placed upon the congregation. The arrangement is not sustainable on several levels, and the whole thing breaks down.

The mighty Five were falling; pride had set in, and it had become a power game. Surely, the churches and ministries that needed guidance continued to need guidance, and thus more and more control from the top down. What appeared to be a solution became a problem.

## Acknowledging the errors

One Saturday when I was exiting San Quentin prison after a baseball game, I ran into Bob Mumford at the East Gate. We recognized each other and stood still for a moment, both wondering what to say. It was the first time we had seen one another for a couple of decades; now we were face to face.

Bob reached his hand through the iron gate and grabbed mine. We spoke for a few minutes, and before I left, he handed me his card and invited me to his office. Within a week I called and made an appointment. We had a wonderful time of reconciliation. Bob was very open about the errors of the Shepherding Movement and did ask for forgiveness, which I was heartened to extend.

Looking back, I do not blame anyone; what the Five did I likely would have attempted myself had I the opportunity. Concerning the pastor who had submitted himself to Bob and left our small association of churches, I might have done the same if I had been in his shoes. The Five were godly men and perfectly positioned to mentor and guide. They must have been appalled at what they saw happening to the Jesus People, especially when the dark sides became apparent.

A lesson learned.

# Chapter 39

# Pastoring
Jesus People

The Church of the Open Door's composition varied, but a substantial part of the membership was twenty-to-thirty-something with not much on either side of that age range. Coming on the heels of the free love counterculture, one could only expect that the Church of the Open Door would be impacted by the sex, drugs, and rock and roll mentality. Within a relatively short time, however, ordinary middle class folks filtered in. After all, we were the edgy, Spirit-filled, controversial new church with a band and everything.

There were a number of pastors leading the church, even some with a seminary education, such as Mike Riley, Roger Hoffman, Jim Smith, and others. (I was the only one who had been a pastor, but I was far from knowing what I was doing.) Beyond them were many more we considered to be 'elders,' who were responsible for various aspects of the activities. Our monthly leadership meetings grew so large we had to rent banquet rooms in large restaurants to accommodate everyone.

It was a complicated operation. There were the Christian houses, the bookstores, the Bible studies in the schools, the Tuesday night Bible studies, the Sunday evening 'body life' meetings, the evangelism efforts, and pastoral care. Throughout the seventies I kept up a regular schedule for the Marin Christian Counseling Center. In addition, Love in Action, the ex-gay ministry, was going gangbusters.

After the Novato, San Francisco, Petaluma, and Pt. Reyes

churches began, there were even more demands on my time. Each church had its problems, normal problems for sure, but they were time consuming and stressful. Our churches were developing their own particular styles of worship, traditions, and ministries. The leadership was largely theologically untrained, and none of them had much exposure to a congregation that was charismatic in orientation.

My pastoring skills were minimal, and I left that important work of visiting the sick, checking in with congregants, and lending an ear and a hand into their lives to the Christian house leaders, the Tuesday night Bible study teachers, and the Sunday evening Body Life leaders. My job, as I saw it, was to be a teacher of the Bible and a preacher of the Gospel. My organizational ability was marginal but passable. I spent most of my time studying, writing (during the seventies I wrote fifteen books, only five of which were published), and counseling. It was clear to everyone that I depended on others to do the bulk of the pastoral ministry.

The Shepherding Movement, as I explained in detail in the previous chapter, posed the greatest difficulty I experienced in the 1970s. At first I was on board, an ardent fan, but as time wore on I saw the downsides of it and began to pull away. Most of the other leaders in our little church planting enterprise differed from me, and a tension developed that separated us. These differences meant that I became isolated from the kind of fellowship I needed.

## Fast Forward to the Present

Now several decades removed, I must admit that the events of those days still cross my mind. The relationships with the other pastors and elders were mostly never mended, except in a superficial manner. By way of compensation or distraction, I decided to pursue a doctoral program at a Presbyterian seminary and thus began to distance myself from those who were connected with Golden Gate Seminary and the leaders of the churches of the Open Door. I did this deliberately, but the pain never went away, although it is now little more than an unpleasant memory.

Surprisingly, now that these memoirs are being prepared and I have had reason to contact many of the old gang, relationships are being restored. Frankly, I would never have attempted any book about the JPM if it had not been for Katie. For years she has been after me to get my story out, and only last year did I agree to it. And I have to admit it has been painful; going over that history and the good and the bad of it has at times gotten to me emotionally. Nearing the end of the process now, I am glad it is all happening. Before me is the hope that what is presented here will help others in coming years to understand the light and dark sides of awakenings and revivals.

One thing more seems to fit into this chapter and that has to do with the counsel Moishe Rosen had given me during the early years of the JPM. He advocated my pursuing higher academic degrees with a view to being a teacher in a Bible college or seminary. He also warned against beginning a church, thinking that would be a distraction from the kinds of ministry we were engaged in, ministries that were obviously bearing much fruit. Rosen's vision was for a para-church ministry that focused on evangelism. And this vision was, of course, realized in Jews for Jesus. Moishe never intended to found a church. He felt that people who were reached through Jews for Jesus would find their way into churches as a matter of course.

I did not necessarily ignore his counsel; it simply did not work out that way. To a considerable degree, after going through all that I have, I wish I could have been able to abide by it. Now, however, I'm ambivalent, because I still pastor a church and enjoy the work. Along with having the opportunity to preach and teach, I also get to do the writing I love so much. Perhaps it is that Miller Avenue Baptist Church is an anomaly and is far less stressful and disappointing than the years of Church of the Open Door in San Rafael. I may make some folks unhappy with what I have just written, but this is the truth.

# Chapter 40

# The Beginning of the End of the JPM

The year that marked the ending of the Jesus People Movement in my view, at least in Marin County, was 1972, the same year Church of the Open Door was founded in San Rafael. It may be that the JPM had not reached some places in America yet, and based on what I have seen and read, it did not impact England until the mid 1970s. More about that later.[1]

The flood of awakening converts who came into newly established churches like the Church of the Open Door in San Rafael, reached its pinnacle in the early 1970s. It was now time for mopping-up operations. Yes, this a military term used for what happens after a major battle has been concluded.

I did not know at that time that awakenings began and ended. Many of us had assumed that, in the years prior to the JPM, the visible church had withered and died, even becoming resistant to the moving of the Holy Spirit. We expected revival would continue as a matter of course. When the 'deadness' we knew from before and had witnessed in many denominational churches crept into our own meetings, it was worrisome and fostered the idea that it was due to 'sin in the camp'. In 1990, as I started to look back and re-evaluate, I had to admit that the charismatic gifts, especially speaking in tongues, had begun to

---

1    In my book, *Awakenings in America and the Jesus People Movement*, published in 2012, I make an argument for the JPM meeting the qualifications for being a genuine American awakening.

fade away in and around 1972. Even prophecy, words of wisdom, words of knowledge, healings, and miracles[2] drifted slowly away. What did continue, however, and actually increased, was the ministry of casting out of demons, which was really a part of the mopping-up operation.[3]

## Our Use of Prophecy

Prophecy is a subject that needs a little more attention here. The charismatic gifts practiced among the Jesus People principally were speaking in tongues, healing, and prophecy. Prophecy turned out to be much more problematic than speaking in tongues, at least for those of us who rejected the idea that tongue speaking was the chief evidence of true conversion. Opportunities for healing via having hands laid on by the elders continued and proceeded fairly smoothly.[4] In our ministry in Marin, tongues were fine, no big deal. But prophecy had its own brand of usefulness.

By useful, I mean we could get people to do what we wanted. "Thus saith the Lord," or, "God gave me a word for you," or some-

2    See 1 Corinthians 12:1-11.

3    I began speaking in tongues in 1968 and continued to do so until about 1975. This was not a conscious decision of mine, it simply happened. For a time I still tried to do it, but it was forced and no longer had a spiritual nature to it. Over the years, there is nothing I have so much examined as my speaking in tongues, almost to the point of obsession. I have concluded that the gift was genuine, as were the others – miracles, healing, words of wisdom and knowledge, and yes, even prophecy. I remain of this opinion, although most people who embrace a Reformed theology like I do are cessationist, meaning that the gifts of the Spirit, particularly the so-called power gifts, have ceased to be given to us now that we have the fullness of Christ and the New Testament.

4    At Miller Avenue Church we continue to pray for healing with anointing with oil and the laying on of hands, as we see precedent and warrant for this in the New Testament, including in James 5:13-15. In addition, we also offer the ministry of the casting out of demons, both of which we do on Sunday evenings.

thing similar, were the words or formulae we used. I must admit I misused prophecy and that it was commonly done among us. The elders would circle a person who desired direction from God, and direction he or she surely got. At some point, I began to record and track some of the more directional 'words' and discovered they failed to materialize. Hmmm. False prophets in our midst! Should they be stoned?

By around 1977, I made a serious attempt to understand what prophecy should look like and how it should be undertaken for a New Testament church. My conclusion was that, having the fullness of God's revelation in Christ, each Christian being a priest with the indwelling of the Holy Spirit, and having the actual written Word in hand, prophecy was for us a declaring of the Word of God already revealed in Scripture and Scripture alone. I came to that conclusion then and am still firmly holding to that understanding.

## Signs of the End

Now, back to the ending of the JPM. Surprisingly, even conversions tapered off. Baptisms of large numbers of new converts at a time were seldom held, and Joyful Noise disbanded. My personal focus was on counseling, writing books, getting more education, helping build up Love in Action (the ex-gay ministry), and pastoring a very demanding church. The reader will notice I did not mention my family, and this because the press of people and events meant that the family got lost in the shuffle, to some degree. Oh, to be able to revisit those years!

The early years of the Church of the Open Door were marked by power struggles in the leadership, which was one of the lesser reasons that the single San Rafael congregation was divided into five in 1975. The roaring fire to reach the lost was reduced to a flicker, and now the concerns were money and positions of power. It almost seems sacrilegious to bring this up, but however much we would like to avoid such thinking, that is what happened. Over the years I have had many a conversation with those who had been outside the power structure yet witnessed it directly. It was painful to hear the things that were said about me. Yes, I am guilty of engaging in the political battles to maintain prestige and authority. And the striving for money! We who had been Jesus freaks living on next to nothing, were now marrying, having children, and wanting to buy such fleshly things as cars, clothes, and homes. How ungodly!

The deck was reshuffled a number of times, and attempts were made to bring back the glory and the excitement. Mostly this was done through prayer, fasting, exercising church discipline, and a renewed emphasis on the gifts of the Holy Spirit. Courses on discovering one's spiritual gifts were coming out by any number of Christian publishers, but they did not seem to help. In fact, those courses usually created more confusion and disagreements than they helped people get into active ministry.

The so-called praise bands formed, new worship music was written, and the volume was turned up. And this was years before the church growth movement got under way. The dark sides of the awakening were about to emerge.

# Chapter 41

# David in London

David had disappeared into The Family. Almost immediately, I began receiving letters from him post marked from some little town in Texas. It turned out he was at COG's Texas Soul Clinic, a ranch-like property owned by Fred Jordan.

David made the best case he could for me to join up with The Family. I learned later that those letters were nearly dictated by his 'shepherds' who rode herd on him during the early months. I kept every one of them.

Only a few of those 'evangelistic' missives arrived in the mail, then nothing. The next communications were different; David began to sound like he was being mistreated. Knowing David, he had discovered the real nature of COG and was beginning to challenge the leadership. (David had grown up in lockups in California and had spent two years in a federal prison; no one would be pushing him around for long.) I reasoned that it would only be a while before he either fled the scene or was booted out.

Unhappily, very unhappily, David's wife and children were also pulled into the ranch there in Texas. Though we have talked about that period, I could tell he did not want me to probe him much on what happened to his family. To this day I know little of it, but what David went through, what he is yet experiencing, I can only imagine.

## My Own Cultic Experience

Beginning about 1988, while pastor of Miller Avenue Baptist

Church in Mill Valley, I began a workshop on cult recovery; it continued for six years. Each workshop consisted of 26 sessions, and I repeated it twelve times. I placed ads in the Marin Independent Journal and the San Francisco Chronicle inviting people to the workshop and was shocked at the response. There were Mormon and Jehovah's Witness elders, ex-Catholics, Pentecostals, fundamentalists of various sorts, Baptists, and folks I knew well, drop outs from the Church of the Open Door.

One of the reasons I started the cult recovery workshop goes back to 1977, when I began a doctoral program at San Francisco Theological Seminary in San Anselmo, a Presbyterian institution, and my major professor was Dr. Louis Rambo. He happened to be one of America's foremost experts on cults and conversion.

In 1978, Lou told me that Church of the Open Door had a pronounced cultic nature to it, and his actual words were blunt: "Church of the Open Door is a cult." The next week I brought him a copy of our statement of faith, which Lou examined but explained to me that, while our theology was orthodox enough, our ecclesiology or methodology was not. Lou explained what he meant. By the time I finished listening to what he had to say, I was shocked to the core. He actually put into words what I had been feeling for years. Indeed, the cultic nature he observed was what I had seen in the Shepherding Movement, yet I was unable to see that I was mired in something similar.

Our primary trouble was the use of intimidating and manipulative tactics on people who were vulnerable, people who thought they were hearing from God through us. We had everyone believing that God spoke through the leaders of the church as well as the Bible. This communication came through words of knowledge, words of wisdom,[1] interpretation of tongues, and especially prophecy. He was spot on it, and I knew I was guilty, and more so than anyone else. I was the senior pastor, and everything that happened was essentially on my watch. So I

---

1    See 1 Corinthians 12:7-10.

began making attempts to correct our methods, only to run into a brick wall. Other leaders did not see things the way I did, and I couldn't blame them. I experienced rejection, which effectively further isolated me.

## Back to David

When David linked up with COG he had no way of knowing how twisted David Berg was becoming. My replies to David's letters were likely not too helpful to him. Then there was another, much longer, period of silence.

One day, I think in 1974, I received a letter from David written from Upper Norwood, a suburb of London.[2] He had escaped out of the COG, but his family was still in and staying in an unknown location. My speculation is that David had been traveling in Europe hoping to find them; leaders of The Family were skilled at making people disappear. We exchanged a few letters, and then he sent one requesting that I come to London to help with a group of Jesus People from Wisconsin who were performing music at U.S. military bases across Europe.[3] The band was called Shepherd and was performing a rock opera called Lonesome Stone, developed with David's input.

Somehow David had met and become friends with Kenneth Frampton,[4] a big time real estate owner who later helped the

---

2    David will be writing about this period in his life, which will be published. Not being sure of the details I will skip most of it and relate only what happened to me.

3    The background for this is long and involved, and David, in his account of the JPM, will detail this far more completely than I am able to do.

4    This is another long and involved story I don't remember well. I did have an office in one of Mr. Frampton's buildings in South Bromley and met numbers of people who were engaged in smuggling Bibles into the countries behind the Iron Curtain. And it was then that I met George Verwer who began Operation Mobilization. On several occasions I was a guest of the Verwers, who lived in a Frampton property in South Bromley, and learned of the incredible missionary work OM was and is engaged in.

Wisconsin youth group come to England. Due to David's recommendation, Mr. Frampton, who was one of the most wonderful and gracious Christians I have ever known, invited me to come to London and help pastor the Wisconsin folks.

My first trip to London lasted six weeks, and I never saw the sun once. I was staying in a big old house in Upper Norwood, just a block or so from the gravesite of Charles Haddon Spurgeon, although I did not at the time know who he was. I was in the house's top floor, the fifth floor, and no light or heat ascended all the way up there.

David was playing the role of Stone in the rock opera Lonesome Stone. Stone was a young hippie trying to find himself but was finally found by God, and at the Churchill Theatre in London, I saw a live show for the first time. Following that we got on a train to Liverpool and more performances of Lonesome Stone. The theatre was next door to the place where the Beatles started, and it was a popular nightclub at that time. Shepherd played there one evening; the place was jammed with kids, and that excellent band played some of the best Jesus music I had ever heard.

That six week period, although I was cold to the bone the whole time, led to several more trips to London and establishing a mission[5] from Church of the Open Door, Open Door Commission,[6] something I had instigated a couple of years before.

Quickly, we gathered some people and began to do street evangelism all over the city, mostly in the popular tourist loca-

---

5    Some of those who led in this mission were Roger and Ava Hoffman, Carol Pohl, and David Philpott -- an Englishman and no relation to me, though we are Facebook friends.

6    One of the efforts of the Open Door Commission was to establish a church in Mexico City. Jim Smith, a Golden Gate Seminary graduate, and a very fine preacher and teacher, led the way in this. I made several trips to Natividad, a barrio on the eastern edge of Mexico City, where Jim planted the church. The adventures encountered are worthy of a middle length book, but what I remember most was a certain taco stand and preaching a sermon entirely in Spanish.

tions like Trafalgar Square and Piccadilly Circus. To this day I receive communications, mostly by way of Facebook, from some of those Londoners who responded to the Gospel during that period.

David Hoyt must be considered one of the most significant personages of the Jesus People Movement. While I stayed mostly in San Francisco and Marin counties,  he took the awakening to southern California, back up to the East Bay, then to southern states, eventually nine of them. Yes, he fell into the hands of a notorious cult, but he never gave up being a follower of Jesus. And it was David, who more than anyone else that I am aware of, took the JPM to England, many parts of England for that matter.

As I look back on my Christian life, some fifty years of it now, I have observed that, although Christians stumble, fall, and make a mess of things, still those genuinely converted will, by the grace of God, get back up and continue following Jesus.

# Chapter 42

# The Dark Sides Emerge

The terms 'Dark sides' and 'wild fire revival' are generally synonymous, but I prefer to call them dark sides. They usually, but not always, follow on the heels of genuine outpourings of the Holy Spirit.

The first great awakening, 1735-1742, involving Jonathan Edwards, George Whitefield, the Tenants, and many others, had its dark sides, yet no one denies it was the real thing. The second awakening, roughly 1798 to 1825 or 1835, depending on how Charles G. Finney is viewed, certainly had its dark sides, which can still be felt two hundred years later. The third, from 1857 to 1859 (and some say this one continued through the Civil War), was perhaps the cleanest of America's awakenings, an assessment I accept. But this fourth awakening[1] was anything but clean, and the dark sides of it continue. I wonder if we have yet to see the worst of it, and this is being written in 2014.

Let me clearly state that I do not delight, to any extent, in the presence of the dark sides. Neither can I close my eyes to them and pretend that they, or some aspects of them, are a continuation of the fourth awakening or even, as some suppose, a fifth awakening or 'wave'.

It is difficult to know where to start describing events and how they yielded unwanted results, because the whole busi-

---

1   In *Awakenings in America and the Jesus People Movement*, I make the case that the JPM meets the criteria of a genuine awakening.

ness is so complex. Perhaps I saw some of it while still pastor of Church of the Open Door, from which I resigned in 1980, due to my divorce and the events surrounding it. The Sunday morning services changed from a focus on teaching and preaching to music and more music. The 'worship' was relegated only to when the praise and worship band was on stage.

I think it is biblically correct to say that, when the Holy Spirit moves in power, there is no need for humans to add to it. Two or three are gathered, Jesus is present, and that is enough. With just two or three – wherever, whenever, or whoever – miracles might happen.

As the awakening waned, the desire, or maybe the need to ratchet things up came imperceptively at first, then deliberately. I had no idea how much worse it would become.

## Some Necessary Background

I had begun studies at San Francisco Law School in 1980, assuming that a divorced pastor had to change careers. I was right in the midst of law school, had already developed a substantial legal support business with a partner,[2] and was ready to get my license as a private investigator, when an old friend, Prince Altom, pastor of what was then called Corte Madera Community Church, invited me to join him. I set the legal business aside to go back into the ministry. The American Baptist Churches of America, the oldest Baptist body in the USA, understood that is was possible to be restored to ministry, and they took a chance on me. In 1984 I began reviving and reorganizing the First Baptist Church of Mill Valley. After ten months we reopened the closed

---

2    This was Terry Cuddy, who spent eighteen years in a federal prison for bank robbery, was pardoned by Jerry Brown, the first time Brown was governor of California, who then proceeded to obtain a license as a private investigator. It was a real Humphrey Bogart kind of operation. I wrote a book about 33 adventures that came my way titled, Serving in Marin. Not published yet, but on the schedule.

doors of the church under the new name of Miller Avenue Baptist Church. Thirty years later I am still pleased to preach the Gospel to non-believers and the Scripture to believers.

## The Church Growth Courses

In 1987 the American Baptists asked me to attend a church growth program at Fuller Theological Seminary in Pasadena. My brother Bruce was a cop in Pasadena (later the chief of police there), and I stayed with him in his home in Glendale, while I attended what I see now as something rather dangerous.[3]

The beginning and the advanced church growth meetings, one year apart, each lasted five days. There I heard John Wimber teach about signs and wonders, and I was absolutely appalled to hear his instructions on how to manipulate a congregation using music, lighting, and other effects, to get people to where they felt the Holy Spirit was visiting them. I also had opportunity to talk with C. Peter Wagner and Charles Kraft, among others, while at Fuller.

Church growth and church planting was what it was all about. And I do not blame anyone for desiring those things. The JPM was long gone, but the memories of the experiences of it were still fresh in the minds of many. Would we love to see those days again? Any Christian would answer immediately and loudly, YES!

Human engineering, meaning applied psychology and sociology, was what I was hearing at Fuller. How to get people excited? How to fill the pews? How to meet human needs? On and on they propounded, with apparently little or no idea that a genuine awakening depends on the moving of the Spirit of God. The ideas expressed were all motivated by the notion that proper means could make awakening happen. I saw the error then, and

---

3    I realize there are those who will disagree with me on this point, but I must report what I thought both then and now.

I had not begun to even consider Reformed theology.

The Emerging Church or the 'seeker-friendly' church developed along the lines I saw and heard at Fuller. Meeting needs, reaching people where they are, targeting specific groups, blending into the culture, and becoming as inoffensive as possible was the litany for church growth and church planting. Cultic in terms of recruitment? Yes, I believe so. Full disclosure? No, not even close. If the Gospel, that offending Gospel that calls attention to our lost and eternally dangerous condition, is not presented, then you can expect the full flowering of a toxic, cultic mentality.

Next came the Toronto Vineyard happening with Rodney Howard-Browne from South Africa. The Laughing Revival, the Toronto Blessing – such a big splash and magnet, drawing local pastors who ran up to Toronto to get the 'anointing.' The anointing, the anointing, the anointing – this was it. Power to command even God's blessing! More, more, and more.

Then it spread like wild fire and landed where I could observe it, at Bethel Church in Redding, California. I went there to see it for myself. Enough has been written about that and about the Kansas City Prophets, International House of Prayer, and MorningStar in North Carolina. I suppose I would have succumbed to the pull if I had not experienced the Jesus People awakening and learned something of the other awakenings in America's history. Moving and grooving to the beat, dancing and swaying 'in the spirit', talking to angels, even to Jesus. Frankly, it is not that much different from shamanistic rituals, Santerían bembes, or Wiccan journeys.[4]

## Spiritual Battles

It is not surprising that the devil should show up. We see this

---

4    Soon to be released by Earthen Vessel Publishing is *The Soul Journey: How Shamanism, Santeria, Wicca, and Charisma are Connected.* The connection is the trance state or altered states of consciousness, upon which all of these pagan, neopagan, and even Christian oriented practices or religions depend.

in the Book of Acts. Jesus warned of it. Paul experienced it. John in Revelation predicted it. In a sense, it is business as usual. The enemy rushes to the holy fire to put it out or pervert it. I have in my mind the backfire, set in the direction of a fire out of control. Whatever metaphor is employed, the picture is one of confusion, deception, and error.

Our God is a sovereign God, and He will do what He will do and allow what He will allow. The enemy is essentially powerless and can only go so far. Christians may pray, preach, and plan for revival and awakening, while at the same time recognize that the mighty wind of the Spirit moves where He will.

# Chapter 43

# What I Wish I Had Known Then

Although awakenings were mentioned in Church History classes at seminary, I did not learn much about them then. I wish I had known that they had beginnings and endings, that they were unusual and not normal, that they were completely a work of a sovereign God, and that they were not always wonderful and joyous events from beginning to end.

Oddly, it never occurred to me that I was involved in an awakening while it was happening. It is not that I was a brand new, right out of the box, Christian. My conversion was in 1963, I had preached occasionally before I got to seminary, was pastor of a church, and had a couple years of seminary under my belt. The trouble was that when the conversions and miracles began, I thought it had to do with my faithfulness and boldness to be a witness. Yes, I thought it had much, though not all, to do with me, that somehow I was specially used of God. The false view I had of myself and what I was seeing made for a kind of personal pride and a judgmental attitude toward others who were not as 'sold out for Jesus' as I was.

"Normal times versus awakening times," is language I borrow from David Martin Lloyd-Jones and Iain Murray, two of the most knowledgeable people on this sort of thing. They distinguish between the two, emphasizing that most of the time for most Christians, we experience normal times. We plan, pray, and preach for an outpouring of God's Spirit, but such efforts cannot produce or guarantee it. Charles G. Finney taught exactly the opposite. Due to the seeming success Finney is reported to have had at the tail end of the second awakening in America, 1825 and on, most evangelists who came later tried to copy him. The essence of Finney's ideas is that revival depends upon Christians. Even in the midst of the JPM, I thought this was correct. If someone had worded it as, "Philpott, do you think you can force God's hand?" I would, of course, have said, "No." The fact is that I was never confronted with such a challenge, so I did not think those thoughts. The prevailing attitude was that people were responsible for revival.

This leads straight to the question, just who is in charge? On the other hand, who would argue that humans are? The concept of a sovereign God who will do what He will when He wants was essentially foreign to me. I recall an evangelistic campaign by Southern Baptists called, "I Found It." I was then pastor of Excelsior Baptist Church in Byron, and local Baptist associations all over California were holding Billy Graham-style, evangelistic, outdoor meetings. We pasted "I Found It" bumper stickers on our cars, went door to door, handed out flyers, conducted long prayer meetings with fasting, and promoted the program as best we could. This was in 1968, right when the JPM was under way, and I was fully behind it. The advertising paid off, or rather, it sparked a negative response, as cars started sprouting bumper stickers that read, "I never had it," "I lost it," and "I am not looking for it." The results were rather dismal and disappointing, and we wondered why.

'The glorious times' were not completely apparent to me during the JPM. My memories of the conversions and miracles are somewhat over-shadowed by the devastation that followed. It is difficult to account for this. Why is it that God would allow for the dark sides of awakenings to compromise the outpouring of His Spirit? Jim Jones, The Way International, The Family, Manifested Sons of God, and many others – what about them? There were also the divisions between those who spoke in tongues and those who didn't, and between those who submitted themselves to the Shepherding Movement and those who didn't.

The wild fire that looked innocent enough at first continues to haunt the Christian community now. It is only when I look back on America's other awakenings that I begin to understand. Without question, the first two awakenings saw all kinds of serious mischief emerge during them and following them. This is without dispute.

## What is this Phenomenon?

There is a spiritual war going on. Whether the devil attacks or counter attacks is unknown. But the reality of the warfare is entirely clear. The same scenario is observed in Scripture. Martin Luther's great hymn, "A Might Fortress is our God," says it succinctly. Luther, leader of the greatest awakening the Church has ever known in its history outside the Bible, fought the devil and won some battles but lost others. Perhaps what we observe in the JPM is simply how it is in spiritual warfare.

Another thing I have learned that I wish I had known then: I am vulnerable to deception. I am most at risk when I suppose I am above it all. It is abundantly evident to me that I must keep close to Jesus and His Word. I want to be sure that what I hold to be true is clearly stated in all of Scripture – Old Testament,[1] Gospels, and records of the early Church like Paul's, John's, Peter's, James', and Jude's letters. In addition, I value the traditions and consistencies of the Church throughout its history.

Rightly or wrongly, I am not impressed by those who say, as we often did, that they are "sold out for Jesus." The Children of God used that phrase a lot and convinced many young Christians that the churches they were involved in were luke warm at best. Members of The Family, on the other hand, were so on fire they left everything behind, sold their possessions, and hit

---

1    In regard to the Old Testament, I want to see collaboration in all three of the major sections, Torah, Prophets, and Writings.

the road to win others. Some of this is biblical, but it was taken to extremes and used as a kind of guilt weapon to upset the lives of vulnerable people.

I am not going to buy into a claim that God is doing something new in the last days. Prophets are proclaiming new revelations, supposedly confirmed by miracles and success in attracting large followings. We have had enough of the Mohammeds, Joseph Smiths, Russells, David Bergs, and so on.

Jesus Christ is God become flesh, full of grace and truth. That is enough for us.

# Chapter 44

# The Core Message of the Jesus Freaks

Joyful Noise began singing a song entitled, "One name under heaven whereby we must be saved," in 1968 or 1969.[1] The index finger pointing upward meant 'one way' and is based on John 14:6: "I am the way, and the truth, and the life. No one comes to the Father except through me." I believed that then, and I believe it now.

For the Jesus People, Acts 4:12 said it all: "And there is salvation in no one else, for there is no other name under heaven given among men by which we must be saved."

Campus Crusade for Christ's The Four Spiritual Laws booklet was widely used in street evangelism. Simple and clear, it was perhaps a bit 'dumbed-down' from the perspective of a much older Christian. My favorite way to present Christ is called "The Roman Road," which I still use. It starts with Romans 3:10: "None is righteous, no, not one." The next stop is Romans 3:23-24: "For all have sinned and fall short of the glory of God, and are justified by his grace as a gift, through the redemption that is in Christ Jesus." It is a short distance from there to 6:23: "For the wages of sin is death, but the free gift of God is eternal life

---

1    Not sure, but I may have written this one, or perhaps it was David Hoyt. I have seen the song listed as written by others, but that was typical of the JPM. The authorship of songs, some written by David Hoyt and myself, became common property and finally, when included in music books, would be claimed by someone or other rather than as "unknown."

in Christ Jesus our Lord." Now a U-turn is required back to 5:1: "Therefore, since we have been justified by faith, we have peace with God through our Lord Jesus Christ." Often the last stop was Romans 10:9-10: "If you confess with your mouth that Jesus is Lord and believe in your heart that God raised him from the dead, you will be saved." Currently, I go back to 8:30: "And those whom he predestined he also called, and those whom he called he also justified, and those whom he justified he also glorified." At the end of this road, there is no dead end.

## The Essential Doctrine

Our emphasis was not self-improvement; it was not a self-help movement. We were not trying to find ourselves, fix the planet, or foment a revolution. We were not intent on changing the world in a political sense. The bare essential had to do with salvation, which was impressed upon us to be the only thing that mattered, when all was said and done.

I will never forget the title of one of Bob Hymers' sermons, "Eternity, eternity, eternity, where will you spend eternity?" Wish I had a recording of it.

This utterly exclusive doctrine was our banner, even in the midst of a generation that was becoming highly syncretistic, tolerant, and inclusive. The Jesus People were upfront; it was Jesus and Jesus alone who could rescue from an eternity in hell.

Sociologists have adequately described the 1960s. The size of the counter-culture that was wildly embracing eastern religions and occult practices and concepts was mushrooming. It was cool to be a Buddhist, even cool to stand on a street corner as a Hare Krishna, chanting and begging for money. Anton LaVey, the founder of the Church of Satan in San Francisco, was celebrated. Some in the Haight Ashbury looked down on me, because I had not expanded my mind by dropping acid or equivalents.

I was reluctant to identify myself with a Christian church, since it was not hip to be a Baptist, especially a Southern Baptist, so I referred to myself as a 'follower of Jesus'. As the song said, "Jesus is just all right with me." For others, He was only all right as long as He was simply another in the pantheon of spiritual gurus. But when some of us proclaimed Jesus as being absolutely the only way to the Father, the response could just as likely be a punch in the mouth as anything else.

I believe I have adequately framed it: Hippie Jesus was tolerated but the Jesus of the Bible was not. Still, the conversions came by the thousands and more than thousands. How could this be explained? It was the power of the Holy Spirit, who convicted the unholy hippies intent on nothing more than sex, drugs, and rock & roll of their sin and then powerfully revealed to these blinded and hardened sinners Jesus as Lord and Savior. Now that is a miracle of the first order, while other miracles like healing, words of knowledge, even multiplication of food, simply cannot compare.

Not all conversions were genuine conversions, of course, but the large majority were, and this is stated on the basis of my personal experience. Having spent my life pretty much in one place for most of the Jesus People Movement and beyond, I have been contacted (mostly through Facebook) by a host of those who were brought to Christ in the JPM, and one of the first statements, whether by phone, email, or Facebook is, "I am still trusting in Jesus."

Some described themselves as having made "shipwreck of the faith,"[2] even for fairly long periods of time, but God would not leave them as castaways. It is one thing to trip or fall, but it is the mark of true conversion to get back up again and continue along the narrow way.

Jesus remains, now and forever, the only name under heaven whereby we must be saved.

_____

2    1 Timothy 1:19 is the reference here and some interpret it to mean a loss of salvation. My experience, and other biblical evidence, causes me to think otherwise.

# Chapter 45

# Radicalized Youth Gone Wild?

Youth are more easily radicalized than mature adults; that is, if adults do, in fact, mature.

It is largely, but not totally, accurate, that the JPM was youth-oriented. The hippies on the streets and the kids in high schools and colleges were most often under age 30, and the slogan was not to trust anyone over that age. In the Bay Area, the rebellious baby boomers, those born around the ending of WWII and further, broke loose and followed their hearts, or another organ, and did everything their parents warned them against. Does this also explain the Jesus People Movement?

In the Bay Area it didn't take a sociologist or demographer to see that large numbers of young people were out on the streets agitating for and against one thing or another. It was in the midst of all this that the JPM began. A detractor might easily conclude that there was no real spiritual component to the JPM, that is was merely the drugs, sex, and rock and roll culture gone wild in a different direction. And I will concede that the JPM was so tarnished, which should not be unexpected.

The first three national American awakenings, according to my reading of them, cut across the board age-wise. Whole families were impacted in these revival events, not merely the young. In the third awakening of 1857 to 1859, the main venue was the businessman's noon prayer meeting, so there were probably not many disaffected youth in the bunch. Young people were obviously involved in the first three awakenings, but they were not the primary participants.

My experience in the San Francisco Bay Area was that adults, parents mostly, including many mature adults, were also involved in the JPM. During the early days when the Bible studies in the schools were going on, I also conducted studies in the homes of actual church going folks of all ages. It did not take long before a variety of people, even some grey-headed types like I am now, were a big part of the awakening. And I can say from what I saw across the country in the late 1960s, that the same thing was occurring elsewhere. It may be that the young made more headlines than others or were more visible, but my observation and experience is that the JPM was not strictly for the young.

Because the JPM was a 'movement' and received a growing amount of media coverage, there were some involved who were not genuinely born again of the Spirit of God; after all, anyone can walk through the front door. False conversion was and always is a big issue; as my ministerial work has evolved, I have become more and more aware of this phenomenon. This interest led to the writing of my first book in the second stage of my 'literary career' entitled, *Are You Really Born Again?* published by Evangelical Press in 1995. My working title had been, *The Mystery of Conversion*, and it was a discussion of the nature of both true and false conversion.[1] As in any awakening, the Holy Spirit works powerfully to save, but the enemy of God is active as well.

## Hearing Now from other JPMers

Fast forward now to the present day. There are starting to be conferences and gatherings of Jesus freaks converted during the JPM. Locally, Scott McCarrel has taken the lead to organize such gatherings. Scott organized one small event already and others

---

1    Earthen Vessel Publishing is soon to bring out a third edition of the book, hopefully in 2014, but the second edition is available now.

are planned.[2]

Let me summarize what I have been seeing and hearing from grey-headed ex-JPMers: Some of the Jesus freaks held on faithfully over the long haul; some made 'ship wreck' of their faith for a period of time and have come back strong; others went their way and, in my view, gave evidence to the fact that their 'conversion' was not genuine. I would like to be more generous than this, but those are my observations.

As I prepared this last chapter, one verse kept coming to mind – Philippians 1:6, and it seems like a proper ending for this memoir: "And I am sure of this, that he who began a good work in you will bring it to completion at the day of Jesus Christ."

---

2    Scott's email address is: Scott McCarrel (MCCARRELS6@aol.com)

# Photos
## of Jesus People
## Then and Now

O n the following pages are photos of those who are mentioned in the pages of the Memoirs chapters, arranged somewhat alphabetically. Some we found online, some were sent to us by the subjects or their relatives, and some we had in our own archives. Please allow us some leeway in the dates indicated, since it was not always possible to determine these absolutely. We hope you will enjoy seeing the people you remember or always wondered about.

**Stephanie Adams (2014)**
In front of Sproul Hall at University of
California, Berkeley Campus

**Dennis Bennett**

DAVID BERG AKA MO / MOSES

**Don Basham**

EARLY BERACHAH HOUSE BROTHERS, SAN ANSELMO, CA

**Baptism at the Russian River**
**1969**

**Jim and Dacie**
## Durkin

**Lynn Rosen Bond &**
**Alan Bond - 1973**

Elders of Church of the Open Door - Bay Area - c. 1974
First Row: Kent Philpott, Doug Cahn, Mike Barrett, Bob Burns, ?
Second Row: Mark Buckley, Bob Gaulden
Third Row: Terry Jenkins, Beverly Igo, John Buckley, Frank Heinrich, ?
Back Row: Mike Riley, ?,  Bruce Arnold, Geoff Tachet, Frank Worthen, Jim Smith

**Mark and Kristina
Buckley**

Lonnie Frisbee

Kenneth P. & Pauline Frampton

Gaylord Enns

Lyn and Alan Bond -
2007

**Lonnie Frisbee Singing**

**Oliver and Mary Louise
Heath**

**Robert L. Hymers, Jr.**

**David Hoyt**

**Roger Hoffman**

Oliver Heath,
Paul Bryant,
Kent Philpott
1969

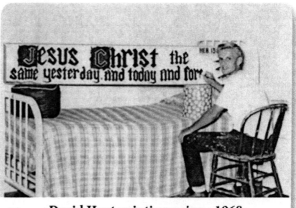

David Hoyt painting a sign - 1968

**David Hoyt playing "Lonesome Stone" in Europe early 1970s**

**Robert Hymers and Steve Gollnick
Easter Demonstration 1972**

Hindu Temple where Kent
found David Hoyt 1967

David Hoyt & Kent Philpott
San Rafael, CA - 1968

JPM Demonstration in front
of Occult Bookstore c. 1971

**Rev. Bob Lewis ordains
Kent Philpott
1966
Byron, CA**

**Kathryn Kuhlman
c. 1970s**

**Holy Hubert at Sproul Plaza,
Berkeley, CA**

"Holy" Hubert
Lindsey

Kent with Bob Lewis
c. 2000

Kathryn Kuhlman
Grave

Pat Matrisciana

**Mary K. and Chuck
Mancebo
1978**

**Mary K. & Chuck
Mancebo (2010)**

**Scott McCarrel**

Kent with son Vernon at Russian
embassy protest against poor
treatment of Jews - 1972 or 73

**Bob Mumford**

Kent interviewed at demonstration in SF
c. 1971

**Kent - 2007 with wall photo of a younger man!**

**Kent and Katie - December, 2012**

**Kent and Bob Burns**
**Miller Avenue Church 2012**

**Kent and David - 2007**

**Scott McCarrel, Kent Philpott, and Gaylord Enns
2014 at Miller Avenue Church, Mill Valley**

**Derek Prince**

**Ed Plowman**

**Moishe Rosen**

**Mike and Mona Riley**

**Rick and Megan Sacks - Sausalito - 1969**

**Kenny Sanders in Easter street demonstration
c. 1973-4**

**Mary and Ken Sanders**

**Charles Simpson**

**Chuck Smith**

**Residents of Soul Inn**

**Jack Sparks c. 1970**

**John Wimber**

Jesus People's Temple of Still Waters, Atlanta

**Frank Worthen**
Young Boy

**Pat and Jerry Westfall**

**Pat Matrisciana**

**Cliff Silliman with Kent**
c. 1970

**Zion's Inn Group of Brothers**
**July 4, 1969**

Early Young Ladies at Zion's Inn
with Kent's Family

# Introduction to the Bios

Somewhere during the process of writing down these remembrances of what happened in my part of the JPM, I thought it might be important to invite people who had been mentioned in the body of the book to provide a short autobiographical sketch. I asked Stephanie Adams, who is a member of the Miller Avenue Baptist Church where I am pastor, and who was actually converted during the JPM while a student at UC Berkeley, to oversee the collection of the biographies. One by one they came in, but for those people who were no longer living, Stephanie went to work gathering the components and composing.

The bios sent to us by the named individuals or their relatives have not been modified or edited in any manner, unless we were specifically instructed to do so. However, I did read each one and found some content to be interesting, to say the least.

A strong case could be made for adding several dozen more bios. If I am energetic and courageous enough to attempt a future edition of the memoirs, these can be added then. If this book finds its way into the hands of others who were involved in the JPM and want to be included in a new edition, please read below.

Bios can either be emailed to Stephanie, or she may be contacted by phone:

Stephanie Adams 510.685.8788

stephanieadams@me.com

See the next page for the components to provide for your bio:

## Bio Components

1.  Name
2.  Birthdate and Place
3.  Where did you grow up?
4.  Education and/or military service
5.  Marriage and Family - optional
6.  Conversion - brief description
7.  Your personal involvement in the JPM
8.  Any special memories
9.  What about now - activities and involvements - optional
10. Contact info if so desired and/or a website
11. Any concluding comments
12. Optional: a photo or two, from then and/or recent (as big as possible, as close to 300 dpi as possible)
13. If you write your bio out, please keep it short, two pages max.

Thank you.
Kent

# Don Basham
## 1926-1989

Donald Wilson Basham was a Bible teacher and a Christian author. He was born on September 17, 1926 in Wichita Falls, Texas. [1] His parents were Henry Joseph Basham (1895–1974) and Eileen Hicks Basham (1896–1973). [2] Donald Basham was raised in Wichita Falls in a Baptist home, but later joined the Christian Church (Disciples of Christ). He attended Midwestern State University and Phillips University.

While at college, he met Alice Rolling who was also born and raised in Wichita Falls. They married in 1949 and had five children; Cindi, Shari, Glenn, Lisa and Laura. Cindi, one of his daughters, married Dick Leggatt who later became the president of Derek Prince Ministries. [1]

Following the reported miraculous healing of a close friend, Basham and his wife, Alice, experienced a spiritual awakening that led them to leave a career in commercial art in 1951 and to enter the Christian ministry. Basham was ordained as a Disciples of Christ Minister in 1955. He became involved in the Charismatic renewal in 1963. [1]

After the publication of his first book, Basham left the pastorate in 1967 to commence a freelance writing and traveling ministry. He traveled extensively in the US and abroad (Jamaica, England, Ireland, Germany, Italy, Austria, Yugoslavia, Hungary, Israel and New Zealand), teaching on subjects such as the Holy Spirit, deliverance, spiritual authority and faith. Basham's deliverance ministry resulted in some notoriety. In the 1970s,

Basham's and Prince's teaching on deliverance and practice of public exorcisms had a significant impact on the charismatic movement. His stance that a Christian could be demonized also caused some controversy amongst Pentecostals. [1]

Basham was one of the now infamous "Fort Lauderdale Five" (a group that was affiliated with the Shepherding Movement), submitting himself to Derek Prince as his personal shepherd. Donald was also the editor of the monthly magazine, New Wine. The end of the publication of New Wine was difficult for Basham, who had invested much into the magazine's ministry. In September of 1987, Basham was diagnosed with prostate cancer. There were also many difficulties regarding the Shepherding Movement. His disillusionment over some of the more negative aspects of the Shepherding movement, along with the cancer diagnosis contributed to a battle with serious depression that eventually required hospitalization. In 1988, he suffered a massive heart attack. Thirteen months later, on March 27th; 1989, Basham died in Elyria; Ohio, after suffering another heart attack. [3]

References

1. http://en.wikipedia.org/wiki/Don_Basham
2. http://www.findagrave.com/cgi-bin/
   fg.cgi?page=gr&GRid=86398658
3. Google search on "Don Basham obituary"

# Bio 2

# Ern Baxter
## 1914 - 1993

In 1914, William John Ernest (Ern) Baxter was born into a Presbyterian family in Saskatchewan, Canada. Today, he is probably best known for his involvement in the Shepherding Movement and also for the profound influence that he had upon Christian communities of not only the United States, but also Australia and the United Kingdom.

As a boy, he was raised as a Pentecostal. In his teenage years, he went through a period of disillusionment regarding his faith in reaction to his perception of an excess of religious legalism.

Ern later developed a serious case of pneumonia. Apparently, there were two things that God used to bring him back to Christianity – first, a miraculous healing of the pneumonia and second, the words of a friend: [1]

"Ern, being a Christian isn't about what you do for God, it's about what God in Christ Jesus has done and will continue to do for you."

On May 24, 1932, William John Ernest Baxter entered the full-time ministry as a musician traveling across Canada with a companion. Ern and his companion attended a conference in Trossachs, Canada, where Ern received the baptism in the Holy Spirit. "Trossachs was an unusual conference as the delegates were not Pentecostal in the classic sense – they were seeking the experience of the Holy Spirit. This was Ern's first exposure to what was to become a central passion in his life and ministry – Word and Spirit or Reformed doctrine and charismatic life and power. The morning after he had been baptized in the Holy Spirit he said God spoke to him and called him to the ministry saying, 'I want you to preach My Word'"[1]

In 1947, Ern joined forces with another traveling evangelist, William Branham. Branham approached Ern and told him that he had been praying and had met the angel of the Lord who had told him to invite Ern Baxter to become his companion and manager. Ern and William worked together for seven years during which time Ern saw some of the greatest miracles, signs and wonders. [1]

Ern did not limit himself to the role of conference speaker. As an active member of the Shepherding Movement, he was dedicated to mentoring. The Shepherding Movement (sometimes called the "Discipleship Movement") was an influential and controversial movement with its main emphasis on the "one another" passages of the New Testament, and the mentoring relationship described in 2 Timothy."[2] Ern took on 12 pastors (affectionately calling them his "Timothys") to mentor and support. Each of these men would travel to meet him in his home, first in Mobile, Alabama, and then in San Diego, California, to spend time hearing him teach. [1]

Ern had a profound preaching and teaching ministry. He was a preacher's preacher. His teachings have been recorded and are being distributed via the Internet. [3]

References:

1. http://en.wikipedia.org/wiki/Ern_Baxter
2. http://en.wikipedia.org/wiki/Shepherding_Movement
3. http://brokenbreadteaching.org/Ernbaxterpage_files/Ern Baxter Page.html

# Bio 3

# Dennis Bennett
## 1917 - 1991

The Reverend Dennis J. Bennett was born in England on October 28, 1917. He was raised in California. Reverend Bennett has been featured in Time and Newsweek magazines and is notable for having been one of the first charismatic ministers. He is the author of several Christian books. [1]

In 1960, Father Dennis Bennett was the Episcopal priest at the conservative St. Mark's Church in Van Nuys, California. During his sermon on April 3, he had the audacity to tell his congregation that he had received the Baptism of the Holy Spirit. [2] Now, 1960 was several years prior to the time at which one could say that the Charismatic Movement "officially" started, so his admission was particularly shocking to the church officials and the congregation.

Quoting from Acts 2:4: "They were all filled with the Holy Spirit and began to speak with other tongues, as the Spirit gave them utterance."

After Dennis shared that he had received the Baptism of the Holy Spirit, it appears that many of his congregation had this same empowering experience. This was his flock and he wanted them to know that God had more in store for them, so he told them (to his own disadvantage). [2]

After this, Dennis was asked by some of the vestry to resign. Not accustomed to such battles at church, he decided that his experience was too valuable to fight over. As Rector and chief pastor he did not have to resign, but he decided it was the best action to take. [2]

"After this explosion in his church, the story was carried in the local newspapers; various wire services picked it up, and the news swept the country. Dennis was not a person who sought to be in the public eye and in fact did not enjoy it. But there was no way to escape it, especially when Time carried the story, and then Newsweek." [2]

Soon after having left the church in Van Nuys, Father Dennis moved to Washington State where he became the pastor at St. Luke's in Seattle. He, his wife and three children began a new life with a new loving congregation. Tragically, in 1963, his beloved wife, Elberta, died. His book Nine O'clock in the Morning is dedicated to her. [2]

After three years of being a widower, Dennis married Rita Reed. He was forty-eight and she was thirty-two. They traveled much of the world together in their ministry and wrote books and newsletters together. [2]

"Being an early leader in what became known as the Charismatic Renewal was not an easy task and certainly not a contest one would enter if one wanted to be voted most politically correct. But Dennis set his heart on living for God and did that to the last day of his life, November 1, 1991." [2]

References:

1.   http://en.wikipedia.org/wiki/Dennis_Bennett_(priest)
2.   http://emotionallyfree.org/DBbio.html

# Bio 4

# Greg Beumer
## 1949 -

Greg Beumer was born on July 30, 1949 in Kodiak, Alaska. According to Greg, "the reason for that is that my dad happened to be in the navy and that's where he happened to be when I was born."

In February of 1969, Greg was attending a junior college in the Bay Area, the reason being that "college was a good place to sell drugs and it kept my parents off my back because my parents thought an education was just the greatest thing in the world for a person."

He had a group of five or six friends, his "druggin' and drinkin' buddies." This group would get together on weekends to engage in erudite discussions about alcohol and other things when one evening in February, the subject turned to God.

"One weekend, we were drinkin' and doing that kind of stuff and we started comparing notes on the things that we'd done and things that we'd tried like re-incarnation and eastern stuff when Dale said maybe we should look at the Bible. I'd never paid much attention to it. I believed there was somebody up there keeping it all together; I didn't know more than that and didn't need to know more than that."

"We decided we'd get together on Tuesday night and we'd all go find a Bible and read it and see what it had to say. Tuesday night came and we all brought a couple cases of beer and we sat down and started reading. We agreed that it made sense to start at the beginning, so we started reading Genesis, but it got real confusing."

"But there is a God and He has His ways; I'll never forget it. It's easy to look back on it and to see God's hand in it."

Greg's buddy, Dale, said that he had heard that God would talk to you out of the Bible. "Yeah but He ain't doin' a good job in Genesis." They therefore decided that the thing to do was to throw the Bible down on the floor and "wherever it opens, that's what God wants us to read. Of course, we'd had too many beers by then."

They threw the Bible onto the floor and it opened to the Gospel of John which states:

"Jesus answered and said unto him, Verily, verily, I say unto thee, Except a man be born again, he cannot see the kingdom of God."

"It didn't mean much to me at the time, but it is amazing that it opened to John."

The group concurred that the idea of being born again was "kind of sketchy." They decided that they needed to call in an expert witness.

As it happened, four of the drinking buddies played music together and the woman who sometimes booked their band into high school gigs often spoke to them of Jesus. She would tell them that God loved them but she never pushed any dogmas on them so she was cool. Her name was Betty Peterson. She would feed them because she knew that all their money went into drugs and band equipment. She brought them cinnamon rolls, which "when you're stoned are pretty big – they are huge – about two feet square and two feet high."

The druggin' and drinkin' buddies invited Betty to come over on Tuesday. "We got a hold of her and she was more than happy to come over and explain 'this born again stuff' because it was kind of sketchy."

That night, five out of six of the buddies gave their lives to Christ – Greg was the one who did not. That night, Betty suggested that Greg go home and go to bed and that when he woke up in the morning, he should just ask God who Jesus is and he should ask Jesus to make Himself real. When Greg woke up, he spoke to Jesus, saying, "Jesus – I don't understand who You are or what You've done. Please help me understand."

Then, he walked to school for classes; it was another beautiful California day in February. Along the way to classes, a friend greeted him saying, "Man, you look really peaceful and calm today. What are you on?" Greg responded, "I'm not on nothing and I don't have nothing to sell." This same sort of encounter happened between classes several additional times.

He didn't really think about it until classes were over and he was on his way home. At that point, he realized that something was different about himself – something that was so strong that even casual observers noticed it and felt it worth commenting on.

He told God, "Okay I can tell something is different. Thank you for touching my heart and I take it as an answer to whatever I asked You about this morning. I haven't been doing too good running this. You know my track record; it's one ditch or tree after another, so You can take over. I don't understand it; I don't understand what You want to do, but I know that You're real and thanks for making Yourself known to me." God seemed to say, "This is the peace you're looking for; this is the love you're looking for."

Greg didn't have experience with church so he and his friends just invited Mrs. Peterson over every Tuesday. She was happy to explain the Bible to them. They stopped drinking beer and they would "drag people over" and tell them about God. He said it was automatic and no one had to tell them to do this.

Later that spring, Greg ran into a friend from high school – a young man who had told him about Jesus and planted some seeds about the gospel years ago. His friend took Greg to San Francisco to a particular coffee house. This is where Greg met Kent Philpott, Paul Bryant, and Oliver Heath. Kent, Oliver and Paul were opening a house for recent converts, people who had come off the streets and had come off drugs. "It was a unique time – I would not trade those days for anything... the relationship and closeness to God – and just watching Him do what He said he would. It was just a blessing to be around all that."

In 1969, Greg moved to Spokane, Washington. In Spokane, he worked with an evangelist group where he met a woman named Debby. They had worked together for four years when God said "you have to talk to that girl about marrying you." He said, "no, no, been there, done that. I'm just here to serve You." "But God has a way of squeezing you in to the right place at the right time." Debby and Greg have been married for almost 40 years and have four children and five grandchildren. "God has blessed us with them and He has done as he promised in drawing them to Himself."

Greg says that he believes the ministry to which God called him is to be someone who proclaims. He spent ten years traveling around the country, telling people about Jesus. Greg and his band would play music in parks and tell people about Jesus. Greg wrote and performed the song entitled You'll Never get to Heaven on LSD. They trusted in God and watched as God provided everything they needed.

He also spent ten years with a prison fellowship until God said "change of plans" and then led Greg to the Union gospel mission working with the celebrate recovery group.

In recalling the phenomenon of the Jesus People Movement, Greg states, "I didn't see it coming. I didn't know it was a movement until probably somewhere in the early '70s when Time magazine said it was a movement, so that officially makes it a movement, I guess."

"It was just something that happened and it happened in the Bay Area and I was there to be a part of it. I remember going to that coffeehouse and running into Chuck Smith and Lonnie Frisbee and they were doing the same thing as us – going to parks and singing and telling people about Jesus."

"Looking back on it, there is something else that strikes me, and that is Mrs. Peterson. One day she took me and Dale to Grove Street in Oakland. We pulled up in front of a storefront church and went in to meet twelve little black women, who comprised the whole church. Mrs. Peterson said, 'These ladies have been praying for you. I just thought you guys would like to come down here and share your testimonies to let them know that their prayers were being answered.'"

The women said that they had been praying for hippies for a long time and would like to hear our testimonies of how we had been drawn to Jesus. They prayed for the most unlikely people – they prayed for the people who were living that life style in the '60s of free-sex, free-drugs and a lot of music."

"We gave our testimonies ... You know a crying woman is a hard thing to take, but twelve of them..... (sigh) and they were all just tears of joy. They prayed and I'm sure glad they did."

# Lyn Rosen Bond and Alan Bond

## 1951 - and 1953 -

L yn Rosen was born to Moishe and Ceil Rosen on October 18; 1951, in Denver, Colorado. Moishe Rosen, (at a later date), would become active in the Jesus People Movement in the Bay Area and would become the Founding Executive Director of Jews for Jesus.

Prior to Lyn's third birthday, Moishe and Ceil became Christians and they went almost directly into ministry in Los Angeles, reaching Jewish people for Jesus, so Lyn was raised mostly in Los Angeles, but also in suburban New York. Moishe and Ceil moved to San Francisco in 1971, while Lyn was away at college.

In 1973, Lyn received her Bachelor's degree, and later that year, her Dad and several others signed a paper making Jews for Jesus a legal non-profit corporation.

Lyn met her future husband, Alan, while they were attending college in Oklahoma. A few months after Lyn graduated, Alan "followed her out to California" (in Alan's words). Prior to his move to San Francisco, Lyn and Alan were corresponding and Lyn was shocked when he wrote to her, saying, "Jesus was a good teacher whether or not we believe that He is God."

She had attended church with him and thought he was already a Christian. Lyn states that, "I had come to faith as a six year old or in first grade Sunday school at Church of the Open Door in Los Angeles. Now at 21 years of age, I was horrified to be so close to falling in love with a man who didn't know Jesus as Messiah." After reading Alan's letter, she prayed, "God – don't let him come out to California unless he's going to get saved."

Alan flew out to San Francisco in June of 1973 and Lyn picked him up at SFO. She told him that she could never marry him, and he thought to himself, "Who's asking?" He imagined that she was saying that she couldn't marry him because he wasn't Jewish.

While living in the Bay Area, Alan got to know Moishe and some of the early people who would become part of Jews for Jesus. They befriended him and witnessed to him about the love of Jesus.

Then, one day, Alan was hitchhiking from Terra Linda to Corte Madera in order to attend a Jews for Jesus Bible Study. Of all people, Kent Philpott picked him up. Kent was also on his way to a Bible Study and noticed that Alan was carrying a paperback. When Kent mentioned the Bible, Alan was quick to correct him, saying, "I'm not a believer."

In Lyn's words, "Kent's interaction with Alan was one of the experiences God used to tear down a misconception Alan had held of what Christians were like. Kent called Alan 'brother' even though Alan had explained that he was not a believer. Previous to that, Alan had held the opinion that Christians were close-minded and associated only with other Christians. The way Kent interacted with him helped Alan see that not all Christians are the same."

After the Bible study, Lyn picked Alan up and drove him to the house where he was staying. They were sitting on the kitchen floor when Alan volunteered, "I would have given my life to Jesus that night, but there had been no invitation. Lyn replied, "You know, you could do it now; you don't need to be in a church." Alan replied that, "If I were to pray right now, you would probably think that I'm not being sincere and praying just to please you." She felt inspired to respond, "Isn't that just an excuse?" So he prayed to ask Jesus to "be his Savior and to save him from himself."

Lyn suggested that he call someone and tell them what he'd

just done, so he decided to call Lyn's sister, Ruth. When he told Ruth, she responded with, "Praise the Lord. You know that I have been praying for you and tonight I was at a Bible study led by Kent and we all prayed for your salvation."

Lyn and Alan were married on June 8, 1974, in the same church in Mill Valley where Kent Philpott is currently the pastor.

Moishe recruited Alan a year later to serve the Lord through Jews for Jesus and he has been serving full-time since November 1975.

Lyn and Alan will be celebrating their 40th wedding anniversary in June. They can be contacted at JewsforJesus.org.

# Paul Bryant
## 1945 -

The term, "Jesus Freak," referred to someone who loved Jesus more than you did. Back in 1968, in San Francisco, those who were witnessing for the gospel on the street were labeled "Jesus Freaks."

There were three of us, all of whom were students at Golden Gate Baptist Theological Seminary: Kent Philpott, Oliver Heath, and myself. We started "working the streets of San Francisco."

We were the counter culture to the counter culture. We were in a social revolution at the time of the Vietnam War and the rise of social non-conformity.

Whatever my parents said must have been wrong because they were all conformists. They lived in a "bubble." The highest "good" was "alikeness." Good people went to church and did their duty on Sunday. More faithful good people tithed and were involved in church activities.

But all of us who were Jesus Freaks felt like there was a disconnect between the institutional church and real Christianity as explained in the Bible and lived by Jesus. Whatever Walter Cronkite said on the news each evening was absolute truth. There were only three networks at the time. They all spoke the same "truth."

Oliver and I moved down near the Haight in the Richmond District of San Francisco. People started coming to Christ. Most everyone was doing drugs, like LSD and marijuana. But harder drugs like cocaine and heroin also started showing up. I remember, in 1969 going to Golden Gate Park, Speedway Meadows, in San Francisco where there was a free concert with The Grateful Dead and The Jefferson Airplane. An estimated 250,000 people were there. There was a thick haze of marijuana smoke that lingered over the whole concert.

Much was going on during the concert, such as small groups that formed for sex and "enlightened" conversation. I felt like the whole world as I knew it, and the world as it had existed up to that time had changed that day and it was frightening. That concert encapsulated those times for me. All conventional wisdom was thrown away, and from now on, truth would be defined only by what we "felt." Since that time it seemed as if the world has crashed and has not recovered.

I started a "house" ministry in San Anselmo, Marin County, called Berakah House. Its purpose was to help new Christians who were coming off drugs and the hippie life style. We were all finding our way through the pages of scripture. Jesus Freaks believed the whole Bible to be true and infallible. We rejected institutional Christianity as we saw it. The goal of the Christian is "to be conformed to the likeness of his Son," (Romans 8:29). That is what Christianity is all about. As we saw the church at the time, it was all about the institution surviving this new day that had come upon us. Most Christians saw Christianity in terms of duty and tasks. The Charismatic movement was also on the rise at the same time. We were attracted to that because of the freedom of worship mostly and the emphasis on the gifts of the Holy Spirit. Mainline Christianity in America has pretty much rejected the gifts of the Holy Spirit, believing they ceased when the last "apostle" died. We did not believe and still do not believe there is any Biblical basis for the belief that the gifts of the Holy Spirit have stopped.

I graduated from Golden Gate Baptist Theological Seminary in 1972, and married my wife, Lana. We had just had our second child. A few of us decided to start a church in San Anselmo. We rented an old chapel building from The San Francisco Theological Seminary for this endeavor. This old stone building was made of granite and it was over a hundred years old. We attracted the hippies, druggies, and the affluent. (Marin County was the wealthiest County in the country at the time.) We called the church Grace Church. We also met in homes during the week. We saw church as simply life together and that the church was what family was suppose to be like.

Living faithfully to the Bible was hard and despairing at the time for me. Older guides were hard to find. But much was going on in the Bay Area. The Spirit of God was moving in the Bay Area and throughout the country. Much was happening in Southern California too with the startup of Calvary Chapel. Ralph Moore, who was the father of the Hope Chapel movement, would later become one of my best friends.

There is also a need to mention Moishe Rosen, the Founding Executive Director of Jews for Jesus. Moishe passed away a few years ago. I remember him speaking one day at Golden Gate Baptist Theological Seminary at chapel. He was the Executive Director of The American Board of Missions to the Jews. He had already heard about us and wanted to see what we were doing on the street. He loved it and felt like "God is in this." He wanted us to come to New York City and do street evangelizing. So we did. Soon he quit the American Board of Mission to the Jews and started Jews for Jesus. He moved to San Francisco. Until he passed away, he loved San Francisco, the Bay Area, and all of the chaotic change going on in its society. For him it was a great opportunity for the gospel. Jews for Jesus now is the largest mission organization to the Jews in the world.

Something needs to be said about the ripple effect of all of this. Fast forward to 1982. My wife and four young children and I moved to Hawaii. Within two years, we became part of a small startup church by the name of Hope Chapel. The founder and pastor was Ralph Moore. He had taken a small Foursquare Church in 1972 in Harmosa Beach, California and he grew it to 4,000. It was a cell-based church. There were several hundred small home groups which he called "mini churches." Ralph never "worked the street." He employed the same methods that Chuck Smith at Calvary Chapel did. What he saw was how the world can come to Christ. Just preaching at a congregation will never do. For Ralph, it was investing his learning, experience and character into the lives of men. This included teaching faithful men to teach others (2Timothy 2:1-2) and sending them out to rely on the Holy Spirit to work through them, not to control them, but to empower them, and encourage them to do the great commission. There are now are over 1,000 Hope Chapels around the world.

Some of the best of the Jesus Movement migrated to Hawaii. What has happened since 1982 in Hawaii is indeed remarkable. Ralph Moore, in conjunction other leaders from many other Christian denominations brought their leadership skills to Hawaii. Since then, the Christian population of Hawaii among evangelicals has grown from 4% to 25% of the population, according to George Barna. It is the only state in the country in which the Christian population is growing faster than the population at large. A big evangelical church in Hawaii in 1982 was maybe 300. Now there are many congregations with multiple thousands.

# Mark Buckley
## 1950 -

Mark Buckley is a native Californian, born in San Francisco on January 10th, 1950. He attended Terra Linda High School and the College of Marin. On August 12, 1973, Mark married Kristina Kenner. Mark is the oldest of eight children, and father to Matthew, Philip, Kelly, and Kathryn, and a grandfather of four children.

Mark heard the Bible taught verse by verse for the first time during the Jesus movement in 1970. According to his own recollection:

I heard the gospel in a way that helped me open my heart to the Lord in

San Rafael in 1970, after Larry Bresnan a high school friend shared his faith with me. We sang contemporary worship songs while we sat on couches, chairs, or the floor in homes filled with people seeking the Lord for the first time in their lives. The leaders gave invitations for people to commit their lives to Christ in almost every Bible study we held. There were people making commitments to accept Jesus as their Lord and Savior at almost every meeting. We took teams of people to evangelize on the streets of San Francisco, San Rafael or Novato every week for many years. We passed out broadsides created by Jews for Jesus, and gospel tracts.

Mark was involved with groups that started what came to be known as Christian General Stores in San Rafael, Novato, San Francisco and Petaluma. These stores were gathering places where people could purchase Christian books, Bibles, and music. They were places where Christians would go for counseling and for direction in locating churches or fellowship.

Mark was one of elders or pastors of the Church of the Open Door in San Rafael. In 1975 he founded a branch of the church in Novato, California. He was involved in starting mission outreaches in London and Mexico City.

In February 1984, Mark and his family moved to Phoenix on account of Matthew's asthma. In September of 1984, he founded the Living Streams Church in Phoenix.

Mark Buckley is currently the senior pastor of Living Streams and the president of Grace Association, a network of Phoenix area pastors and leaders.

He leads Living Streams by working with a team of pastors who oversee the churches and ministries. They are governed by a board of elders and work closely with churches and ministries throughout the Valley of the Sun (Phoenix metro area).

To learn about Mark's ministry or to download sermons, you can visit his website at www.Livingstreams.org.

# Bio 8

# Bob Burns
## 1956 -

Bob Burns was born on February 18, 1956 in Burlingame, California, the fourth of five brothers in an Irish-Catholic family. Their father was a fireman for the city of San Francisco. Bob grew up in San Francisco, and San Rafael, and graduated from San Rafael High School, San Francisco State University, and the Golden Gate Baptist Theological Seminary.

Bob became a Christian, as he says, "at the tail end of the Jesus People Movement", on April 1972. He met Kent through a Bible study group at San Rafael High. Bob says, "I saw something in those days that was totally different than what can be seen today." Bob was convicted by the whole-hearted commitment he saw in the Jesus people group that met on his campus. They were very up-front and unashamed about their faith. Bob often felt he wanted to join them but was afraid of what people would say.

In those days, Bob, like most others didn't realize how unique those times were. Identifying with the "counter culture," Bob thought the Jesus Movement was "just part and parcel of being open to new things as counter culture ideas."

Bob recalls that throughout the year of 1971, he "kept running into Christians who were very outspoken and confident about Christ in their conversations with him." Once when he was hitchhiking, a car pulled over to pick him up. He recognized the people in the car and thought, "Oh no - it's all these Jesus Freaks picking me up." Just then as the car pulled away from the curb, Mary, who sat in the front seat in front of him, turned around 180º, cracked a big smile and asked, "So Bob, have you given your life to Jesus yet?" Everyone in the car, it seemed, gave Bob an earful for the duration of the ride.

Bob didn't want to commit to Jesus because he was afraid of being labeled a "Jesus Freak". He struggled with this for about a year. Then, one day, Hugo, a friend of Bob's, struck up a conversation with him about Christ. He pulled out a pocket Bible and started reading pertinent verses to him. He invited Bob to pray to become a Christian. Bob was hesitant and told Hugo that he "had loose ends to tie up," (meaning that he didn't want to change his life). Hugo asked, "Why not let Jesus tie up those loose ends for you?" Bob could not disagree. Just then Hugo called out to his friend, Keith, in a loud voice right there in the hallway at school. "Bob wants to give his life to Christ," Hugo said.

Bob says, he didn't really pray that prayer that day, he was so distracted by the crowds of people milling by. But later, as he walked down the hallway to his next class, he made the decision that he stick this Christian thing out to see if there was any truth in it.

That night as he prayed alone in his room, Bob says, "it was as if the room filled up with the presence of God... like liquid love. I had a sense that I was meeting someone who was intimately related to me, but whom I had never known before. This experience put me on a completely different trajectory, that I would remain we me for the rest of my life."

# Bio 9

# Jim Durkin
## 1925 - 1996

In many ways Dad's story is similar to the generation that lived through the depression and WWII. He was born Nov 12 1925 in an Irish neighborhood in Chicago an only child of a first generation Irish immigrant father. He lived with his parents and maternal grandparents. By age 15 Dad was orphaned, moving from relative to relative until he joined the Navy.

During the war years Dad was in the officer training program. To become an officer you had to have a college degree, so he began what was called the V-12 Navy College Training Program at the University of Louisville and completed his College years at the University of Washington in Seattle this also corresponded with the end of his enlistment in the Navy.

Honorably discharged but finding no work in Seattle he and a friend traveled to Hoopa CA., to find work in one of the lumber camps. Although in during his time in college someone would occasionally witness to him it was in the lumber camp that 2 men in particular began to focus their witness on dad. One night Dad was the assigned to a sort of guard duty over the camp while the other men went into town. Lying on his bed he began to ask if what these two men were saying was real. If there really was a God who cared about him would He make himself known? He said immediately this incredibly warm sensation began to surround him first it was like it was all around him. Then it was like it what over his whole body and finally it was like it was in him. That night he opened his heart to receive the Lord. I remember him saying often I couldn't wait for his now two brothers to come back so he could tell them that he got saved.

Mom and Dad met sometime later in the Assembly of God Church in Hoopa. Mom a graduate of Northwest Bible College in Seattle was serving with her older sister as interim pastors in a little Native American church in Weichpec CA. a town just a few miles away from Hoopa. They were married in May of 1947 and moved to Blue Lake, CA, where they served as the pastors of an Assembly of God church.

Between the years of 1947 and 1967 Dad and Mom served as an Assembly of God minister in Northern California and Oregon. He also tried his hand as an insurance salesman, used car salesman, door to door salesman and ultimately as a real estate broker.

In 1969 While Pastoring a small independent church Licensed by the Full Gospel fellowship of Churches and Ministers international and at the same time trying to build their real estate business dad was approached by a group of Jesus People traveling up the coast. They felt the Lord had directed them to Eureka and wanted to establish a base from which to evangelize. With some misgivings dad let them use an old storefront building with apartments overhead he had just purchased. "The Whosoever Will House" began to see a number of new converts joining and wanting to grow in God they began attending the church dad was pastoring.

A few miles away another early pioneer in the Jesus People movement, Ken Smith had purchased an old Coast Guard Lighthouse outpost station. Wanting to get away from the fog and damp weather of Northern California and being drawn back to Hawaii. Ken approached dad about purchasing the Lighthouse Ranch and moving these young disciples that by now had outgrown "The Whosoever Will House" out to the ranch. In the latter part of 1970 that transaction took place and dad began going out to the ranch to minister. A year later dad and mom moved to the ranch.

Seeing the hand of God in something completely new Dad decided that things would not fit in the old paradigms of the organized church. As a result he formed a corporation called Gospel Outreach that would own the ranch and be the foundation of whatever God would do in and with this new generation of young disciples.

In 1972 the first "teams" were sent out to Coquille OR., and Anchorage Ak. The teams as we called the were as few as 3 or 4 couples and a few singles to over 20 or more "sent out" to move to a city for the purpose of bringing the Gospel to that city. Over the next decade 100 teams were sent out throughout the US, Europe, Asia, and Central and Latin America.

It would not be a complete picture into the life of Jim Durkin without understanding that He and Dacie were a real team Although He had much more of the public image he would not have been able to continue on in what God had called him to do if it had not been for the strength of a woman who became mom to a generation of young believers.

Dad passed on January 12th 1996 2 months past his 70th birthday. His legacy continues not in an organization he built but rather in the hearts of the thousands that came to Christ and sat under the anointing and teaching of a man and woman who allowed God to mold them.

[Written by Jim Durkin, Jr.]

# Bio 10

# Gaylord Enns
## 1945 -

Gaylord Enns was born on August 17th; 1945, in Corning, California. He grew up on a farm, in the Capay farming district, which is near Orland, California. His parents were Christians, so Gaylord grew up in a Christian environment and made a childhood commitment to the Lord.

His commitment weakened during a dark period of time from around age 13 to 18, but he made a conscious adult commitment at age 18. This was right before going off to college. He attended Bethany Bible College in Santa Cruz and he attended Chico State.

He and his wife, Patti, married, in January of 1969. They have a son and a daughter.

Gaylord started his ministry in 1967 at Chico State University. He did a full-time Christian ministry with a Christian organization on the campus. It was around 1966 when Chico seemed to have been discovered by and invaded by "the Hippies". By 1967, Gaylord was hosting meetings in his apartment. The famous evangelist, Mario Murillo, came to Gaylord's apartment and spoke on occasion. Many Hippies came to know Jesus.

One of the people to be saved was Bob Maddux. After becoming a Christian, Bob came to live with Gaylord, and in the summer of 1968, they opened a Christian commune, Ivy House. They lived there and ministered to new converts for four years. At the height, there were 35 people living in the commune at once. Over the years, the commune housed 100 young people.

One of Gaylord's memories of the Jesus People Movement is that there was "an amazing flood of people who came to know Jesus. It started with street people, then college and high school kids." It's funny, but like everyone who was involved in the Jesus People Movement, none of us seemed to appreciate the enormity of it at the time. Gaylord says that, at the time, he thought it was just a phenomenon of Chico. (This writer, having moved to the Bay Area from Boston, believed that it was just one of the differences between the East Coast and the West Coast.)

Gaylord recalls that there were "many miracles, conversions, answered prayers and material needs being met. Lots of extraordinary things happened." One of the things that he said has impacted him the most was the "selflessness and sacrificial love that people had for one another."

After his ministry at Ivy House, Gaylord became the youth pastor of a congregation in Chico. In 1972, he became the associate pastor, and in 1980, the senior pastor. He served as senior pastor until 2003, at which time, he founded the Servant Leadership Network, which is an organization that works with pastors and next-generation Leaders. In 2009, he released a book, Love Revolution: Rediscovering the Lost Command of Jesus.

If you wish to contact Gaylord, his e-mail address is gaylord@ gaylordenns.com

# Bio II

# Lonnie Frisbee
## 1949 - 1993

onnie Frisbee was born on June 6, 1949 in Costa Mesa, California. He is notable as an American Pentecostal evangelist in the signs and wonders movement of the 1970s and 1980s and for having been at the forefront of the Jesus Movement.[1]

He grew up in a single-parent home, received a minimal high school education, and was exposed to various unsavory characters during his childhood. He suffered a rape at age eight.[1]

During his teenage years, Lonnie developed an interest in art and cooking, winning awards for his paintings. At the young age of fifteen, he became a part of the drug culture and entered the gay community of Laguna Beach. At age eighteen, he moved to San Francisco with the hippies and flower children in the "Summer of Love." He described himself as a "nudist-vegetarian hippie."[1]

Lonnie did things that were highly unusual. He used to make a habit of reading scripture while on LSD. During one acid trip, he had "a vision of a vast sea of people crying out to the Lord for salvation, with (himself) in front preaching the gospel."[1]

In San Francisco, while attending the San Francisco Art Academy, Lonnie made the acquaintance of people from Haight-Ashbury's Living Room mission. He reportedly used to talk to them about Jesus in conjunction with UFOs. He practiced hypnotism and spoke about dabbling in the occult. Eventually, with the help of God, his ideas were straightened out and he became one of the most dynamic Christian leaders of the Jesus Movement.[1]

Lonnie Frisbee was one of the first street Christians in Haight-Ashbury. Soon after his conversion, he helped to establish some of the first Christian Communes.[1] He was called "the quintessential Jesus freak" and was featured in Life and Time magazines in articles documenting the "Jesus Movement" throughout North America.[2] From 1968 to 1971, Frisbee made thousands of new converts with his dynamic God-Given abilities to witness to the counter-culture of hippies and surfers.[1]

Lonnie worked together with Chuck Smith and John Wimber to establish the Association of Vineyard Churches and Cavalry Chapel. In 1971 Frisbee and Smith parted ways because of ideological differences. Smith "discounted Pentecostalism, maintaining that love was the greatest manifestation of the Holy Spirit while Frisbee was strongly involved in theology centering on spiritual gifts and New Testament occurrences."[1]

Frisbee had often struggled with a tendency toward homosexuality and he was the first to admit that homosexuality is something that God considers to be a sin. He was forthright in admitting that he had struggled with this throughout his life. Many of the churches ostracized him because of his same-sex attraction.[3]

". . . Lonnie Frisbee was not a perfect person, but he never claimed to be one either. He was honest almost to a fault and he never tried to be something he wasn't. He struggled with drugs and sexual urges that he deemed sinful for most of his life, but he loved the Lord and he loved other people. Lonnie had a rough life, but because of this strange bisexual hippie from Laguna Beach, thousands (and possibly millions) of lives were changed and .. the full extent of his impact will never be known. . . ."[3]

Frisbee tragically died of AIDS on March 12, 1993. ". . . his funeral depicted him as a man who loved Jesus but tragically fell victim to his own vices. Before he died, Lonnie made sure that it was known that he forgave all those who had ostracized him and shunned him in the past. Despite being mistreated and despised by the churches he helped found, he wanted it known that he forgave them." [3]

References:

1.   http://en.wikipedia.org/wiki/Lonnie_Frisbee
2.   http://www.kqed.org/arts/programs/trulyca/episode.
     jsp?epid=152173
3.   http://benevolentbaptist.wordpress.com/2013/03/12/
     the-forgotten-hippy-remembering-lonnie-fris-
     bee-and-the-jesus-movement/

# Oliver Heath
## 1945 -

Oliver N. Heath Jr. was born in Atlanta, Georgia on January 30, 1945 to Dell and Oliver N. Heath Sr. Oliver Sr. was in the Air Force, so the family ended up having to move frequently from one military base to another.

Oliver grew up in a Christian family and he made a personal commitment to the Lord while in college. He received a Bachelor of Science from Auburn University, a Master of Divinity (MDIV) from the Golden Gate Seminary and a Masters of Education from the University of Mobile.

It was at the Golden Gate Seminary in Mill Valley, California that Oliver became friends with Kent Philpott, a fellow-student there at the time. Kent asked Oliver to work with him in a church that he was pastoring not far from the Seminary. Not long after that, Oliver went to Switzerland to persue additional studies.

He returned to California in 1967, the "Summer of Love," and reconnected with Kent. Oliver, Kent, and Paul Bryant began witnessing to the young people who had come to the Golden Gate Park and the Haight Ashbury district by the thousands. Many of those that they witenssed to gave their lives to the Lord. With all these new Christians needing care and discipling, they had to come up with a plan for these young Christians. Paul & Oliver convinced the pastor of Lincoln Park Baptist Church to let them use part of the facility to house these young men. They got cots and blankets from the Salvation Army. The new converts "camped out" here. It came to be known as "the Soul Inn." Every night, there was a Bible study. The disciples were provided with food and a place to sleep and help finding jobs.

By 1969, communal living had become commonplace among the "Hippies". New believers continued the practice and Christian Communes were proliferating. Kent and Paul oversaw communes in Marin County. Oliver and his wife Mary Louise oversaw communes in San Francisco under the name of Harvest House. As the ministry grew soon a Free Store was added, as well as and the publication of the street news paper, the Oracle, which contained news of the movement, and Bible teaching.

In 1971 the Lord spoke to Oliver saying, "You can keep your hair and your beard or you can keep your ministry." In addition to that the Lord had been speaking to Oliver about basing the ministry in the pattern of the New Testament Church. The communes were phased out leaving only twelve people. They became the foundation for a new church---Calvary Fellowship. They rented a building (an abandoned bar) at the corner of Haight and Ashbury Steets. Sunday mornings, there were church services with a children's service available and mid-week, they held Bible studies.

In 1978, Oliver and his family moved to Mobile, Alabama. Oliver and Mary Louise have four children: three sons and a daughter, and 5 grandchildren. He is pastoring at the Covenant Church of Mobile. His contact information is oliverheathjr@gmail.com and the phone number of the church is 251-639-9020.

# Bio 13

# Roger Hoffman
## 1947 -

Roger Hoffman was born into a Christian home. His maternal grandfather was a Southern Baptist lay-preacher and church planter. Roger attended Sunday school, church and youth groups on a weekly basis. He went to Vacation Bible School and youth camp every summer. When he was eight years old, he gave his heart to the Lord, was born again and was water baptized. As a youth, he was taught to read the Bible and to pray every day. By his mid-teens, reading the Bible and praying were a regular habit for him.

At age 16, Roger attended a camp for high school seniors and college students at Glorietta; New Mexico, a Southern Baptist facility. He and the other students heard missionary speakers all week, and, Roger says that after one of the services, he knew that the Holy Spirit was dealing with him about serving the Lord full time. That evening, he answered the call to the ministry.

In his second year at junior college and in his first year at the university, he served as the president of the Baptist Student Union. During the summer of 1969, he served on a BSU summer mission team, working in churches in Northern California, leading Vacation Bible schools and summer camp programs.

Paralleling his involvement with the Baptist Student Union, the Lord was gently leading him into a deeper walk with Him and drawing him into uncharted territory. One of Roger's concerns had been that the church did not seem to measure up to the church that he read about in the Bible. He wanted to see the gap closed. As a teenager, he had asked his grandmother about the passages in 1 Corinthians 12-14 concerning the gifts of the Holy Spirit. Her answer had been encouraging; she just said, "They're there in the Bible, aren't they?" This had helped to open a door in inquiry for Roger.

While at the university, and while also involved with the Baptist Student Union, Roger became involved with Inter-Varsity Christian Fellowship and Chi Alpha, the Assembly of God student group on campus. Roger felt that something was missing from his Christian walk and sought the Lord concerning the baptism of the Holy Spirit. Within a few months, Roger says that God answered his prayer. The scriptures were alive to him and his prayer life became more fervent. Roger received a boldness to be a witness for the Lord.

After graduating from the university, Roger enrolled in the three-year postgraduate Master of Divinity course at Golden Gate Baptist Theological Seminary in Mill Valley, California. While at the seminary, he was persuaded by a friend to help him start an independent charismatic church in the area. The Lord blessed them and within a year and a half, they had a church of about a hundred people. Another ministry merged with them, and before long, the congregation grew to about three hundred. They conducted Bible studies, ran ten residential discipleship houses, and a food co-op. They also did counseling and ran seminars on drug abuse at the local schools.

Eventually, Roger was led by the Lord to start missions. The first team was sent to Mexico City. Roger and his wife led the second team to London, England. They spent over seven years in London doing street evangelism, establishing a residential discipleship house, pioneering a church and raising up leadership. They also started a national ministry to help people who were coming out of the homosexual lifestyle.

In 1986, Roger and his family returned to California. He took over the pastoral work of one of his churches that had experienced a crisis in leadership and spent the next eight years in that church bringing stabilization.

Roger is currently the pastor of the Penngrove Community Church in Penngrove, California.

# Bio 14

# David Hoyt
## 1945 -

David was born in Los Angeles, California. His childhood and early adulthood would have to be characterized as having been turbulent, as he was in and out of the Juvenile Justice and Corrections System from ages 9 to 21.

## Testimony

In the spring of 1966, David moved to San Francisco to continue his search for truth and God. Up to this point he'd taken correspondence courses through Self Realization Fellowship with Guru Paramahansa Yogananda, and read extensively about The Fourth Way, Daoism, Zen-Buddhism, Eastern Mysticism and other esoteric writers. For 2 years he engaged in a daily routine of meditation & prayer and was a vegetarian. Moving to SF he hoped to make the right decision and settle on a spiritual path to follow.

When Swami A.C. Baktivedanta set up a Krishna Temple in the Haight, David began attending regularly. In the fall of 1966, he was initiated by Swami A.C. at the Krishna Temple on Frederick Street, given a Hindu name, and became one of Swami's early San Francisco devotees.

Shortly after his initiation, David met Kent Philpott, who was at that time a student at the Golden Gate Baptist Seminary. Kent engaged David in spiritual dialogue. David understood that most religions and teachers claim their way to God, is the one true path.  Regardless of his Krishna (Hindu) commitment, he remained curious about Jesus Christ's role in human history.

On-going conversations with Kent about Jesus Christ sparked recollections of other voices, both past and present.  Just prior to moving to San Francisco, a neighborhood friend who had shared food with him over the months took him to the bus station on moving day. As they were saying goodbye his friend said, "Jesus is God's Son, the true Christ.  Be careful not to be misled by imposters."

David's deceased grandmother was also a Christian.  She used to take him to the local Methodist Church when he was a boy.  She'd told him about God and his Son, Jesus Christ, and about his two great-grandfathers, who were Christian clergymen.

More recently a nun, an older man, and a little old lady had told him about Jesus Christ.  The little old lady had followed him into the Krishna Temple and was visiting with him until the temple commander entered the room and heard her talking about Jesus. Abruptly he rushed to her, grabbed her by the arm and pushed her out of the temple, causing her to fall on the sidewalk. David helped her to her feet, and she turned, walking slowing down the street.  David rebuked the temple commander, telling him he was a heartless human being.  This wasn't the first time they'd clashed.

Despite the honor of having been invited by the swami to be part of the temple core staff of four individuals, unresolved questions lingered in David's mind: "Who can forgive human sin? Why do Krishna followers put out food and flowers before wooden idols? Why does Swami dodge and avoid any questions about Jesus Christ by changing the subject?"

These questions intersected with the time frame of having made Kent's acquaintance, and shortly afterwards, meeting Timothy Wu.  It was the spring of 1967 and the Haight District was becoming more dangerous and dark.  To David, even the Krishna Temple was beginning to look like another dead-end of human origin.

One evening after a Bible discussion at the Krishna Temple, a confrontation between David and Timothy arose regarding God and the exclusiveness of Christian claims. This incident led to Timothy giving an unusual prophecy and challenge to David. This challenge and two visions about being deceived got David's attention. His prayers intensified with a focus on Jesus Christ's identity. Was Jesus Christ a gifted teacher and miracle worker, or was he these things and also the true Son of God, God's Messiah? David sensed God was near (Jer. 17:10, II Chron. 16:9).

While praying for a breakthrough, David was simultaneously experiencing a gradual dismantling of the Krishna Consciousness mindset and he followed Timothy's urgings to, "stop chanting and ask God for the truth." On a cool morning, about 7:15 AM, in the middle of a Krishna worship service, a fire and panic broke out in the temple. Those in attendance fled. David and a few others who lived at the temple stayed behind. Venturing down the stairs to the basement where the fire was, David heard a voice say the same words twice, "Call on me now." Frozen on the stairs a silent prayer was offered, "God, If Jesus Christ is Your Son –reveal it to me (Jer. 33:3)."

David recalls, "Immediately I was flooded with a powerful presence of light that seemed to permeate every part of my mind, body and spirit. Intuitively I knew it was God. He was accepting and forgiving me and Jesus Christ's Spirit was revealing this. Jesus Christ was the true Son of God and he had been raised from the dead (John 1:12-18, Hebrews 9:11-15, Jer. 17:14)!

That day David was invited to live with Kent and his family at Golden Gate Baptist Seminary.

## In David's own words: Jesus People Days

What followed was an amazing journey of following Jesus Christ in ways similar to what I read about in the book of Acts. I was baptized in water in the name of God the Father, Jesus Christ

His Son and the Holy Spirit. I studied the Bible and prayed daily. I participated in worship, was filled with the Holy Spirit and told others about Jesus Christ whenever I went (Matt. 3:11, Acts 1:5, 1:8, 2:1-4). A witness in my spirit confirmed my salvation as I practiced these things (I Cor. 2:7-10. God's grace and presence was strong (Acts 4:33). My life along with others who'd received Jesus Christ was being transformed (II Cor. 5:17-21).

We were called 'Jesus People' by those on the street. It was in our DNA to share our faith. We were not ashamed of God, Jesus Christ, the Holy Spirit, the Bible or the gospel message (Romans 1:16) God gave us boldness in sharing the good news, carrying our bibles, handing out tracks and engaging people in dialogue at parks, beaches, high schools, colleges, universities, Juvenile Halls, city jails, honor farms, prisons and the streets. While we were doing this, miracles took place on a regular basis. The most frequent miracle was people opening their heart to Jesus Christ. For this to occur there were often accompanying miracles like people coming down from a drug they'd taken, or deliverance from a demonic spirit, physical healing, or mental confusion being removed (Luke 9:1-6, Acts 8:4-8).

We prayed in advance of going, while among those in need and after every outing (Joshua 1:9). We asked God to speak through us and guide our steps to those we were intended to speak with. We realized that spiritual miracles were God's doing. He honored faith and took the truth we presented to people and applied it to their heart and need. If what they heard was mixed with faith and openness of heart – something mysterious from God would happen (Acts 8:26-40). Our outings weren't always what we hoped for. Sometimes people would yell, spit, curse, or try to hit us (John 15:18-19). We encountered evil and the devil regularly. We stood our ground in the authority of Jesus Christ. Demons would get roused, causing a scene. Shop owners would get upset because of all the commotion in front of their stores. Anything could happen (Mark 5:1-20, Ephesians 19:23-34). The Lord went with us and consistently backed up our words allow-ing us to bear spiritual fruit (John 15:14-17). Surprisingly, there was an absence of other Christians harvesting in most of these venues.

"My food," said Jesus "is to do the will of him who sent me and to finish his work. Do you not say four months more and then the harvest? I tell you, open your eyes and look at the fields! They are ripe for harvest. Even now the reaper draws his wages, even now he harvests the crop for eternal life, so the sower and the reaper may be glad together (John 4:34-36)."

When a street person or drug addict came to believe in Jesus Christ, they needed to get off the streets and established in the faith. Most street converts didn't have a job, or place to live. If they had a place to live it was usually a drug infested flat, or building filled with demonic activity. This need, led us by faith to establish discipleship houses (Hebrews 11:1). With very little money or resources we leased properties, houses, storefronts and small ranches. In time we'd expand to open coffeehouses, restaurants, book stores and start a variety of small businesses which provided work for a growing number of young Christians. We also started Christian music groups/bands, newspapers, developed theater teams and wrote songs and tracts about God. The notion of not caring about people who were in need of help was unacceptable to Jesus People (Matthew 25:34-46, James 2:14-24). We sent out teams to carry the gospel of Jesus to venues throughout the USA, Europe and into the world (Matthew 28:18-20).

Our message was Jesus Christ's miraculous life and teaching, death on the cross payment for human sin and resurrection from the dead – conquering the power of death for all who would believe (Romans 5:6-11, 6:8-11, I Cor. 15). God did many things that were not humanly possible (Luke 18:27). When Jesus spoke about the necessity of taking up our cross and following Him, losing our lives for Him, we took these words seriously (Luke 9:23-26). We asked God to help us understand His Word. Many Jesus People were diligent students of the Scriptures, reading, studying and memorizing to become better equipped to witness, for personal growth and group edification (2 Timothy 2:15, I Peter 2:2, Hebrews 4:12-13, Psalm 119).

My fondest memories are of the special people God put in my life in JP days and the Christian house ministry teams of: 'Home for His Glory', Upper Streams, House of Judah, Jesus Family Beulah Hill London, Wythenshaw Outreach - Stockport / Manchester UK, the Lonesome Stone Theatre Company – England / and a handful of friends from Church of the Open Door.

## Problems We Encountered

Jesus People struggled with the baggage they brought; emotional and mental issues, past and present sins, previous demonic activity and substance abuse, etc. We were constantly engaged in a raging battle between the flesh and the Spirit (Gal. 5:16-23). Four central weaknesses in the JP movement were: (1. Misuse of authority by young leaders. (2. Character and moral flaws in leaders. (3. Not enough seasoned older teachers and leaders who could have provided stability for the avalanche of new Christians. (4. Several cults deceived and devastated JP ministries; 'The Children of God' aka 'The Family' was by far the worst. I joined them for a time losing my first family and many close friends.

## Summary

The Jesus Movement was God's spark of light, truth and love – woven into the larger hippie movement that was destined to fail in living up to its promise of 'Peace and Love' – with drugs and evil running the show. The Jesus Movement was God's way of redeeming a 1960's binge of unrestrained free-love, experimentation with drugs, old world religions, witchcraft and the like – with the evil-One cloaked, masquerading himself in the background – seeking to destroy people's lives. The Jesus Movement was used to infuse the established church with new life, new music, worship and discipleship wherever it was welcome.

**David E. Hoyt:**

» 40 + yrs. Christian Service: In Missions, Pastorates, Correctional & Hospice Chaplaincy
» Undergrad Equiv. Ashland University, English / Correctional Counseling / Theater
» Master of Divinity / Pastoral Care / Counseling / Chaplaincy
» Ashland Theological Seminary - Ashland, Ohio.
» Ordained with: The Brethren Church & Church of the Open Door

# Robert L. Hymers, Jr.
## 1941 -

Robert L. Hymers, Jr. was born in Glendale, California in 1941. He is known for his passionate protests against abortion, and for leading several protests against the movie, The Last Temptation of Christ. Dr. Hymers is the founder of the Baptist Tabernacle of Los Angeles. He is the author of several books and his word-for-word sermon manuscripts, as well as videos of his sermons, can be found on his website and his videos on YouTube. Hymers and his wife, Ileana, are the parents of two sons.

Dr. Hymers is a graduate of the Los Angeles City College (1968), the California State University at Los Angeles (1970), Golden Gate Baptist Theological Seminary (1973), the California Graduate School of Theology (1974), the San Francisco Theological Seminary, Presbyterian USA (1981), and the Louisiana Baptist Theological Seminary (1989). He also holds an honorary Doctor of Literature degree from the Louisiana Baptist University (2003).[1]

While attending Golden Gate Baptist Theological Seminary, Hymers confronted some of the professors over their rejection of the full authority of the Bible. Hymers is a strong advocate of the complete reliability and inerrancy of the Scriptures. He answered the professors' attacks on the Bible in the seminary student paper, The Current, when he was the editor.

In the 1980s Hymers led several provocative anti-abortion demonstrations. In one of these demonstrations he even went so far as to call upon Christians to pray that God would remove by death one of the Supreme Court justices who was responsible for supporting the "Roe v. Wade" decision to legalize abortion. He later gave a public apology for this prayer, saying, "I wish I had not done that and I would never do it again." He still maintains a strong commitment to the pro-life movement, and gives at least one major sermon on his website against abortion each year. Hymers compares abortion to Hitler's massacre of the Jewish people in World War II.

Over the years, Hymers has had to deal with various attacks on his ministry. This would not be deemed unusual for someone who is an outspoken Christian, as he is. In Hymers' own words,

A preacher who takes a strong stand against abortion and other evils in our society, and preaches a strong Gospel, will be vilified by hate mongers...Every preacher understands that there are bitter, disgruntled people.[2]

Dr. Hymers remains the Senior Pastor at the Baptist Tabernacle of Los Angeles. His word-for-word sermon manuscripts, and videos of his sermons, go out on his website in over 28 languages to over 180 nations. He is the author of 15 books, and his congregation in the civic center of Los Angeles is comprised of more than 20 ethnic groups. His video sermons are translated sentence by sentence from the pulpit in Chinese and Spanish on his website at RLHSERMONS.com, and on YouTube.

**References:**

1. http://en.wikipedia.org/wiki/R._L._Hymers,_Jr.
2. http://www.drrlhymersjranswershiscritics.com

# Kathryn Kuhlman
## 1907 - 1976

Kathryn Johanna Kuhlman was born on May 9, 1907 in rural Concordia; Missouri, to German farmers, Joseph and Emma Kuhlman. [1, 2]

A childhood friend described Kathryn as having "large features, red hair, and freckles. She wasn't dainty or appealingly feminine in any sense of the word. She was taller than the rest of 'our gang,' gangly and boyish in build, and her long strides kept the rest of us puffing to keep up with her." [2]

Kathryn herself deemed that she was just "an ordinary person." [2]

One day when Kathryn was fourteen, while at church with her mother, she began to shake all over. A weight of conviction came over her, and she realized that she was a sinner in need of salvation and forgiveness. She slipped out from where she was standing, went to the corner of the front pew and sat weeping. At that moment Jesus lifted the weight from her shoulders and entered her heart. [2]

At the young age of seventeen, Ms. Kuhlman, and Kathryn's older sister, and her sister's husband began an evangelistic tent ministry. [2]

In 1928, Ms. Kuhlman had a ministry in Boise, Idaho, in what was called the "pool hall mission." In 1935, she founded the Denver Revival Tabernacle. It was here that she met the handsome, married, Texas evangelist; Burroughs Waltrip. There was quite a scandal. He allegedly left his wife to marry her. Soon she realized her mistake and got a divorce. However, it was too late; this fiasco was the undoing of everything that she had worked for so diligently. People stopped attending her services and her ministry collapsed. [2]

In the wake of this disaster, Kathryn decided to re-commit herself to God and she never wavered again in answering His call. She began daily radio broadcasts and had a weekly TV program called I Believe in Miracles. [1]

Between the 1940s and the 1970s, she held "healing crusades," in which thousands of people received spiritual and physical healings.

This author had the privilege of attending several of her services at the Oakland Auditorium and was an eyewitness to the miracles. During the course of one of these meetings, this author recalls her as having said the following:

You know, often a male evangelist will ask me "What do you think you're doing? This ministry is a job for a man, not a woman." And I reply that I absolutely agree with them. I don't believe that I'm God's first choice. I believe that He called several men to this ministry before me, but they all refused Him.

"The world called me a fool for having given my entire life to One whom I've never seen. I know exactly what I'm going to say when I stand in His presence. When I look upon that wonderful face of Jesus, I'll have just one thing to say: 'I tried.' I gave of myself the best I knew how. My redemption will have been perfected when I stand and see Him who made it all possible." [2]

-- Kathryn Kuhlman

**References:**

1.   en.wikipedia.org/wiki/Kathryn_Kuhlman
2.   http://www.godsgenerals.com/person_k_kuhlman.htm

# Robert D. Lewis
## 1929 -

R obert Lewis was born in Little Rock, Arkansas on August 26, 1929. Leona Lewis was born on May 2, 1929 in Arcadia California. She grew up in the Mojave Desert, where the government had recently opened a rocket-testing base. Bob was a marine stationed at the rocket base.

In 1946, some friends of Leona brought Bob to her house for a visit. In 1948, Bob and Leona were married.

Bob was honorably discharged from the Marines in 1951. He attended a college in Arkansas, and after graduating, moved to San Francisco, where he attended the Golden Gate Baptist Theological Seminary. He was a trustee at the Seminary. While attending the seminary, he was also a pastor at the First Baptist Church of Fairfield, California. Bob was Kent Philpott's pastor and Kent became a Christian in 1963 through the preaching of Pastor Lewis.

Pastor Lewis is known as the "Singing Pastor." He has a beautiful tenor voice and has made several records.

Robert and Leona currently reside in Upland, California. They have five children, fifteen grandchildren and twenty-five great-grandchildren.

Note: When the above information was collected, Pastor Bob was dying in a hospital in Pomona and Leona was ten miles away in Upland, California and unable to visit her husband. She was able to speak for a few minutes with Stephanie. Leona said her husband often spoke of Kent.

Following is an email response from a woman who attended First Baptist Church, Fairfield, under Bob Lewis' pastorship:

"My family moved to Fairfield in 1956. We joined First Baptist. I was twelve. Bob Lewis came after V. B. Brazill resigned. Bob and Leona were a young couple with children. Bob was a passionate preacher! He loved his people. He was active in the community. He was a city councilman. He attended our football games. He was at the bowling alley. As a youth, I was glad to see my pastor where the kids went!

Bob built our sanctuary. It was full every Sunday. We had to add folding chairs in the isles. He also started several mission churches: Temple Baptist, Grace Baptist and Calvary Baptist. I believe he also started a Spanish mission.

After Bob resigned First Baptist and became a pastor down south, he got a call to come to Temple Baptist. Their membership had dropped to about fifty people. He saved that church and they had to build a larger building.

Thank you for caring about Bob. We loved him and are sorry to hear he's not doing well." -- Carlanne Barrett

# Bio 18

# "Holy" Hubert Lindsey
## 1914 - 2003

Hubert T. Lindsey was born in Georgia in the year of 1914. The Lord Jesus Christ called him at the age of fifteen. Hubert was not sophisticated or self-confident and responded in a Moses-esque manner. He explained to God that he would not be able to serve Him very well because his memory was so poor. Indeed, Hubert would reportedly go to the store to purchase an item for his mother and upon arrival at the store, would not be able to recall what the desired item was. The Lord assured Hubert that he would do just fine; He made it so that Hubert was able to memorize the entire New Testament in just six months' time.

Hubert knew that he was to become a preacher but his father was not thrilled with the idea and declared that he did not want a preacher in the house. He threw Hubert out. Hubert worked in the coal mines of Kentucky and the logging camps of Louisiana until he had saved up enough money for an education. He attended the Southern Baptist Seminary in Louisville, Kentucky, where he received a Master's Degree and later taught Greek.

In 1965, Dr. Hubert Lindsey moved to Berkeley. It was Hubert's daily practice to preach on the campus of the University of California. His audience was mostly hippies and hapless students who were minding their own business, on their way to and from classes. One could venture to say that almost every student at Berkeley (and the population numbered over 27,000) knew who Hubert was. It was hard to miss him. He would stand outside the administration building, in Sproul Plaza, near the Student Union, and vociferously and toothlessly (that's right - his teeth had been punched out) proclaim the gospel. He was a fixture at the campus. Hubert had his own inimitable style of spewing phrases like "Bless your dirty little heart" and "You godless, fornicating, hell-bound sinners." This did little to ingratiate him to the passersby but it certainly caught their attention.

The student population duly named him "Holy Hubert." This was a name that would stick for decades. Holy Hubert is still in the memory of most of the people who lived in Berkeley during the '60s and early '70's. The results of informal interviews confirmed this; five out of six of the interviewees remember Hubert.

Having been an eye-witness to Hubert's interactions with the Berkeley citizens and having later been an acquaintance of Hubert, I believe that the reports of his interactions with riotous mobs are over-stated. Most of the time, Hubert interacted with "normal" students, whose main goal was to study and learn, albeit, specifically to not learn anything about God, but, nonetheless there was usually not more than an occasional sneer of protest or a nasty hand signal. Sometimes, heated arguments would arise.

The reports of riotous confrontations are certainly legitimate as well and are given the emphasis that they have been given because of the gravity of the situations and the ensuing injuries to Dr. Lindsey. However, the non-violent encounters were the more common of Hubert's interactions with the student population.

Dr. Lindsey is credited with having established twelve Baptist churches, and having written five books. He is considered by some to have been the father of the Jesus People Movement on the West Coast. He certainly played a part in spear-heading the movement along with many other men and women of God. God sent Holy Hubert to a key location of the movement and sent him at the time that it was all just getting started.

Hubert was somehow both loved and hated. Perhaps he was

hated because he was so outspoken and was incredibly stubborn, but loved because even though his personality came off as less than polished and often offensive, those listening to him could tell that he was a tunnel for the love of God. Reportedly there was an incident in which a Hell's Angel punched Hubert and broke his jaw and told Hubert that he hated him. Hubert responded (broken jaw notwithstanding) with "God loves you."

Hubert suffered much as a warrior in the fight against evil. He was shot at while in the pulpit in Kentucky; he was beaten by Hell's Angels; he was stabbed and he was blinded. Twice he miraculously regained his sight, but blindness returned 18 years after the attack.

Sadly, Holy Hubert died on March 30, 2003, blind and in a wheel chair, but still going to campuses to preach repentance. God Bless your clean heart, Holy Hubert!

- Stephanie Adams

# Bio 19

# Mary K. Mancebo
## 1947 -

**W**hile serving time in the Federal prison in Long Beach for smuggling drugs, a group called Addicts for Jesus spoke and I (Mary K) accepted Jesus at that time. Things really changed in my life. I was serving a six-year sentence but through some unknown circumstance (I know now it was the Lord), my sentence was changed and I was released in three months.

I was born January 22, 1947 in Columbus, Ohio. Moved to California in 1961 when my mother remarried my step-father and he was stationed at Camp Pendleton. I attended Oceanside and Vista High School. I attended some college until the drugs took over.

I met Chuck Mancebo at a Bible Study while living at Zion's Inn in San Rafael, CA. We have been married 43 years and have two children (Chuck also has a daughter who was born during the Vietnam War in Thailand – which is a story in and of itself). I was told early in my life that I could not have children and there are 8 grandchildren in our lives and they are a wonderful blessing.

Our first child was born in Modesto one month after moving from San Rafael for Chuck's job. Another child came three years later after several miscarriages. That is when God told me my quiver was full.

I stayed home with my children until our son graduated from high school. I did work part-time to be able to send the kids to Christian School and only worked when they were at school.

I went to work in the school district office when our daughter was in tenth grade. I was still home with her most of the time because she was involved in cheerleading at high school and practiced a lot. Our daughter married in 1997 and had her first child on month after getting her four-year degree from college. She now has three children (15, 13, 10) and has been a stay-at-home mom until just recently. Our son went to two years of college and then has been working in law enforcement since he turned 21 years old. He was married in 2000 and they have two boys. Chuck's daughter lives in Washington and she has three children.

After leaving Zion's Inn, getting married, and moving to Modesto we have been very involved in church. In 1989 we moved to Chuck's home town of Atwater and now have a small almond orchard. After moving to Atwater some people in our church were missionaries and they had a big impact on our life. Chuck started doing short-term missions trips to help with communications in remote villages in the Peru jungles. He has been doing them every year since about 1991. I have gone on two trips, one with Chuck and one with another group while he went to Africa. He has been to many remote places around the world and has worked with many people groups.

Several people have influenced my life over the years as I have grown as a Christian. In the beginning Kent Philpott at Zion's Inn kept me pointed in the right direction after coming from a life of dealing, selling, and using drugs. I learned to be able to be strong and grew as a new Christian.

I got involved with the Jesus movement when I realized I needed to get my life in order and get off drugs and away from my past lifestyle. I can remember going to a lot of Bible studies while living in Zion's Inn with several other girls who had come off the streets or were runaways. One girl was only 14 years old. I was the oldest girl in the house at the time. It was a great time because I was getting what I never really had growing up in my family and seeing the love that comes from living your life for Jesus.  The people living in the houses went and passed out tracks, witnessed to people in the North Beach part of San Francisco, and carried picket signs stating "Jesus is the Way" and many other Christians sayings of that time.  We also went to parks to witness, and even went to some Christian rock concerts. This was not just a time of fun but a time of learning.  Had I not been involved in the JPM, I do not think I would be here today writing about my life.  I saw many people come and go from the Christian homes in the Bay area where I was involved and a few really grew and went on to be strong Christians.  But it seemed to me that more left the movement than stayed.  Those who stayed were reaching out and bringing others into the movement.  We were earnest in our turning people to Jesus.  There was a singing group that Kent gathered of people from the houses in the area. I was in that group, "Joyful Noise" and we went around talking at schools about drugs and the effect on lives and then telling the students about how we kicked the habit with Jesus.  That sure has changed today.

Being a former drug addict (heroin), the testimonies given at the schools often made a big impression on the students.  I have been able to share with many people after that at schools, churches, and other groups.  I even spoke at my daughter's high school FCA and that had an impact on her as she had never heard my full testimony.  It was a blessing to be able to share with the younger people.  Several parents called after the talk telling how much impact it had on their child's life.

# Pat Matrisciana

## 1939 -

**p**atrick Matrisciana was born on March 17, 1939 in Texas. His father was a meteorologist for Pan American World Airways (Pan Am). The family moved quite a bit. At the end of World War II, Pat and his family moved to the Bay Area. Then, in 1949, they moved to Tokyo, Japan where they lived for 3 and a half years. Then they moved to Washington State. In 1955, Pat attended High School in Bangkok, Thailand. When they returned to Washington, he graduated from Kent Meridian High School. He then went to work at Boeing Aircraft as a mechanic. Pat attended the University of Washington and graduated with a BA.

While Pat was in college, he had a variety of interesting jobs. He was a commercial fisherman in Alaska, a lifeguard in Seattle and he worked at a cannery in Washington. He became a teacher of history at the same High School from which he had graduated.

In graduate school at the University of Washington, Pat's roommate was Fred Dyson, who is now the Republican state senator in Alaska. When they were roommates, Fred was part of the Campus Crusade for Christ and was praying for Pat. Pat became a Christian through the Campus Crusade for Christ.

In 1971, Pat joined the staff of Campus Crusade for Christ and became the state director of the branch for the state of Oklahoma. Pat was the co-founder of Athletes in Action, an offshoot of Campus Crusade for Christ, the purpose of which is to "use sports as a platform to help people answer questions of faith and to point them to Jesus."

Pat worked closely with Bill Bright and Chuck Smith of the Campus Crusade for Christ. He believed it was essential that there be a gospel outreach to the Radical Left at Berkeley. He, along with Fred Dyson and Jack Sparks, worked to reach the Berkeley Marxist revolutionaries and hippies. He was active in evangelism and formed five halfway houses in the Berkeley area. He placed a strong emphasis on Bible Studies and the publication of literature. He formed several organizations, including the Christian Liberation Front, which published the newspaper, Right On.

Pat became a dominating force in the free speech movement at Berkeley with an outreach to thousands of individuals. He worked closely with other groups, including groups with which Kent Philpott was involved. Pat's outreach was unique. Others at Berkeley, such as Holy Hubert and Mario Murillo, had no specific "target audience." Pat filled a gap by putting his focus on those who were Communists, people into eastern mysticism, those involved in Satanism, SDS (Students for Democratic Society), the Chinese Red Guard (etc.).

Roger Heyns was the Chancellor of the University of California at Berkeley from 1965 to 1971. In his retirement speech, he said that for years, the Free Speech movement had been dominated by the Radical Left, but that it was now dominated by people called Christians.

During the years of Richard Nixon's presidency, many felt deceived by the political establishment and felt leaderless. The Hippy anti-war movement exploded. Pat was active in presenting the gospel to this part of the population at Berkeley. He saw that the media was biased against Christians and that it was largely pro-Marxist. He decided that he needed to get involved in the media and worked in the motion picture business as early as 1969. He produced the movie Son Worshippers, which was about the Jesus People Movement. In 1978, he founded Jeremiah Films.

Jeremiah Films produces movies that "promote patriotism, traditional values, and the biblical worldview of [the] founding fathers" of the United States. It has produced films that investigate subjects as varied as terrorism, paganism, evolution, Mormonism, Seventh-day Adventism, abortion, Halloween, Islam, Christianity, Cults, the occult, Jim Jones, Jehovah's Witness, and the Clinton presidency and scandals surrounding Gennifer Flowers and the alleged murder of Vince Foster. [1]

In 1996, Jeremiah Films distributed a film entitled The Clinton Chronicles, which contains a list of people who were linked to the film and who either died mysteriously or who were murdered. [1]

Also, in 1996, Jeremiah Films and an organization called Citizens for an Honest Government, produced a video called Obstruction of Justice: The Mena Connection. It claimed that two police officers with links to former Arkansas governor, Bill Clinton, were implicated in drug trafficking, two murders, and a cover-up of the murders. The police officers sued Matrisciana for defamation and won an award of $598,750. [1]

However, in 1999, the award was overturned after Matrisciana appealed to the United States Court of Appeals for the Eighth Circuit. He won in appeals court, the three-judge panel saying: "Campbell and Lane, being public officials bear the burden of proving statements made by a defendant are false, and they failed to meet that standard." The judge said a public figure plaintiff must also prove malice and they did not. 4 The decision of the Eighth Circuit court was a victory for the first amendment of the Constitution. [2]

Pat views his motion pictures as "weapons for spiritual warfare." One of his guiding principles is:

Ephesians 5:11 - Have nothing to do with the fruitless deeds of darkness, but rather expose them.

Jeremiah films is still in business, being run by Pat's son.

Pat Matrisciana is currently living in Florida and is working in the field of renewable energy.

## References:

1.   Jeremiah Films - Wikipedia, the free encyclopedia
2.   1st Amendment winsvictory in court

# Scott McCarrel
## 1951 -

### Prologue:

**M**ike made his home in Hawaii - in an avocado tree. To him, it was paradise. He grew his own drugs, ate fresh fruit and dove in the Pacific to spear fish. But, one dark night, Mike's paradise came to an abrupt end. The previous day, a sorcerer had given him a candle and had told him that he should meditate on it. Mike rubbed sticks together, lit the candle, and was doing his best to meditate. He started hallucinating and having terrible visions of creatures and monsters.

That was it. The next day, he packed up his few possessions and started hitchhiking to the airport. A large Hawaiian guy picked him up. After a few miles, the large guy started talking about not liking "long-hairs" and started talking about cutting people up with knives. Mike noticed that there was a machete on the dashboard of the Hawaiian's truck. In panic, he realized that this guy could do him in and no one would even be the wiser. In sheer desperation, having no other idea as to how he could save himself, Mike reached into his backpack and pulled out a New Testament, which had been given to him prior to his arrival in Hawaii.

He opened it to Matthew 24, which is one of the passages concerning the coming of the end of the world, and started reading out loud. Amazingly, this same guy, who Mike thought only minutes before, was going to do him in, pulled over to the side of the road and started crying. He then took him to the airport and gave Mike money for the flight home.

Mike went straight to Chico; California, to the Ivy House, a Christian Commune. He knew something powerful had happened when he had read that passage from Matthew and he wanted to find someone who could help him understand it.

## Scott:

Scott McCarrel was born on September 12, 1951 in Oakland, California. He grew up in Lafayette and attended Chico State University. While at Chico State, Scott would go to parties where he would frequently see an old friend from high school. His name was Mike. Mike would attend the parties and share the gospel.

After four or five times of listening to Mike, Scott decided that he needed to figure out for himself whether Christianity was real or not. Mike, and Mike's friend, Rich, were planning to go to a Christian farm in Oregon. Scott decided he would go along with them on an "exploratory journey." He withdrew from his classes and said good-bye to his friends and his girlfriend. Mike, Scott and Rich left for Oregon in an old green Dodge Colt.

The trip was truly incredible; God was active in an undeniable manner each day of the "exploratory journey."

On the first day of the trip, Mike and Rich said they needed to stop off at Mount Shasta to visit with a cult group who lived at the top of the mountain. They wanted to share the gospel with them. They stopped at the bottom of the mountain to get directions on how to find these mountain people. When they got to the top, Mike and Rich were in the front seat, and Scott was in the back. Mike turned and said, "This is probably going to be a little intense." Scott said to himself, "What am I doing here?!"

It was the end of October and it was freezing cold. The three of them got out of the car and started looking around for people. There was no one in sight, and there were not even any cars going up or down the mountain. Mike kept saying, "God – I know you have us here for a purpose." After a half hour, Scott said to God something to the effect of, "Right, God – You want us up here in the middle of nowhere freezing to death."

After another half hour or so, they walked back to the car and one of them looked down through the trees and saw smoke some distance away. They started walking down to see who it was. They came to a clearing with trees all around it. In the middle of the clearing were two girls, kneeling at a campfire with Bibles open to Matthew 24. They had just prayed, "God – if You are real, send someone here to explain this to us because we don't know what it means." Enter the three amigos. The girls looked at them and broke down crying.

Now, a question – who, other than Mike, could have been a more appropriate candidate for God to have sent to this particular scene for the purpose of explaining Matthew 24 ? Mike knelt down and shared not only Matthew 24, but the whole gospel.

On the second day of their journey, the three stopped at a church in Salem, Oregon. Scott says he didn't know what an altar call was, but the pastor gave one and Scott went to the altar. He doesn't remember what the pastor was saying, but Scott broke down in tears. When it was over, he says he was completely different.

The next day, they arrived at their ultimate destination, the Freckle Face Christian Farm in Myrtle Creek, Oregon. Scott stayed there for two months.

When he got back to Lafayette, one of the first things he did was to go to his girlfriend's house. He knocked on the door, and when she opened it, he said, "It's over between us. I'm a Christian and everything is different." She replied that she as well had become a Christian during Scott's absence. So, as Scott says, "We started all over again."

He and Andi Ann have been married for 42 years and have four children. They currently live in Lafayette. When asked what he particularly recalls about the Jesus People Movement, his answer is that "it would have to be the extreme caring that we had for one another."

Scott has been busy trying to re-connect with individuals who were involved in the Jesus People Movement. He would enjoy hearing about your experiences, especially those that could be classified as "lessons learned." Please feel free to visit Scott's website -JesusPeopleLessonsLearned.org.

# Bob Mumford
## 1930 -

**B**ob Mumford was born in 1930. He came to the Lord at the young age of 12, but soon thereafter strayed from Him. When Bob was 13, his parents divorced and Bob had to quit school and work to help support his mother and five sisters. [4]

At 20 years old, he joined the U.S. Navy as a Medic. He would go with his Navy buddies to the bar and end up preaching to those in the bar the necessity to repent of their sins and come to Christ. Even then Father God was pursuing him! [4]

In 1954, while on leave from the Navy, Bob attended a church service one evening. He was overcome by the conviction of the Holy Spirit and literally ran to the altar. After Bob had been away from God for 12 years, the Lord cleaned up his heart and gave him new purpose and direction, calling him specifically to "Feed My people." [4]

After completing his High School education in the Navy and then graduating with a Bachelor of Science from Valley Forge Christian College, Bob attended the University of Delaware and then received his Masters of Divinity degree from Reformed Episcopal Seminary in Philadelphia. [4]

Over the years, Bob Mumford has served as a pastor, as Dean and Professor of New Testament and Missions at Elim Bible Institute. In 1972, he founded Lifechangers, Inc. to distribute his teaching materials all over the world where he has traveled extensively to some 50 nations as an international conference speaker. His materials have been translated into more than 20 different languages. [4]

Bob has written for major Christian periodicals in the United States and abroad. He has published twelve books including: Take Another Look at Guidance, The Purpose of Temptation, Dr. Frankenstein & World Systems, and The Agape Road. His writings have been translated into 25 different languages and distributed around the world. [2]

Mumford was one of the "Fort Lauderdale Five," which was the group that founded the "Shepherding Movement" in the 1970s. It was an influential and controversial movement within some British and American charismatic churches. The doctrine of the movement emphasized the "one another" passages of the New Testament, and the mentoring relationship described in 2 Timothy. [3]

In an open letter from Pat Robertson to Bob Mumford, dated June 27; 1975, Robertson said that he found cultish language like" submission" rather than churches, "shepherds" not pastors, and "relationships" but not Jesus. Pat Robertson banned the CGM leaders and erased all tapes that included them. Robertson used CBN to pronounce the shepherding teaching 'witchcraft' and said the only difference between the discipleship group and Jonestown was 'Kool-Aid.' Kathryn Kuhlman refused to appear together with Bob Mumford at the 1975 Conference on the Holy Spirit in Jerusalem. [3]

In response, Mumford made a public statement in which he admitted that he had not heeded earlier warnings about doctrinal error. "While it was not my intent to be willful," he said, "I ignored their input to my own hurt and the injury of others." ...He admitted that there had been an "unhealthy submission resulting in perverse and unbiblical obedience to human leaders." He took personal responsibility for these abuses, saying that many of them happened under his sphere of leadership."[3]

Bob continues to be a Bible teacher with the unique and powerful gift of imparting the Word of God with authority, clarity, personal application and humor. Today he is considered a spiritual "Papa" to thousands of Christians worldwide who have attributed their spiritual growth and determination in serving the Lord to Bob's ability to help them understand the ways of God and His Kingdom. [2]

His ministry has been to prophetically proclaim and teach the sufficiency of Christ Jesus and His Kingdom in a manner that promotes reconciliation and unity in the body of Christ. Bob seeks to bring about personal spiritual change and growth in the lives of believers, regardless of denominational persuasion. [4]

Bob and his wife, Judith, currently reside in Ft. Lauderdale, Florida. Bob, who is now 78, is the director (along with his son, Eric), of a ministry called Lifechangers.

If you would like to receive information on Bob Mumford's ministry, Lifechangers, you can contact him at:

Lifechangers
P.O. Box 3709
Cookeville, TN 38502
U.S.A.
lc@lifechangers.org
www.lifechangers.org
931.520.3730 / 800.521.5676   [2]

**References:**

1.  http://jonrising.blogspot.com/2008/12/bob-mum-ford-at-78.html
2.  http://www.lifechangers.org/about_lifechangers.php?bio=1
3.  http://en.wikipedia.org/wiki/Shepherding_Movement
4.  http://www.amazon.com/Bob-Mumford/e/B001JSBFMO

# Derek Prince
## 1915 - 2003

Peter Derek Vaughan Prince was born in Bangalore; India, of British parents on August 14, 1915. He was an international Bible teacher whose daily radio program, Derek Prince Legacy Radio, was broadcast to half the population of the world in various languages. These languages included English, Arabic, Spanish, Croatian, Russian, Malagasy, Tongan, Samoan and four dialects of Chinese. He is probably most noted for his teachings about deliverance from demonic oppression. [1]

Derek's teachings are considered to have been distinctly non-denominational. Derek Prince Ministries operated under the slogan "Reaching the unreached and teaching the untaught." Derek Prince Ministries continues today and its mission statement is, "Derek Prince Ministries exists to develop disciples of Jesus Christ, through the Bible teaching of Derek Prince." The vision is to reach the peoples of the world in a language they understand, with the Bible teaching of Derek Prince, using every type of media and all forms of distribution, regardless of the economic means of the recipients. [1]

In describing what his life was like, Derek said, "I was born into a family of 'empire builders'. My father, Paul Ernest Prince, was an officer in the Queen's own Madras Sappers and Miners, his commission signed by Victoria's own hand. My mother, Gwendolen, also born in India, was the daughter of Major General Robert Edward Vaughan. Her brother, a Punjab Lancer, later became a brigadier." [1]

When Derek was five, he said goodbye to his father, his nanny, and his Indian playmates and he boarded a ship to England to live with his grandparents. Those early years shaped Derek's character and the course of his life. Even though he was the only son and the only grandson, he was expected to behave like a good soldier. His grandparents were kind to him, at the same time training him to excel in whatever he did and to be prepared to carry on the family military tradition. [1]

As a young child, he learned to entertain himself. He says, "I always had friends, but I enjoyed my own company most." When he discovered the world of books, he began his search to find out what life was about. [1]

At the age of nine, Derek was sent off to boarding school, leaving his grandparents whom he loved dearly. From that time on, all his teachers and associates were masculine. In the school system of that time both class work and sports were highly competitive. He participated enthusiastically and successfully in sports, and academically, he was usually at the top of his class. His early training in diligence and thoroughness enabled him to maintain that position. [1]

When he was thirteen, his headmaster entered his name in a competitive exam for a place at Eton College, and he was one of the fourteen boys of his age to be enrolled as king's scholars in the election of 1929. Like other boys his age, he had begun to study Latin at the age of nine and Greek at ten and was writing and translating verse in both languages by the time he was twelve. As he studied the classics, he became more enthralled with the realm of ideas and was drawn toward philosophy with a specialization in logic. At the back of his mind was always the tantalizing question: What is the real meaning and purpose of life? [1]

Derek's academic career was interrupted abruptly by World War II. On the basis of his philosophical convictions (not wanting to bear arms) he chose to enter the forces as a non-combatant and began as a private in the Royal Army Medical Corps. [1]

While in the army barracks, Derek, (a self-proclaimed agnostic) started reading the Bible simply as a philosophical exercise. One day in July 1941, Derek had what he described as a supernatural experience, a meeting with Jesus. "Out of this encounter" he later wrote, " I formed two conclusions: first, that Jesus Christ is alive; second, that the Bible is a true, relevant, up-to-date book. These conclusions altered the whole course of my life. I had found what I was searching for! The meaning and purpose of life is a Person!" [1]

In 1946, while serving in Palestine, Prince met Lydia Christensen, a Danish woman who ran an orphanage in Ramallah. Lydia had adopted eight girls (six of whom were Jewish). Despite the fact that Lydia was 25 years Prince's senior, they married. Prince strongly supported the establishment of the State of Israel, which he saw as the fulfilling of Biblical prophecy. In 1962, the Princes moved to Canada, and from there, to a pastorate at Peoples Church in Minneapolis, becoming US citizens. From here they moved to Broadway Tabernacle in Seattle. During this time, Prince was becoming widely known through his cassette-tape Bible lectures, and he became involved with the Full Gospel Business Men's Fellowship International. [1]

Lydia Prince died on October 5th, 1975. Derek later married Ruth Baker on October 17th, 1978. In 1981, they moved from Florida to Jerusalem where they lived six months out of the year. Derek and Ruth traveled extensively in ministry up until the time of Ruth's death on December 29th, 1998. Derek's radio program, which had begun in 1979, has been translated into more than a dozen languages and continues to touch lives. His gift of explaining the Bible and its teachings in a clear and simple way has helped build a foundation of faith in millions of lives. Derek's nondenominational, nonsectarian approach has made his teaching equally relevant and helpful to people from all racial and religious backgrounds, and his teaching is estimated to have reached more than half the globe. [1]

In 2002, Derek said, "It is my desire—and I believe the Lord's desire—that this ministry continue the work, which God began through me over 60 years ago, until Jesus returns." Derek's ministry continues today. [1]

Prince has authored over 50 books. He pioneered teaching on such groundbreaking themes as generational curses, the biblical significance of Israel and demonology. Derek Prince passed away in his sleep on September 24th, 2003, at his home in Jerusalem of heart failure following a prolonged period of declining health. [2]

### References:

1.  http://en.wikipedia.org/wiki/Derek_Prince
2.  http://www.derekprince.org/Articles/1000088212/DPM_US/About_Us/The_Passing_of.aspx

# Bio 24

# Mike Riley
## 1947 -

Mike Riley was born in August, 1947 in Gridley, California. Gridley is a city in Butte County, in the Sacramento Valley area. He grew up in Gridley and attended Gridley High School in 1965, and Chico State in 1969, where he received a BA in social sciences. In 1976, he attended the Golden Gate Baptist Theological Seminary, earning his MDiv (Master of Divinity).

When he was 13 years old, he attended a Christian Camp in Santa Cruz, California at the Missions Springs Conference Center. On a Friday night, he answered an altar call and gave his life to Jesus.

Jesus called Mike to move to the Bay Area. Mike viewed himself as a "valley kid who didn't even like the Bay Area." He felt like a country boy who moved to the big city.

In the early '70s, Mike met Kent Philpott and Bob Hymers at the Golden Gate Seminary. The three of them, along with a college buddy of Mike's, Roger Hoffman, started working together doing in-house ministries. On Friday nights, they would go into San Francisco and evangelize on Broadway. They ran Bible studies throughout Marin County on high school campuses.

In August of 1972, he opened the Church of the Open Door in Mill Valley, California. In 1974, the church moved to San Rafael. Mike is married to his wife of 40 years, Mona, and they have three adult children. He is currently the pastor of the Church of the Open Door in San Rafael, California.

# Moishe Rosen
## 1932 - 2010

**M**oishe Rosen, the founding executive director of Jews for Jesus, is considered to have been the most flamboyant and controversial Jewish minister of Christianity since the Apostle Paul.[7] According to evangelical leader, Vernon Grounds, "When Moishe Rosen came into a city there was either a revival or a riot." [5]

Mr. Rosen launched Jews for Jesus in 1973 and turned it into the largest messianic Jewish organization in the world, with branches throughout the United States and in ten foreign countries. [6] The success of Jews for Jesus stirred the wrath of Jewish leaders, who denounced Rosen as a cultist and fought back through groups such as Jews for Judaism. [5]

Martin Meyer Rosen (aka Moishe Rosen) was born in Kansas City, Missouri on April 12, 1932. His boyhood nickname was Moishe (pronounced moy-sheh), Yiddish for "Moses," meaning "drawn from the water." When he was an adult, Martin officially changed his name to Moishe. [6]

Moishe grew up in an orthodox Jewish family in Denver, Colorado. He is quoted as having said about his home town, "I grew up in a neighborhood where most of the people were Jewish. If you walked into the grocery store, or the shoemaker, or the barber, you expected to hear Yiddish." [7]

Moishe's parents, Ben Rosen and Rose Baker Rosen were Jewish immigrants from Eastern Europe. Although his father regularly attended an Orthodox synagogue, Rosen described his father as irreligious and claimed that his father viewed religion as a "racket". [4]

While going door to door selling numbers for house addresses, Moishe met Ceil Starr, whose parents were even more orthodox in their Judaism. Moishe and Ceil attended the same high school and they were married in the summer after their graduation. Shortly after their marriage, Hannah Wago of the American Board of Missions to the Jews led Ceil to the Lord. In an attempt to refute his wife's Christian ideas, Moishe studied the scriptures and pamphlets that Ceil left conspicuously around the couple's home, but when he couldn't disprove Ceil's beliefs, she became instrumental in leading him to the Lord.

As recounted by Susan Perlman, a longtime assistant, Moishe gathered his family together to tell them the news: "I've been studying the Bible lately and I've decided that Jesus is really the Messiah. We've all been wrong and I wanted you to know that I'm going to believe in Him and follow Him and give my life to Him."

The response that came from his father after hearing that announcement was jarring: "You can just get out of my house and don't come back until you've given up this Jesus business!'"

The rejection by his family "didn't deter him from following his destiny," Perlman wrote. "If anything, it brought him closer to his Messiah, who was 'despised and rejected' by so many. Moishe immersed himself in the Scriptures and never wavered from being a forthright teller of the truth of the gospel. He actually came to discover that he loved to tell others about Y'shua."[1]

"It wasn't because I thought Christianity was nicer than Judaism," he told the Los Angeles Times in 1985. "Nor was it because I wanted to renounce my birthright, as many have said. Basically, I accepted Jesus because, after searching the Scriptures, I found Him to be true." [2]

Estranged from his parents at age 21, Mr. Rosen moved to the East Coast to study theology at New Jersey's Northeastern Bible Institute. He was ordained a Baptist minister in 1957. He

led Hebrew Christian congregations and worked for 17 years
for the American Board of Missions to the Jews with the aim of
spreading the gospel. [2]

In the summer of 1970, Mr. Rosen moved to San Francisco,
the time and place in which the

"Jesus People" Movement was picking up a full head of
steam. Apparently Mr. Rosen was particularly impressed by
the anti-Vietnam War activists, whose communication skills he
adopted. He was a street-preacher in the Haight-Ashbury district of San Francisco where he drew thousands of Jewish people
from among the youthful seekers of the counterculture era. [5]
An important part of his message was that one could believe in
Jesus without giving up Jewish culture. [6]

Mr. Rosen was quick to poke fun at himself and the incon-
gruity of his ministry. Rosen often quipped: "I'm overweight,
overbearing, and over 40. What am I doing leading a youth
movement?" [7]

Mr. Rosen's organization has long engendered turbulent,
often vitriolic, debate; and has often had to go to court to secure
permission to hand out its literature. The group has been repeatedly condemned by leaders of mainstream Jewish organizations.
[6]

Quoting from the "Jews for Jesus" website: [3]

> Our name tells who we are, who we stand for and what
> we do. Everything is right up front! While we might have
> chosen a less controversial name, Jews for Jesus is the
> one that most quickly, easily and accurately lets people
> know who we are and what we are about.

In direct contradiction to the above quote are the assertions
made by Rabbi James Rudin, the senior interreligious affairs
adviser of the American Jewish Committee, an international
Jewish advocacy group, who said of Mr. Rosen's organization: [6]

We have truth in advertising and truth in labeling in the
United States. And the people should know that they [Jews for

Jesus] really are Christian missionaries. I would have had much more respect for him, and for his organization, if they had just come out and said, 'We are Christian missionaries, trying to convert Jews.

To his critics, Mr. Rosen responded with the kind of wit for which he was known. As he said in an interview with The Fresno Bee in 1994, "If the Jews didn't need Jesus, why didn't He come by way of Norway or Ireland?" [6]

To further quote the "Jews for Jesus" website: [3]

Sometimes people ask us, "How long has Jews for Jesus been around?" We love that question because it gives us the chance to grin and say: "Since 32 A.D., give or take a year." The joke reminds people that a minority of Jewish people have always believed and proclaimed the gospel, and that we follow in that same tradition.

Actually, "Jews for Jesus" began as a slogan. In the late 1960s a moving of the Holy Spirit brought thousands of cause-oriented young people to faith in Jesus, many of whom were Jewish. As for our organization, Moishe Rosen officially founded Jews for Jesus in September of 1973. Rosen, a veteran missionary to the Jewish people, was the executive director of the mission for 23 years. He revolutionized evangelistic methods and materials with his creative approach to communicating the gospel, and we believe he was the foremost strategist and tactician in the field of Jewish evangelism.

Mr. Rosen's books include *Jews for Jesus* (Revell, 1974; with William Proctor); *The Sayings of Chairman Moishe* (Creation Press, 1974); and *Share the New Life With a Jew* (Moody Press, 1976), written with his wife. Moody Press published the couple's first book, *Christ in the Passover*, (originally in 1978; the latest publication year is 2006).

Throughout his life, Mr. Rosen continued to observe many Jewish customs. Associate Executive Director of Jews for Jesus, Ms. Perlman, said that Mr. Rosen held seders at Passover, fasted on Yom Kippur and officiated in the marriage of Jewish couples under a huppah, the Jewish wedding canopy. She also said Mr. Rosen had left instructions that he wished to be buried in his tallis, the traditional Jewish prayer shawl.

Mr. Rosen succumbed to cancer at the age of 78. He died at his home in San Francisco. [6]

"You can take from me everything but my Jewishness and my belief in God," he once said. "You can say I'm a nuisance, a Christian, out of step with the Jewish community, but you can't say I'm not a Jew." [2]

### References:

1. Art Toalston (May 20, 2010) "Jews for Jesus founder dies," *Baptist Press.* Retrieved 11/25/12.
2. Emma Brown (May 21, 2010). "Moishe Rosen, 78; founded evangelistic group Jews for Jesus". *The Washington Post.* Retrieved November 30, 2012.
3. "A Brief History of Jews for Jesus - History and Timeline" - Jews for Jesus  Retrieved Nov. 26, 2012.
4. Moishe Rosen - Wikipedia, the free encyclopedia. Retrieved November 30, 2012.
5. Elaine Woo (May 23, 2010). "http://articles. latimes.com/2010/may/23/local/la-me-moishe-rosen-20100523". *The Los Angeles Times.* Retrieved November 29, 2012.
6. Margalit Fox (May 22, 2010).  Moishe Rosen, 78, Dies - Founder of Jews for Jesus - Obituary (Obit) - NYTimes.com *The New York Times.* Retrieved November 28, 2012.
7. Ruth Tucker (May 21, 2010) "Remembering Moishe Rosen" | *Christianity Today.* Retrieved November 29, 2012.

# Bio 26

# Rick Sacks
## 1948 -

I was walking down Haight Street in San Francisco on a Friday night. There was a very small vacant storefront occupied just for the evening by some very straight guys wearing neckties and inviting people in for free coffee and donuts to hear about Jesus. I was barefoot and did herbal teas and brown rice, so the food had zero allure, but hearing about Jesus did. I invited the spirit of Jesus to dwell in me and I asked forgiveness of all my sins against God and fellow humans and stood up a different person. As I walked the streets during the next several days, telling people about what I had experienced, I found another who thought he was also the first in two thousand years to have this mystery revealed. Then there were two more. And a few more. In short order I was part of a tribe that God had chosen to know Him and we read the Bible and asked Him to explain it to us and to show us what to do and whom to talk to. We learned to talk to God as a friend and listen as He spoke back to us. The days were filled with what seemed miraculous events and all our needs were provided for.

I was born in Boston, Massachusetts in January 1948.

I went to high school until I completed the tenth grade and then spent some time in the army and did some college years later.

My family being Jewish, rejected the message and sent me off wanting nothing to do with this new level of my disgracing them. My grandfather's wife opened the door handing us our coats and told us to leave and never return. That was the last time I saw my grandfather. Years later, I was able to speak with my dad, but the subject of Jesus remained closed...that was not an option if I wanted to have any relationship at all. My mom came to know Jesus in her late seventies. My sister did in her forties and is a believer.

I have been painting and carving signs since 1970 on a full time basis. I served an apprenticeship for many years and worked in sign shops until striking out on my own in 1977. I consider it an absolutely tremendous gift to be able to discover the passion I have for letters and graphics and making things with my hands and working with tools and pleasing others with my abilities and financially supporting my household.

Megan and I have been married going on forty-six years. We work together daily. Our kids understand the model of being business owners and servants and doing our passions. We can speak about God's love to customers and friends on the phone or in our shop freely. We enjoy our home and community and when we travel we can't wait to get home. We enjoy our kids and their kids. We still have a friend group with a core of those we lived with back in the Haight St. days. God truly knit us together. We've tried to integrate into the established churches over the years, and have been with several for over a decade. Only one delivered the depth of caring and unity and families sharing lives like we knew living communally with our original group. We have a core group of close friends and extend love and outreach to others. We've seen doctrines sweep through the network of followers with the zeal of a new clothing fashion. I still wear blue jeans and tee shirts, both on my body and in my doctrine.

This was the truck we lived in for several years. [See photo on page 193.] We roamed around finding work and ministry and relying upon the hospitality of friends for shower privileges. This was in Sausalito in '69, after I cut off my hair.

My memories of God choosing a people are numerous and dear. I've seen most leaders choosing to be controllers, and that is very different from how I see and experience Jesus. I've seen God take some very messed up people and use them to accomplish mighty works, yet they continued to not be models of perfection. I've seen compromise and dilution in my zeal over the years when Jesus hasn't returned in the time frame I expected. I've had people thank me for deliverance in their life many years prior, and I wasn't walking in that way any longer, and had my faith refreshed by their testimony.

# Ken and Mary Sanders
## 1950 - and 1953 -

**M**y (Ken's) parents were an interracial couple, marrying shortly after both graduated from Hartford Theological Seminary. These two family of origin dynamics (race and "religion") would play key roles in my eventual conversion. First, being raised during the Civil Rights Movement, I felt the weight of prejudice, racism and segregation. It always made me feel "less than," and much of my childhood and adolescence was spent compensating for feeling inferior. Second, the religious milieu in which I was raised almost inoculated me against the true gospel. My religious experience was not one that was deeply informed by a knowledge of the staggering grace of God--manifested by Jesus' death on the cross for my waywardness. It allowed me to think that I knew what being a Christian was all about, though I really had no idea.

My first attempts at college were a struggle, not the least because of my involvement with the drugs and alcohol. I was expelled from one college during orientation, for drug related issues, and dropped out of another resulting in all F's. Soon after, I left the Midwest and came out to California in 1969 to be closer to the origins of the Counter Culture scene. After a number of disastrous drug related incidents, including an arrest, I headed up towards Canada while out on bail in order to avoid prosecution. On my way up Highway 101, I ran across a Christian on a freeway ramp in San Rafael. I was invited to stay at a Christian commune, and for the first time, I not only heard the gospel clearly, but saw it being lived out in the lives of the community. Shorty thereafter, I confessed my self centered rebellion against God, asked Jesus to forgive me, and accepted his substitutionary sacrifice for my sin on the cross (sin being my wrong doing in God's eyes). The justice required (separation from God because of my sin)  was paid for by the very one who imposed the sentence--God himself, in the person of Jesus Christ (the Messiah). WOW, that was good news.

I (Mary) grew up in a highly explosive family, primarily in terms of my father's anger and my family's reaction to it. As a child my nerves were shattered. I couldn't eat after dark, because that's when my parents' arguing began. It caused me such anxiety that I would not be able to keep food down and my whole body would shake from the unbearable stress. I had a brother who was nine years older and he also got in horrendous fights with my Dad. In between the two of us was a sister, but she was a family secret due to her severe birth defects, so she grew up in a state hospital and no one was to know about her.

This background set the stage for a tumultuous time as a teenager. I was so sick and tired of the tension in my home, and this led to the beginnings of my experimentation with drugs, in order to relieve the pressure. During one LSD experience I thought I was turning into a tree and becoming part of nature. Thank God that the simple desire for tea and toast seemed to snap me out of it. Eventually I got in a little trouble with the police and  remember yelling at them and calling them pigs, as was fashionable by some in those days.

These experiences did get me thinking about life more seriously. I was flipping through the radio one day and I heard a lady quote Jesus saying: "I am the way the truth and the life no one comes to the father but through me." I started thinking about what real truth was but felt she was wrong about there being only one way to God. I thought there were many ways to God and she made me mad. I began going to Buddhist meetings and was told I could get what I wanted by chanting, what teenager wouldn't do that! I did chant, and chanted that my parents would die. Fortunately they didn't. Besides chanting I decided to pray, which created a much more peaceful feeling. One night in Berkeley, CA, before our Buddhist gathering, we began asking people on Telegraph Avenue to join us for the meeting. I invited many, but one person was different than all the rest. Unbeknownst to me I had asked Holy Herbert to come. He was a confrontative street preacher who happened to be walking with his friend Dave Palma. He let me have it full strength, telling me I was a sinner, separated from God, and in need of Jesus who had died for my sins and rose from the dead. He had no idea this message broke into my heart, but Dave Palma saw how it affected me, and prayed with me as I asked Jesus to be my Lord and Savior. This experience was like no other; I felt such a deep sense of the love of God and an amazing feeling of forgiveness, as if I had been carrying a heavy load and the burden had been completely and finally lifted. I was forever changed by the realization that there was a God who actually loved me.

We both look back on our decisions to follow Jesus and realize that God had been drawing us close to Him in many ways that we ignored, or were even unaware of. Though our justification was an act, a punctiliar event in time, we now see our conversion as a process initiated by Him from the moment we were born. The arc of God's love brought us to the Jesus People Movement where the work He had been doing in us, would be chiseled into a more final and defining form.

We both ended up going to a Bible study in San Rafael, CA and became part of an associated ministry that quickly evolved into a series of Christian House Communities, high school bible studies, street ministries and small businesses. We became friends, fell in love and were married in 1971. We had three children between 1975 and 1980. Ken worked as a house leader, overseer of the various ministries, and later as an ordained pastor in an association of churches that grew out of the Christian

Houses. Mary was a stay at home Mom, and a vital and active part in all aspects of the various ministries and, eventually, the church.

As time went on, Ken realized that he wanted more training if he was going to continue with pastoral responsibility, and with the time commitment that finishing college and seminary would take, we both began to consider other options that would require a similar time investment. God seemed to be pointing Ken toward medical school, and Mary toward nursing school, so we both started our studies. Ken was subsequently accepted into the UCSF, School of Medicine, and Mary into the College of Marin's Registered Nursing program. We both graduated in 1987 and moved to Los Angles where Ken finished a residency in Emergency Medicine, and Mary worked in Labor and Delivery. We returned to the San Francisco Bay area in 1990. Mary's love of art led her to the University of Iowa where she earned an MA and an MFA in Painting. Ken worked for 20 years in the Emergency Department at the Kaiser Hospital in Vallejo, CA and retired in 2010. Shortly before retirement, we discovered Grace Church of Marin, a wonderful congregation of people, not prideful or pretending to be perfect, yet a deeply committed group, striving to live out the true implications of the gospel and resurrection of Jesus.

In early 2011 we spent about 6 months with Mercy Ships in South Africa and Sierra Leone, as part of a medical team helping West Africans who were candidates for the type of surgeries the ship offered. That fall we moved to Vancouver, B.C. for a year of studying theology at Regent College.

We look back on our time in the Jesus People Movement as laying a solid foundation in terms of knowing the enormity of Christ's sacrifice on the cross, and in terms of designing a life dedicated to His kingdom. A life based on gratitude for His immeasurable gift (not driven by guilt or obligation-though we are obliged). Many of our closest friends are still those we met forty-four years ago during The Jesus People Movement. Our life has had many struggles and difficulties since, because we are broken people living in a broken world. But the grace of God is surely the glue that holds us together, and provides us with the means to discover a wonderful and meaningful life.

# Cliff Silliman

## 1949 -

My parents divorced while my mom was pregnant with me, and I never met my father, who died when I was sixteen. I grew up in my grandparents' home until the summer of '64, when my mom and I were thrown out, or left, depending on whose story you believe. One older brother is a famous poet, and there are three younger half siblings, one of whom I met for the first time in 2009.

Even though I ran away at age seventeen with a younger girl, we came back after three weeks so I could graduate from Albany High School in 1967. I went to school, so it seemed, so I could then to work at McDonalds and live in a one bedroom cottage in Richmond. We broke up in March of 1968.

Two guys I met while working at McDonalds, Jim and Ernie Ayala, celebrated my breakup by turning me on to meth for the first time. By the end of the summer of '68, I was selling drugs for a living on the streets of Berkeley, starting mostly with LSD, although I had a prescription 'uppers' connection who supplied me with large quantities that I sold exclusively to Hells Angels. I met Linda Fritz when she was brought into my home after my partner found her in a dumpster where she landed after she jump/fell off the roof of a building on Telegraph Avenue.

I was drafted in May of '69 and burned my notice, since I could not be bothered. (Later, after being arrested for selling drugs, I reported to the Selective Service, and they decided I was undesirable for military service.) I was making a ton of money selling LSD and had graduated to selling large quantities, minimum 1,000 tablets at a time, with people established in other cities across the U.S. My personal use had gone through roof - LSD daily along with a growing cocaine habit. In December of 1970, while traveling to Oregon, I stopped at Berachah House and got reacquainted with the Ayala brothers a few days before their double wedding to two women, Linda Fritz and Cathy, whom I knew for a number of years. On the day before the wedding, while helping them move from Christian houses into homes they would be going to, I prayed for the first time in my life, "Jesus, if you are real, be real to me." In about fifteen seconds I was flooded with the peace that passes understanding and knew that this was Jesus showing himself to me, so I prayed, "I am yours, forgive me for all the stuff I have done and people I have hurt." This was on December 11, 1970.

Ten days later, I moved into Berachah House. In August of '71, I became the elder over Berachah House after Ken Sanders moved out to get ready for his upcoming wedding in September.

We had a one-ton Ford pickup and would go out to the highway around 5 p.m. and then again at 6 p.m., pick up hitchhikers and bring them home for dinner, promising them that we would bring them back in the morning to be on their way. On 3x5 cards I kept track of those who prayed to receive Christ and stayed at least two days. From August of '71 until we moved into Thyatira, 500 people prayed to receive Christ with us. A number stayed to become an active part of our ministry, like Richard Dewey, who became one of our crew foremen. We had painting crews, landscaping crews, and construction crews as a means of support for the ministry. We also raised pigs and sold the meat that we ourselves did not use.

Berachah House was on a six acre farm, and besides the pigs, we had a large garden, chickens, rabbits, and goats to provide for the steady number of people that we had coming through. The main house was a two bedroom home with a loft upstairs. It got so crowded that we started living in whatever outbuildings we could, besides the barn and chicken coop for animals. In the summer of '72, we had so many people at one time, that, considering the nice weather in Petaluma, many who stayed with us temporarily slept in the fields. We averaged over thirty-five people most nights with a core group of maybe a dozen.

Our Saturday nights Bible study grew so much that we moved it out of the house and into town to fit the crowds.

I was traveling with Dr. Hymers most weekends, giving my testimony before he preached in Assembly of God Churches all over northern California. I took and finished a correspondence course from Moody Bible Institute. If not traveling with Dr. Hymers most Sundays, you could find me in a local church sharing my testimony somewhere in Sonoma County. During the week I would be giving my testimony in local middle and high schools. The drug problem during that time was so bad, the schools would let us in; they sought any help they could get to stem the flood. The original contact would be through some Christian teacher or administrator. I spoke in history classes, science classes, and at assemblies giving my testimony and answering any questions open and honestly that students had about drugs.

Along with Kent, I was involved in starting the Christian General Store in San Rafael and later the one in Petaluma. We started with a donation from one of the guys who came to Christ after we picked him up on the freeway.

(Kent: I will stop this part here, but it brings up so many thoughts. From my involvement in the start of the Catholic Charismatic movement in Sonoma County in '72, deliverance ministry, street ministry in Cotati and at Sonoma State, and the start of multiple Bible Studies and houses.)

From 1975 to 1985, I was involved in pastoring in Church of the Open Door. Since then I have ministered and been involved in house churches or Four Square churches. My involvement with the Four Square movement is normally in a teaching or pastoring capacity. I am attending a Four Square Church presently.

I can be contacted through cliffsilliman@gmail.com and live in Sequim, WA.

Some regrets from those days include that I was discouraged from going to college, since Jesus was coming back soon. But that peace that passes understanding that came upon me when I prayed in December of '70 has not left, and my faith in Christ is still strong.

# Charles Simpson
## 1937 -

C harles Simpson is a renowned author, Bible teacher, motivational speaker, and pastor. Some of the books he has written are Courageous Living, The Challenge to Care, Ants, Vines and Churches, and Straight Answers to 21 Honest Questions about Prayer. He is know for his humor and his story-telling ability. [1]

Charles Simpson was born in New Orleans in 1937; his father was a Baptist pastor. They lived in the bayous of Louisiana, and then later moved to southern Alabama. [1]

Charles responded to God's call into ministry in 1955 at the age of eighteen, and two years later, he became the Pastor of a small Baptist church in Mobile, Alabama. He completed his Bachelor's Degree at William Carey College, Hattiesburg, Mississippi, in 1959, and attended New Orleans Baptist Theological Seminary. [1]

In 1964, he experienced a profound personal spiritual renewal and began traveling and teaching in churches worldwide. He became widely recognized as pioneer in the modern Charismatic Renewal Movement. In 1969, he became part of the inaugural issue of New Wine Magazine, an international publication dedicated to Christian Growth,. During the next seventeen years, Charles wrote and served alongside other notable Bible teachers on the board of New Wine, including Don Basham, Ern Baxter, Bob Mumford and Derek Prince. [1]

In the 1970s, Charles Simpson, along with Don Basham, Bob

Mumford and Derek Prince, started what came to be known as the Shepherding Movement (also known as the "Discipleship Movement"). Ern Baxter later joined the group. The doctrine of the movement emphasized the "mentoring one another" passages as described in 2 Timothy. The Shepherding Movement was headquartered in Ft. Lauderdale, Florida, and these five men soon became known as the "Ft. Lauderdale Five." [2]

The Shepherding Movement started off on the right track, but eventually degenerated into one of the most controvertial organizations of the Pentecostal Movement. It had a national network of followers who formed pyramids of sheep and shepherds. Down through the pyramid went the orders, it was alleged, while up the same pyramid went the tithes. At its height, an estimated 100,000 adherents across the US were involved in the networks. [2]

Pat Robertson denounced the Shepherding Movement, declaring their teachings to be 'witchcraft' and said the only difference between the discipleship group and Jonestown was 'Kool-Aid.' [2]

Kathryn Kuhlman refused to appear together with Bob Mumford at the 1975 Conference on the Holy Spirit in Jerusalem. [2]

The Fort Lauderdale Five eventually parted company. Derek Prince and Bob Mumford both publicly distanced themselves from the teachings. Derek Prince withdrew in 1983, stating his belief that "we were guilty of the Galatian error: having begun in the Spirit, we quickly degenerated into the flesh." Bob Mumford issued a "Formal Repentance Statement to the Body of Christ" in November 1989. Mumford admitted that there had been an "unhealthy submission resulting in perverse and unbiblical obedience to human leaders." He took personal responsibility for these abuses, saying that many of them happened under his sphere of leadership. [2]

Charles Simpson, who leads a major segment of those who continue in the legacy of the movement, has said that human carnality won out all too often. While many were hurt as some leaders improperly exercised spiritual authority, mostly ignored are those who benefited from the movement and those who continue in its varied expressions today. [3]

Currently, Charles Simpson serves as a spiritual father to many pastors and as a consultant to churches and businesses, traveling and ministering globally. He is the Editor-in-Chief of One-to-One™ magazine, and is a featured writer in every issue. He resides in Mobile, Alabama. [1]

The Jesus People Movement was a fabulous thing that God brought to us and millions of lives were transformed by it. Charles, as well as everyone else who was involved in the Jesus Movement, fervently hopes and prays that the Lord will graciously bring another of his out-pourings to us.

"The 'Jesus Movement' touched millions everywhere. Our Youth Minister, Jerry Beavers and Worship Leader, Gary Browning, reached out to Hippies in Mobile during those same years. Our church was transformed.

The Holy Spirit was moving everywhere and I pray [He] will do so again in that same way."

Charles

**References:**

1.  http://www.csmpublishing.org/ab_bio.php
2.  http://en.wikipedia.org/wiki/Shepherding_Movement
3.  http://thewartburgwatch.com/2011/02/18/
    did-charles-simpson's-"covenant-theology"-influence-
    sovereign-grace-ministries/

# Chuck Smith

## 1927 - 2013

C harles Ward "Chuck" Smith (June 25, 1927 – October 3, 2013) was an American pastor who founded the Calvary Chapel movement. It began in 1965 with a congregation of 25 people. The influence of Calvary Chapel now extends to thousands of congregations worldwide, some of which are among the largest churches in the United States. He has been called "one of the most influential figures in modern American Christianity."[1]

Chuck Smith was born in Ventura, California in 1927, to Charles and Maude Smith. He graduated from LIFE Bible College and was ordained as a pastor for the International Church of the Foursquare Gospel. [1]

Calvary Chapel operated as a cross-cultural missions organization that bridged the "generation gap" as it existed during the Vietnam War period. It was a hub of the "Jesus People" phenomenon. Calvary Chapel was featured in *Time Magazine* for its success among "hippies" and young people. It pioneered a less formal and more contemporary approach in its worship and public meetings. For example, it did outreaches on the beach, and baptisms in the Pacific Ocean. The impact of Chuck Smith and Calvary Chapel on evangelical Christianity is profound, widespread, and largely unheralded. [1] To his ragged following, he was Papa Chuck, and he welcomed them to his church by the thousands, accepting their barefoot, floor-sitting, outdoor-living habits and incorporating their rock music into his Sunday services – an innovation that other evangelical churches as well as mainline Protestant and Roman Catholic churches later adopted. [2]

In 1971, Mr. Smith helped found Maranatha Music, one of the first contemporary Christian record companies in the United States, partly to provide a platform for the Christian musicians and songwriters who performed at his church. The group Love Song, one of the first Christian rock groups, was for a time a kind of house band at Calvary Chapel. [2]

In his 1978 book, *End Times*, Smith predicted that the generation of 1948 would be the last generation, and that the world would come to an end by 1981. He supported his convictions again in his 1980 manuscript, *Future Survival*, postulating that from his "understanding of biblical prophecies... [I am] convinced that the Lord [will come] for His Church before the end of 1981." He conceded that he "could be wrong" but continued in the same sentence that "it's a deep conviction in my heart, and all my plans are predicated upon that belief." When the world continued beyond 1981, many disillusioned followers left the Calvary Chapel movement. [1]

On December 27, 2009, in the early morning hours, Smith suffered a minor stroke in his home and was immediately hospitalized. He recovered and returned to the ministry. [1]

In his church service on New Years Day of 2012, Chuck Smith announced he had lung cancer. In June 2013, Smith's doctors found that his lung cancer had morphed from stage three to stage four. Smith died in his sleep from a heart attack around 3:00 a.m. on October 3, 2013, at his home in Newport Beach, California. [1]

He is survived by his wife, Catherine L. Johnson Smith, four children: Chuck Jr., Jeff, Janette Smith Manderson and Cheryl Smith Brodersen, and five grandchildren. [2]

**References:**

1.  http://en.wikipedia.org/wiki/Chuck_Smith_(pastor)
2.  http://www.nytimes.com/2013/10/14/us/chuck-smith-minister-who-preached-to-flower-children-dies-at-86.html?_r=0

# Bio 31

# Jack Sparks
## 1928 - 2010

Jack Sparks was born in Lebanon, Indiana; on December 3, 1928; [1] a year in which no crossfire hurricanes passed through Indiana. Jack grew up on a tenant farm with his parents, Oakley and Geraldine Sparks, and three younger siblings. [2]

After graduating from high school at age 17, Jack Sparks earned his Bachelor of Science and played football for Purdue. He then received a Master's of Arts at the University of Iowa in 1951. [2]

In 1952, Jack was drafted into the army. In December of that year, he was hospitalized and met a nurse named Esther. They were married in San Antonio, Texas on April 11, 1953. The couple had four children. [2]

Jack received a Ph.D. from the University of Iowa in 1960. The University of Northern Colorado then hired Jack as a Professor of Applied Statistics and the Director of Research Design. In 1965, he became a Professor of Psychology at Pennsylvania State University. While at Penn State, he became involved with an organization called Campus Crusade for Christ and decided to leave his academic post and work in campus ministry. [2] This must have represented a major change for him; leaving a most illustrious academic and professional life for that of campus ministry.

On April 1, 1969; Jack and his family traveled to the University of California at Berkeley where they began what became an eight-year ministry to students and street people. Jack and Esther would witness to students and hippies and offer as much help to them as they could. At one point, Jack's neighbors forced Jack and Esther to move because they didn't like the Sparks family opening their house to hippies and countercultural types for meetings and "crashing" overnight. [2]

The "Christian World Liberation Front" was initially a project sponsored by Campus Crusade for Christ, but soon became reorganized as an independent, nonprofit, nondenominational outreach to the campus and the counterculture with Jack Sparks and Pat Matrisciana serving as the directors. CWLF provided housing and food for the homeless, counsel for drug users, and their own discipleship efforts. On the streets they employed street theater and urged all within earshot to consider Jesus Christ, His death and resurrection. [3]

In that period (the early 1970s) there were several underground and alternative newspapers in Berkeley; Jack Sparks published "Right On", a Christian newspaper. [4]

Jack was the author of many books including Letters to Street Christians, God's Forever Family, The Mind Benders, The Resurrection Letters, St. Irenaios' the Preaching of the Apostles, Victory in the Unseen Warfare, Virtue in the Unseen Warfare, and Prayer in the Unseen Warfare. He was also the editor of The Apostolic Fathers and wrote many booklets, poems, articles, and short stories. [2]

1970 arrives on the scene and it's yet another time for Jumpin' Jack Sparks to make another huge change. Jack, like some of his erstwhile colleagues in Campus Crusade for Christ, had begun to question their method of evangelism. They were leading people to Jesus, but not establishing them in a church, so the people were falling away. They considered that the problem was that there were so many denominations that they didn't know which to recommend. The obvious answer, it seemed, was to point people to the New Testament Church, or the nearest modern equivalent. But every denomination claimed to represent the New Testament Church. So they began a study of church history to see where the New Testament Church had gone, and the trail led them to Orthodoxy. [4]

In 1977, Jumpin' Jack was one of the founders and dean of St. Athanasius Academy of Orthodox Theology in both Santa Barbara and Elk Grove, California. He was ordained into the Orthodox priesthood in 1987. [4] Later in his life, Jack and Esther moved to Alaska to be near their children. [1]

Jack lead a very full life, having received many degrees, having held prestigious jobs, playing football for Purdue, having been a loving husband, father to four children, a grandfather and a great grandfather [1], but most importantly, having served the Lord.

Jack Sparks died in his sleep of a heart attack at age 81 on February 8, 2010, near Anchorage, Alaska. [2]

### References:

1.  Marc Dunaway;  (Feb. 2010) ; Memory Eternal! + Fr. Jack Sparks Antiochian Orthodox Christian Archdioces;  http://www.antiochian.org/node/22274;  Retrieved 12/03/12.
2.  David W. Gill;  (Feb 10, 2010) Virtual Memorials http://www.virtual-memorials.com/main.php?action =view&mem_id=18884&page_no=4; Retrieved, 12/03/12.
3.  The Jesus Revolution, Part 13:The SF Bay Area Jesus People Movement; http://www.earthenvesseljournal.com/ issue04+/articles/Hoyt/Hoyt_14.html; Retrieved November 30, 2012.
4.  Ministry to street people and hippies; http://khanya. wordpress.com/2010/02/15/ministry-to-street-people-and-hippies/; Retrieved 12/3/12.

# Bio 32

# Jerry and Pat Westfall
## 1931 - and 1941 -

**J**erry Westfall is a native Californian, born in West Los Angeles in 1931. He attended Van Nuys High School, and graduated in 1949. In 1957 he attended Baylor University, a nationally ranked Christian University in Texas, and graduated with a B.S. Then, he attended Fuller Theological Seminary in Pasadena, California and graduated in 1963 with a Master of Divinity.

Jerry became a Christian in 1954, at the age of 23. He says,

In 1954, I was completing my last of 4 years in the Air Force. I was stationed near El Paso, Texas, and met some guys while playing volleyball at the local YMCA. They were Christians, but never let on and I wouldn't have known what that meant anyway.

They invited me to spend one weekend with their family, so I did. Little did I know they lived right across the street from a Baptist church. And they attended everything, like all day long. I endured, and decided never to go back. Enough is enough! But I did go back, more and more often, and after buying a cheap Bible, reading about Jesus for 3 months, I joined Jesus, trusted in His work on the cross, and have been as loyal to Him as I am able to this day.

Jerry grew up with a good family, but not with up-front Christian parents. He married a girl from church shortly after his conversion and after his discharge from the Air Force. They had a son, but in 1959, after 4 years, and while Jerry was in seminary, she left, taking their son with her.

In 1961, God graciously brought Pat into his life. They have been married 52 years and have 3 married daughters and 13 grandkids. Pat is a solid follower of Jesus, and has been the miracle wife for Jerry.

In the early 1960's a seed was planted in the hearts of Jerry and Pat through a Christian retreat ministry in Southern California. This was a small country ministry that had found the value of hosting folks away from the business of their usual routine. God worked significantly in such a setting. Both of them were impacted by this fresh retreat approach to ministry. Together they realized that they were somehow destined to do something similar. In 1964, after Pat graduated from nursing school, and Jerry graduated from seminary, with 2-week-old Jane, the Westfalls moved to Mendocino. [1]

In the fall of 1965, after a year of searching for just the right place, God led them to the 20 acres that they now call Antioch Ranch. The Ranch had history, and a lush, overgrown orchard. It had some pasture land, hundreds of Redwoods, and was a nice distance from the fog belt. [1]

The year 1969 was a pivotal year. The Presbyterian pastor of the church that the Westfalls had been attending suggested that they open their 20-acre "home" to the countless searching Hippies flowing into Mendocino. They say that they somehow identified with Moses at the burning bush. Yes, it was the Lord, so they jumped into what was later called the "Jesus Movement." For 11 years, thousands of wonderful and often weird young people journeyed through what they came to name Antioch Ranch. They used the name Antioch after the city in Syria where many of the early Christians found safety and spiritual nourishment. [1]

Pat and Jerry encouraged and taught many of those folks until 1980, when God took them down another turn in the road. They were asked to start a Christian school for a growing number of Jesus Movement churches in the Bay Area. So they packed up their stuff and headed for the big city where they "birthed" and "parented" a Christian school for 7 years. [1]

Presently, Pat and Jerry Westfall are active at the Mendocino Presbyterian Church and are still serving folks by providing vacation rentals on their 20 acres in the Mendocino area.

**References:**

1.   http://www.antiochranch.com/about-us.php

# Victor Paul Wierwille
## 1916 - 1985

V ictor Paul Wierwille was born on December 31, 1916 in New Knoxville, Ohio. He is best known for having founded The Way International.

As a young man, Victor Wierwille attended and was ordained by the Evangelical and Reformed Church (which later became known as the United Church of Christ). [1]

"Wierwille graduated from Mission House College with Bachelor of Arts and Bachelor of Theology degrees. He then studied at The University of Chicago Divinity School and received a Master of Theology in practical theology from Princeton Theological Seminary. Wierwille later studied at Pikes Peak Bible Seminary and Burton College, a non-accredited institution, and received a doctorate in theology. "[1]

In 1942, he ran a radio show entitled Vesper Chimes. This later was incorporated as The Chimes Hour Youth Caravan. In 1955, he formed The Way Incorporated. Later, this corporation became known as The Way International. In 1961, the headquarters of The Way Incorporated relocated to New Knoxville, Ohio on approximately 147 acres of family farmland. [1]

Wierwille authored several books, the most notable being Jesus Christ is Not God. In this book, he claims that he conclusively proves that Jesus was not God in any way, but merely a perfect man. In asserting that Jesus did not have the nature of God, Wierwille denies the existence of the trinity. Wierwille's argument is based on a misinterpretation of John 1:1. [2]

"In the beginning was the Word, and the Word was with God, and the Word was God. " – John 1:1.

He says that the key to interpreting this verse is pivotal upon the meaning of the word "with." He says that "with" does not mean that Jesus was personally with God, but only "in the Mind of God." Therefore, Jesus did not preexist with the Father but was just a thought in God's mind. [2]

The author of empirenet.com then goes on to explain that "Wierwille abuses other Greek words in this chapter of John. ...In addition to disagreeing with all Christian scholars, Wierwille often disagrees with himself. His inconsistency illuminates his manipulative brand of 'scholarship.' " [2]

"Some groups have considered The Way's beliefs, viewed as heretical by a number of denominations, to be evidence of cult status. ...There have also been some accusations about The Way's alleged history of sexual abuse, ...excessive control over members' lives, and brainwashing. ...The anti-cult movement (ACM) attempts to raise public consciousness of what they feel are the dangers of cult membership. They view a cult as a religious or other group that uses deceptive recruitment techniques to lure new members into the organization, and then subjects them to sophisticated mind-control techniques to reduce their ability to think and act individually (brainwashing)." [4]

"Given The Way's high-intensity nature in the 1970s, there were some instances of family members who weren't a part of The Way hiring deprogrammers to illegally abduct their loved one because they believed exposure to these doctrines or the followers was harmful." [4]

"V. P. Wierwille consistently taught that people's own negative believing (fear) make and keep them sick. In Power for Abundant Living, he wrote, 'If one is afraid of a disease, he will manifest that disease because the law is that what one believes (in this case, what he believes negatively), he is going to receive. ...Today I have no fear within me. ...fear always defeats the promises of God. ...'" [3]

V.P. Wierwille succumbed to liver cancer in 1985. The Way International never released this information, perhaps not wishing the believers in "The Way" to think that maybe their leader could have had negative beliefs or fears. [3]

## References:

1. http://en.wikipedia.org/wiki/Victor_Paul_Wierwille (Retrieved 12/26/13)
2. http://www.empirenet.com/~messiah7/rsr_jcwdsway. htm (Retrieved 12/26/13)
3. http://www.empirenet.com/~messiah7/vp_DEATH.htm (Retrieved 12/26/13)
4. http://en.wikipedia.org/wiki/The_Way_International

# John Wimber
## 1934 - 1997

J ohn Richard Wimber was born in Kirksville, Missouri on February 25, 1934. His parents were Basil Wimber and Genevieve Martin Wimber. As a young man, John played the keyboard for a group called the Paramours. [1] He is also credited with having been the manager of the famous rock group, The Righteous Brothers. [3] In May of 1963, John converted to evangelical Christianity. He moved to California and attended a Quaker church in Yorba Linda. According to Christianity Today, he was a "beer-guzzling, drug-abusing pop musician, who was converted at the age of 29 while chain-smoking his way through a Quaker-led Bible study." [2]

During the time in the Quaker church, he led many people to Christ. At one point, he was leading eleven different Bible study groups that involved more that 500 people. [1]

Wimber is most famous for having been one of the founding leaders of the Vineyard Movement, a neo-charismatic Evangelical Christian Movement which is still active today. In the mid-1970s, a group at the church that Wimber was attending became increasingly charismatic and they were eventually asked to leave. In 1977, in association with Chuck Smith's Calvary Chapel, the Anaheim Vineyard Fellowship was born. The new church did not grow quickly in the beginning, but witnessed miraculous healing services. In 1978, the famous evangelist, Lonnie Frisbee made a guest appearance at the church and triggered a huge outpouring of charismatic phenomena and thereafter, the church grew to over 1,500 members. [3]

By the year of 1982, there were about seven loosely structured "Vineyard" churches. In the early 1980s, Wimber assumed leadership of what was to be known as "The Association of Vineyard Churches." Today, almost 40 years later, there are more than 1,500 Vineyard churches worldwide, 550+ in the US, with 16 regions actively planting churches across the country. [4]

John was a fruitful and enthusiastic pastor. He believed in training his church to imitate Jesus and helped thousands to experience intimacy with God. [4]

He seems to have had a very practical view on the baptism of the Holy Spirit. He believed that the baptism of the Holy Spirit occurs upon conversion, but may manifest itself experientially (for example, speaking in tongues) at a later date. [1]

He strongly believed in authenticity and scorned the thought of acting for "religious effect." He is quoted as having said, "I also visited several healing meetings...and became angry with what appeared to be the manipulation of people for the material gains of the faith healer...dressing like sideshow barkers. Pushing people over and calling it the power of God. And money – they were always asking for more, leading people to believe that if they gave they would be healed..." [1]

"I have also seen groups where the expected behavior of the ones being prayed for was that they fall over. This was nothing more than learnt behavior, religion at its worst." [1]

John was actively involved in the Vineyard until his death in 1997. [4] He died of a brain hemorrhage on November 17, 1997 at the age of 63. [1]

### References:

1.   en.wikipedia.org/wiki/John_Wimber
2.   Christianity Today, editorial, Feb. 9 1998)
3.   www.wheaton.edu /isae/hall-of-biography/john-wimber
4.   http://www.vineyardusa.org/site/about/vineyard-history

# Frank Worthen

## 1929 -

Frank Worthen was born in 1929, a year that was, according to Frank, "an exceedingly bad year to be born – the year of the great stock-market crash." He grew up in an old Victorian house in San Jose, California, that his father had purchased for $2,000 with the intention of fixing it up. But the Great Depression thwarted his plans.

In Frank's words, "The house grew progressively darker and uglier as my childhood passed." [1]

Frank's boyhood was fraught with feelings of rejection and inadequacy.

> Not long after Wall Street crashed, my father's salary was cut in half. ...He was able to get a second job. ...In my earliest years, my father was a shadow figure, one who would arrive at the house late at night after I was in bed, and leave before I got up. Occasionally, Father came home for dinner before heading out to his second job. I remember eagerly waiting for him at the gate, longing for his attention. When he finally arrived, he would absently pat me on the head and head for the kitchen. [1]

By the time Frank had reached his teens, he was having serious problems with uncontrollable anger. He even went so far as to commit frequent acts of vandalism against his family's home.

> Fury had seethed within me for years, bubbling up with

every insult, every family battle, and every hurtful rejection. In truth, I was a very disturbed child. Why was I in exile when other kids were out on the streets playing together? Why didn't I have a loving family? Why did my father abandon me? Why did other kids hate me, and what did I do to deserve it? [2]

When Frank was 13, in 1942, his pastor told him "Frank, you are a homosexual." Though Frank knew he was "different" from other children, he didn't know what homosexuality was. "I'd been called different before!" Frank had become a loner – hiding in the attic during his family's constant arguing. "My peers called me names which I later learned meant 'homosexual.'" [3]

For 25 years Frank was exclusively homosexual. At age 44, he says he heard God tell him, "Today, I want you back." "God's voice was so real. [3]

God's voice can sometimes be identified when a thought (positive and good – of course) enters your mind, unbidden and quite the opposite of a thought that you would normally be entertaining.

"Once again, I was crossing the Golden Gate Bridge. Once again, I was thinking about the emptiness and futility of my life, pondering my destiny. Every time I had driven across the bridge's picturesque span in recent days, I'd grown more convinced that it would be remarkably easy and sensible to end it all right there. Then on one particular day, as if out of nowhere, a completely contradictory thought entered my mind: 'If you are willing to take your life, are you willing to give it to Me?'

When I asked myself, 'Where did that come from?!!', the unexpected words repeated themselves in my mind: 'If you are willing to take your life, are you willing to give it to Me?'"[4]

Frank was in turmoil.

It didn't take me long to find problems with the idea. Of course, I'm willing to give my life to God, I thought bitterly, but what good will it do? I knew I couldn't have a relationship with God while I continued to live in homo-sexual sin. ... I flashed back to age 23, when my gay-life-vs.-God conflict had come to a head. I had been in such turmoil, I had honestly been afraid of losing my sanity. I remember taking an afternoon off work and driving through Golden Gate Park. I was so frustrated with God. Lord, I had told him, our relationship is over! You won't change me, and I can't serve You the way I am. This con-flict will kill me, so it's goodbye! [4]

Frank continued with his gay life style, but feelings of hope-lessness, suicide and self-disgust were constantly increasing. His job was going well, but he was getting no enjoyment from working. One day, he left work with the intention of checking out a new gay bathhouse. As he walked down the long corridor out-side his office, he heard an audible voice speak to him, "I want you back!"

This was no still, small voice; it was a shout. It was not a voice I could associate with any of my employees or, for that matter, anyone I'd ever known. I was frightened out of my wits... In that moment, although I was feeling tremendous remorse for my evil lifestyle, a different and profound truth broke through; God had indeed ful-filled His role as Father in my life. He had saved me from numerous life-threatening situations. I had been beaten and robbed several times, yet I had always survived. In my travels, I had once been within blocks of a deadly bombing, and I'd had several harrowing experiences while flying. Now, in an instant, I could clearly see how, time and again, He had protected me. I knew beyond the shadow of a doubt that he was still my Father. [4]

From that moment on, Frank's life turned around. He went on a retreat and read the Bible from cover to cover. He became involved in Bible study groups and Christian churches. He made the acquaintance of Kent Philpott, who had recently started a Bible study group in the Haight/Ashbury, which was in those days, a "Hippy Haven." Kent also did street witnessing and had set up a drug-abuse center.

Frank was in Kent's office one day, and it came up that within the same week, two other homosexuals had independently contacted Kent, each wanting counseling for same-sex attraction tendencies. A group was formed. They eventually came to call themselves Love in Action. [5]

On November 24, 1984, at age 55, Frank married Anita Thomas. About his marriage, Frank says, "Our marriage has been far better than our greatest expectations. The honeymoon continues!" [6]

**References:**

1.   1. Frank Worthen, *Destiny Bridge* (Winnipeg, Canada: Forever Books, 2010), 15 – 17.
2.   2. Frank Worthen, *Destiny Bridge*, 28-31.
3.   3.http://www.crossministry.org/index.php?option=com_content&view=article&id=234:frank-worthen&catid=65:articles-by-tim&Itemid=278
4.   4. Frank Worthen, *Destiny Bridge*, 147-150.
5.   5. Frank Worthen, *Destiny Bridge*, 178.
6.   6. Frank Worthen, *Destiny Bridge*, 240.

# Bio 36

# Stephanie Adams
## 195? -

Dear Reader,

I hope you have enjoyed the biographies and that you have found them to be an encouragement in the Lord. Some of them were sent in just as is by the named person or a relative; some were the result of my research and compilation; and some were written after phone interview input. They were all a wonderful way to know about people I have never met.

Kent wanted me to write about my own experiences with the Jesus People Movement. I wasn't one of the leaders in the movement, as were those about whom I've written; I was merely a participant in the incredible awakening that God brought to the West Coast.

To start, I was born in Boston, Massachusetts. Since I am the author of this bio, I claim immunity from having to disclose the actual year of my birth, notwithstanding the possible option of lying, but this being a Christian book, and all, I can't do that. Suffice it to say I was born in August.

My mother was the director of a Sunday school at the local church in Needham, so for her sake I would go to Sunday school and church, but the foremost impression conveyed to me regarding Jesus was that He was a really nice guy who walked around a lot in the desert wearing a robe and sandals.

I attended a private girls' high school in Brookline, Massachusetts and studied hard, hoping to be able to get into a good college. Toward the end of my senior year, there was one thing that I knew more than anything else: "I had to go to Berkeley."

There was no Internet in those days. I had never been west of New York (unless having been in Chicago as an embryo counts). I had no idea what California was like other than what could have been gleamed from some advice given by some friends of my mother, which was to bring a warm jacket because evenings in San Francisco can get chilly. I can't explain why or how I knew that I had to go to the West Coast.

I graduated high school in May of 1969. At the graduation ceremony, the school presented our graduation gifts in reverse alphabetical order so that I was the last person to receive a gift. I'm sure they did it this way because my gift was by far the best. They presented me with a gas mask.

That was May. In June, I was on a plane for San Francisco. June happens to be the month of the famous Laconia Motorcycle Week in New Hampshire. As it turned out, most disconcertingly for my mother witnessing her firstborn going off to college, about 20 Hells Angels had decided to fly back to San Francisco on the same plane that I was boarding. I recall them as being very disheveled. Their jeans were old and ripped. Mind you, this was a day when torn jeans weren't fashionable. Remember how in those days, you could go into a store and find jeans that looked new and that would even come all the way up to your waist? But I digress.

I arrived safely in Berkeley and loved it as much as I thought I would. I would walk to the campus for classes and hear the beat of the drums of the Hare Krishnas, and I'd walk through Sproul Plaza where Holy Hubert would often be street preaching. He had his own unique style. He would be argumentative, saying things like, "You filthy fornicating sinners...." But I was into being a student and, as such, didn't pay much attention to those things around me. To me, they were just a part of the Berkeley atmosphere, which I loved so much.

In the spring quarter of 1971, I went to the University of California at San Diego on a visitor's pass. One (beautiful) (in parentheses because this word is redundant when the subject is California weather) day in February, I was on the campus, sitting on a patch of grass, leaning against a tree, studying – minding my own business - when a girl came up to me. I remember that her name was Linda. She started telling me about Jesus. I don't recall what she said, but I remember thinking that she seemed sincere and she seemed like a bright person.

The next day, I was sitting in the cafeteria of Discovery Hall, (an appropriate name in view of the change in my life that occurred while I was there). A girl, whose name was Patty, and who just happened to be Linda's best friend, sat down with me and she started telling me about Jesus. I remember thinking the same thing about her that I had thought about Linda; they actually believed what they were saying! I thought if it works for them, maybe I should, at least, try it. They took me to their church, which was affiliated with the Campus Crusade for Christ. I don't remember what was said at church, but when I woke up the next morning, so many things were different in my life.

Then, I came to find out that my roommate at Discovery Hall, Jeanne Davies, was a Christian and she had been praying for me. God had sent Patty and Linda and Jeanne to me, and I thank Him so much for that. I also am so grateful to Him for putting it in my mind that I should go to the West Coast to be part of His great revival.

When my visitor's pass was about to end, I asked the Lord what he wanted me to do. My actual intention was to find out whether I should go back to Berkeley or stay in San Diego. But, the very distinct answer that came back was, "Love the Lord your God with all your heart, soul and mind."

I was almost totally ignorant of the scriptures (well, perhaps completely ignorant of them) and it wasn't until later that I found out that God had spoken the First Commandment to me.

"And thou shalt love the Lord thy God with all thy heart, and with all thy soul, and with all thy mind, and with all thy strength: this is the first commandment." – Jesus speaking in Mark 12:30

In conclusion, I would like to say what I have possibly already said, or at least implied. It seems that no one really knew what was going on at the time. I thought that the fact that God was interacting with people in such a visible manner reflected one of the differences between the East Coast and the West Coast. Gaylord Enns thought it was "just a phenomenon of Chico." Bob Burns thought it was a "counter-culture thing" and that the interest in God was a result of how the counter-culture was so open to new ideas. According to Greg Beumer, "I didn't know it was a movement until probably somewhere in the early '70s when *Time* magazine said it was a movement."

But God be praised for what He did all the way up the West Coast from San Diego to Washington state. Like others have said, we will always remember the love that God imparted to us for one another and will always marvel at the ways in which the Lord engineered circumstances and events so as to have us meet and work together for His glory.

# Index

Notes: Names marked with * have a separate entry in the Bios Section. No entries are logged from within the Bios section.

# Other Books by Kent Philpott

*The Soul Journey:*
*How Shamanism, Wicca, Santería, and Charisma*
*are Connected*

*If the Devil Wrote a Bible*

*Awakenings in America and*
*the Jesus People Movement*

*How Christians Cast Out Demons Today*

*Are You Really Born Again?*
*Understanding True and False Conversion*

*Are You Being Duped?*

*Why I Am a Christian*

*For Pastors of Small Churches*

*How to Care for Your Pastor*

EVP

Available at www.evpbooks.com

CPSIA information can be obtained
at www.ICGtesting.com
Printed in the USA
FFOW02n1157030614
5657FF

9 780989 804110